More advance praise from the experts . . .

Money is too important to ignore—with women outliving men and growing professionally, it's essential that they learn to effectively manage money. In this, her second investment book, Kathy has done a terrific job of demystifying investments and providing the knowledge necessary for women to be money wise.

> **—Kimberly A. Bradshaw**
> Vice President, National Accounts Manager
> American Skandia, Inc.

As some age, the financial issues that pertain to women can become more complex. Kathy Buys does an excellent job of explaining the issues that women face and the intricacies of the financial markets. She provides sound investment solutions that help her clients achieve their financial dreams. Kathy is truly one of the best financial advisors in the business!

> **—Lin Bercher**
> Senior Vice President and Managing Director
> Kemper Funds

A must-read for every woman. No matter what the reader's age, career, or personal lifestyle, Kathy delivers financial solutions and investment alternatives to them that work and make sense! Women who strive for financial independence should not be without Kathy's second masterpiece.

> **—Lynette Sasso**
> Regional Vice President
> AIM Funds

What Kathy Buys' seminar participants say about her:

"I was enlightened. You have motivated me to get on the stick and start more investing. You were great."

"Kathy is a wonderful instructor and is able to relay her knowledge to others in a very understandable way."

"Talk about bonding with the public—Kathy fired us up."

"The only comment I have about the class is that I wish it were longer and would cover more topics."

"Kathy gave us a very dynamic presentation, and I would be interested in any other class she teaches."

"You left the whole group feeling quite empowered. We're ready to go out and 'make our fortune.'"

"What great enthusiasm—I'm inspired to study more."

"Ms. Buys focuses on the needs of the people she's speaking to and delivers clear, informative, and practical information."

"Kathy is a truly entertaining speaker, and her frankness and knowledge make learning a pleasure."

"This is a woman who truly makes the difficult topic clearly understandable."

"Now I finally have the knowledge of what doing nothing is costing me. With her information, I have the foundation to understand what my next move will be. Thanks so much."

"If you're looking for practical, user-friendly information, this is it. I was afraid I'd be lost but found myself able to follow everything that Kathy said."

"Thank you, Kathy, your enthusiasm is contagious. Very empowering. Now I'm ready to exercise my power."

"Kathy made what could a boring, difficult class fun and interesting."

"I will certainly tell others about this seminar."

"Thank you for speaking to our employees. The feedback was very positive and I had several employees who were unable to attend approach me after the session to ask when we would be scheduling another presentation from you. Your session was a great hit."

Invest with
Confidence
A No-Nonsense Guide for
Women and Their Money

Invest with Confidence

A No-Nonsense Guide for Women and Their Money

Kathy Buys

Chandler House Press
Worcester, Massachusetts
1999

Invest with Confidence:
A No-Nonsense Guide for Women and Their Money

ISBN 1-886284-20-2
Library of Congress Catalog Card Number 98-74419
First Edition
   BCDEFGHIJK

Published by
Chandler House Press
335 Chandler Street
Worcester, MA 01602 USA

President
Lawrence W. Abramoff

Publisher/Editor-in-Chief
Richard J. Staron

Vice President of Sales
Irene S. Bergman

Editorial/Production Manager
Jennifer J. Goguen

Book Design and Production
CWL Publishing Enterprises
3010 Irvington Way
Madison, WI 53713 USA
www.execpc.com/cwlpubent

Chandler House Press books are available at special discounts for bulk purchases. For more information about how to arrange such purchases, please contact Chandler House Press, 335 Chandler Street, Worcester, MA 01602, or call (800) 642-6657, or fax (508) 756-9425, or find us on the World Wide Web at www.tatnuck.com.

Chandler House Press books are distributed to the trade by
National Book Network
4720 Boston Way
Lanham, MD 20706
(800) 462-6420

Disclaimer The opinions expressed herein are solely those of the author and are based on the author's personal experiences. They are not intended to be the norm for all investors. Reasonable care has been taken in the preparation of the text to ensure its clarity and accuracy. This book is sold with the understanding that the author and the publisher are not engaged in rendering legal or accounting services. Laws vary from state to state, and readers with specific financial questions should seek the services of a professional advisor. The author and publisher specifically disclaim any liability, loss, or risk, personal or otherwise, which is incurred as a consequence, directly or indirectly, of the use and application of any of the contents of this book.

Contents

Acknowledgments

While my name appears as author, this book could not have been written without the assistance of my friend and co-worker, Heidi Schoenberger. How lucky I am that she is as quick with her mind as she is with the keyboard.

Many women have been involved in the review-and-comment phase of writing this book and have contributed ideas and suggestions that have resulted in a better book.

Lastly, I wish to thank all the women who contributed to Chapter 14, the interview portion of this book. They gave generously of their time and emotions so that others may gain from their experience.

Introduction

Buy this book!

Now that gives you an idea of just how subtle my writing style is and what you can expect throughout the rest of this book. You've got it. Cutting through the investment jargon, this book is a down-and-dirty, roll-up-your-sleeves-and-jump-in adventure. Whether you are a beginning or experienced investor, after you've read the book you'll know a heck of a lot more than you do now. Don't close this book and put it back. Take the plunge and join me in this educational quest!

If you're thumbing through this book, it has no doubt come to your attention that there are as many investment books out there as it seems there are investors. Publishers are no dummies—they know this is a very timely topic. Some of these are actually quite good, depending on your and the author's level of knowledge about the subject. Others are written by the investment journalist du jour or people who think that, because they've bought a stock, they're qualified to write on the topic. That makes about as much sense as saying that since I've taken a pill, I can write about medicine.

I can honestly tell you, this book was written exclusively with you in mind, covering topics you need to know, in a manner that I promise will make sense to you. Any of you who have taken my classes, attended any of my speeches, or read anything I've written know that my real claim to fame is making complex investment issues simple and easily understood. It's absolutely my intention to continue that claim to fame in this book.

As a financial advisor and as a woman, I have a deep and profound commitment to helping women help themselves by learning more about finance. I've simply seen too many horror stories where women have been taken advantage of, have misunderstood what they've been sold, or simply do themselves a great deal of harm by buying the wrong investment. They hurt themselves not because they're not smart but because they're nervous and intimidated and somehow see this as a topic beyond their reach. That is plain and simply not the case—and we're going to prove that in this book!!!

Women historically have considered their best investment friends to be things like money markets, savings accounts, treasury bills, CDs, and credit union accounts. Throughout time we have come to know and love all those "safe" places for our money. Yet if you look at almost any financial book, television program, or magazine, they'll show you that, over time, the worst-performing assets are usually these types of investments. The reality is, we can no longer afford to let our whole financial future rest with those comfortable "old friends."

What I won't do with this book is bore you with a lot of statistics that you probably already know in your mind and understand in your gut. We all know that women make and save less money than men. We also have smaller retirement funds and generally wind up poorer than men. If you've picked up this book, you're already onto the fact that you've got to do something to take care of your financial future and you believe that you can, with some tools, help yourself to overcome many of these depressing statistics.

Here's something to think about right off the bat—9 out of 10 of us will at some point in our life be responsible for our own finances whether we like it or not. About 20% of us never marry and half us who do marry end up getting divorced. If you don't fit in those two categories and have a blissful life with a spouse, it's highly likely you'll outlive that spouse by six or seven years. Thinking of it another way, 90% of us had better get a handle on this stuff, because one way or another we're going to have to deal with it.

Given the fact that we hear these statistics and we aren't a bunch of dummies, what is it that's keeping a lot of us from moving forward with taking care of our financial life? Based on my experience with literally thousands of women, I believe there are two major things that keep us from moving forward in the face of the reality of all of those statistics.

Clearly one of the first hurdles we need to clear is emotional barriers that keep us from wise money management. We somehow have it in our heads that men were born with a magic gene that makes them inherently wise about money and investing. We also believe that this gene is missing in women.

It's no great insight that money represents many different things. If we understand some of our conditioning and the messaging we receive about women and money, we can start shattering some of those myths and get on with our financial life. Once women begin investing, they actually become better investors than men. Until we correct some faulty perceptions, those perceptions become our reality and freeze us in place.

The second thing that keeps us from moving forward is a lack of investment knowledge. Most women have simply never been exposed to investment concepts. Often we are not taught about finance in either our personal or educational background. In my own MBA program, I was exposed to a variety of esoteric financial models but nothing regarding the basics of investments. The assumption was that, as adults, we just know these things. If women have never been exposed to them, how could they know them? By nature, most of us don't like risk and since the unknown is risky, we turn to those tried and true investment vehicles we do know. Back to our "old friends," which tend to be in the low-risk, low-return arena.

Women like to understand things before we invest in them, which makes us pretty smart cookies. Unfortunately, many of us don't take the next necessary step—becoming educated about investments.

The importance of both of these factors cannot be minimized. If a woman has emotional issues and/or feels ill-prepared educationally to deal with investing, she can hardly be expected to leap into that arena. This book will address both issues. We'll come to understand some of why we behave as we do and we'll become equipped with a variety of tools for managing our financial life.

I believe my background with both a Master's in Social Work and a Master's in Business and working in these fields has allowed me to learn a great deal about what some of these factors are and how paralyzing they can be to women. Trust me: by the time you finish this book, you'll be on top of both of them. For now, you're going to have to take that on faith.

When I grew up, we religiously watched *Father Knows Best* on television. Doesn't that title say it all? I also witnessed Lucy Ricardo being constantly condemned by Ricky for her frivolous spending. Great role modeling so far. Her financial priorities were obtaining a new hat or dress. Ricky spent his time earning money and worrying about how Lucy spent it. As we continued in school, we weren't supposed to be as good at math as the boys. Somehow it just wasn't feminine. Interestingly and depressingly, to this day, a lot of that thinking persists. We'll look later at a study that demonstrates "how far we've come."

I know that many of you would rather visit the dentist than pick up and study a book on investing. I'm going to do all in my power to make this a heck of a lot more interesting than the subject might imply. In return, I ask that you work with me to become educated.

To help you, I'm going to use a visual indicator to signal important points. When I clarify an issue or define a term, you'll see a "lovely" caricature of me at the side of the page. These pearls of wisdom will be referred to as "Buys Briefs." You will clearly see that either I have a good sense of humor or I'm an idiot. What else could account for me allowing myself to be portrayed like that?

I've asked a number of people in my classes to give me a question that they would like to see answered and I'm going to weave those into the fabric of the book so that I know I'm answering some of the questions that will be on the minds of a lot of you readers. You'll see lots of these throughout each chapter. Not only will they help you learn, but also I hope they'll keep the book from reminding you of some boring textbook.

We'll start with a chapter that I'm calling "More Than Just Dollars." This is where we're going to talk about some of the emotional/psychological components that we attach to money. We'll learn to understand some of these barriers and why men and women frequently view money matters so differently.

Once we've gained some insight into our emotional baggage about money, we can begin to change our behavior. Now we're ready to move forward to gain the knowledge we need in this area.

I'll start by giving you a simplified way to assess what you currently have and what you need financially. Understanding the major concepts such as compounding, inflation, and tax-deferred growth will give us the groundwork to start to look at our investment options. The next three chapters are devoted to what I call financial building blocks: stocks, bonds, and mutual funds.

An examination of three different investors—conservative, moderate, and growth—will show what specific investments are appropriate to each. A growth investor may be interested in an emerging market, while a conservative investor may prefer utility stocks. You'll see how to categorize different types of investments within a financial pyramid.

The next stop on our educational journey will be to cover asset allocation. Integrating what we've learned in the preceding chapters, you'll see how to structure your assets. Since asset allocation is responsible for over 90% of the return in your portfolio, this is an "absolutely don't miss" chapter.

The next chapter, "Making Your Retirement Years Golden," allows you to project your monthly retirement needs and determine any gaps you may have. You'll see an extensive review of available retirement plans, including the new Roth IRA, and learn an interesting way to withdraw money from an IRA before you're 59½ without penalty.

The following two chapters provide a review of some of the fundamentals of financial planning. The first of these, "Estate Planning," examines wills, a variety of trusts, and powers of attorney. This will allow you to understand and implement those that are appropriate. The insurance chapter actually helps you wade through all the verbiage that no one really understands. We explore life, disability, and long-term care insurance, looking at the pros and cons of each.

Then we're going to look at "life uncertainties"—things that may come up and force you to look at money before you thought you wanted to. Death, divorce, inheritance, or winning that lottery all force financial decisions. If you don't want to go it alone, I discuss types of financial advisors and the fees associated with their services. I provide red flags to help guide you through the selection process.

If we haven't covered everything yet, you'll likely find the remainder in the chapter called "Financial Potpourri." There I address a variety of topics, such as real estate and various types of company sponsored stock programs. We'll look at mortgages and I'll give you information about obtaining your credit report.

Finally comes the chapter I think you'll find most interesting—"Real Women/Real Stories." Here are the true stories of many women dealing with a wide range of financial issues. Ever wonder what you'd do if you won the lottery or found out your husband was a drug addict? The women I profile here share their stories, the lessons they learned, and offer advice to others.

You'll notice many of the chapters in this book are stand-alone material, meaning that you don't have to read the entire book and you don't have to become a financial planning expert. However, reading the whole book will give you an excellent knowledge base that you can use in various situations. The book is not intended to help you get rich quick, but it will provide you with all the information you need to achieve control of and better manage your money.

1 | *More Than Just Dollars*

By virtue of purchasing this book, you're aware that women must take control of their own financial futures, and you've taken a step in that direction. In this book I'll give you what you'll need to become a serious, long-term investor. Having dealt with primarily female clients over the course of my career, I know that it isn't always simply a lack of information that keeps women from making wise money decisions. This chapter addresses some of our emotional barriers as we look at money and investing.

The idea here is not to cast blame on men, women, society, or any other element in the universe. It is, rather, to look at some of the realities that shape our thoughts about our roles as women and our place in the financial universe.

These perceptions may be in conflict with what our intellect tells us we must do. I'm not looking for scapegoats or providing handy excuses. What I'm doing is trying to offer some ideas that may provide insights into our behavior and allow us to become more comfortable with our decisions about money and then move forward.

We Don't Live in the '50s Anymore

When we look at some of our perceptions of money and a woman's role in making financial decisions, it becomes a little clearer why many of us are uncomfortable in this area. It pains me to say that I'm an aging baby boomer and as such I grew up with some very destructive role models in the media. Some of my favorite TV shows when I was young were *Ozzie and Harriet, My Little Margie,* and *I Love Lucy.* If you can remember them, can you name which one of those shows portrayed a financially shrewd woman being an equal partner to her husband when it came to money management? I think not. On the contrary, you watched a series of TV programs featuring women who were totally dependent and utterly unable to handle any aspect of the family's financial life. At the time I thought many of those programs were outrageously funny. Later in life I came to understand how much of our feelings about how things should be were shaped by those programs. I don't mean that they were intentionally sexist and designed to make women look incompetent when it came to money. Sadly, they reflected real-life role expectations. If you watch those old shows today, many of them are still very funny but the reality of today's woman is very different.

Just as television was an influencing factor, what were we seeing in our daily lives? Typically, dad went off to work and mom stayed home. If mom worked, she was apt to be a teacher, nurse, secretary, or clerk. Dad, on the other hand, was frequently involved in the business world, which was somehow magical and endowed him with vast wisdom that was beyond the comprehension of women. In the home, men certainly made all of the money decisions and the women would frequently get household allowances. If the woman was working, her boss was generally a man who made the work-related decisions. In neither the workplace nor the home front was the woman considered to be a major decision-maker.

They Don't Always Treat Boys and Girls the Same

As girls went to school, we quickly started to get the message that girls weren't supposed to be as good with numbers as the boys. It simply wasn't feminine. Little girls were rewarded for being cute and cheerful. Little boys, on the other hand, were rewarded for being smart and strong. Little girls were conditioned to believe that, when they grew up, they'd get married, have children, and be financially provided for. Little boys grew up believing they would be responsible for providing for a wife and family.

Studies show that boys tend to receive an allowance sooner, have jobs earlier, and are more likely than girls to save for highly coveted items, such as cars and stereo equipment. In this process, boys are gaining valuable experience as this teaches them the value and use of money. Thus starts our early role modeling regarding our perceptions of money and our confidence in making investment decisions. These scenarios would certainly not instill a great deal of self-confidence in women regarding their ability to manage money and finances.

If you think this patterning is ancient history, think again. Liberty Financial recently did a study of junior and senior high school students in the Boston area. They found that boys were almost twice as likely as girls to consider themselves very knowledgeable about money and investing. The study further revealed that there was actually very little difference between girls and boys in knowledge levels. Sadly, the perception, although incorrect, that the girls knew less than the boys may become a self-fulfilling prophecy in adulthood. The study concluded that female students need two things: education and confidence.

We carry much of this early imprinting into our adult life. Prior to marriage, most of our money decisions are made by our fathers who take care of us financially. After marriage, our husbands are expected to fulfill the same role. In most families, while women may pay the bills, the man is still the primary wage earner and makes most of the financial decisions. Men make most of the large family purchases and feel freer than women about spending money, often without consulting their partner.

Money and Miscommunication

Money is one of the major areas of miscommunication between men and women. Many people feel that money represents love and a man may feel that he is showing his love for the family by providing material things. A woman, on the other hand, may want the traditional type of love—caring, affection, and romance—more than the material things that money can buy. She wants quality time and family-centered activities. He is living up to his role expectations by being responsible, working hard, and bringing home a paycheck.

A 1996 *Money* Magazine poll found that women worry more about finances, have a gloomier economic outlook, and are more likely to worry more about money than sex. (I know that will come as a big shock to you.) It's easy to see why money is consistently one of the most common issues mentioned as a source of problems in a relationship.

To most of us, money represents control. It's often the case that a woman feels she has no right to demand an equal partnership since it may not be her name on the paycheck. If she does bring home a paycheck and it's smaller, she may believe that diminishes her right to financial equality. Does society still encourage men to provide and women to be provided for? You be the judge.

Make no mistake about it: in our society money defines us. It's painfully obvious that money is the great American status symbol. If society believes that money defines our worth as human beings, it's extremely difficult to see how women can win. We are in fewer management jobs, make less than men for the same jobs, save less than men, amass less wealth, and own less property than men. If that's not bad enough, if a woman gets a divorce, her income drops on average by 50% and we generally retire poorer than men. Is it any wonder that we feel inferior?

Even when women break out of the mold and become highly successful in their careers, they still may have to pay a price. While men frequently express their desire for independent women, many men find it highly threatening when their significant other earns as much as they do or more. A woman with a great deal of financial knowledge may find it difficult to be accepted as equal or superior in investing. This is just not supposed to be her arena. It's been my experience that often women will come to talk with me and begin the conversation by saying, "I'm sorry I'm so stupid about money." I can honestly tell you I've never had a man make that same comment.

How does all of this affect our behavior as investors? Men generally believe they will be able to handle money and investments. Women generally believe they won't. Many men feel that if they lose money in an investment they'll be able to make it up in a future investment. Women, on the other hand, are often so fearful of making the wrong investment choice that they make no investment choices at all. Men who invest successfully give themselves the credit; if their investments do poorly, they tend to blame outside factors, such as changing market conditions. A woman with a successful investment often credits her investment advisor's sage advice and blames herself if an investment goes wrong.[1]

As I said earlier in the chapter, the last thing I want to do is to provide a number of handy "poor me" excuses to keep women from moving forward. It's my hope that, by looking at some of these factors that shape our perception and behavior, we'll better understand the demons that keep us from taking control. Now that we've gained some insight about where we come from financially, let's proceed with overcoming these fears by gaining knowledge so you won't have any excuse for not taking action.

Note

1. "Caveat Gender," Olivia Mellan, *Dow Jones Investment Advisor*, June 1996, page 1.

2 What You Have and What You Need

The title of this chapter focuses on the basics of your financial situation, on the answers to two questions: "What do you have?" and "What do you need?" If your answers are "nothing" and "lots" and if winning the lottery is your financial plan, you need to pay close attention to this chapter.

Let me start this chapter by being totally honest with you and confessing that budgeting is not my strong suit. The more complicated and detail-oriented the budgeting process, the more I dislike it and the less I'm apt to do it. Knowing my philosophy, you'd probably guess that we're going to keep this section as simple as possible—and you'd be correct.

My grandma always told me the road to hell is paved with good intentions. While I didn't have a clue what she was talking about then, now I get the picture. I bet every one of you reading this book had very good intentions at one time about adding to your 401(k), putting money aside monthly, and generally becoming more disciplined with your finances. In real life, we find that our car breaks down, our homeowner's insurance comes due, or the kids need braces. After years in this business, I'm convinced that we generally adjust our spending levels commensurate with our income levels. All of a sudden we discover that, even if we're making decent money and should have extra dollars, we have no idea where it goes.

What You Have

Assets

Asset is anything that you own.

A good starting point to get a picture of our financial life is to see what we currently have. This does not have to involve a complicated spreadsheet and vast calculations. I believe you can do a very simple chart to begin to get a handle on this. Initially take a look at what your assets are.

Cash	_____
Savings Accounts	_____
Money Markets	_____
Certificates of Deposit (CDs)	_____
Government Securities (Savings Bonds, T-Bills)	_____
Bonds	_____
Stock	_____
Mutual Funds	_____
IRAs	_____
401(k) and Other Retirement Assets	_____
Personal Property (Jewelry, furniture, etc.)	_____
Antiques/Art	_____
Vehicles	_____
Real Estate	_____
Life Insurance	_____
Other	_____
Total Assets	_____

Liability is
what you owe.

Liabilities

After you've taken a close look at your assets, now turn to the thing we don't like as much.

Mortgage/Rent	_____
Car Payment	_____
Credit Cards	_____
Personal Loans	_____
Student Loans	_____
Taxes Owed	_____
Short-Term Liabilities	_____
(Bills currently due)	
Total Liabilities	_____

Net Worth is
assets less
liabilities.

Net Worth

After you've listed your assets and your liabilities, you need to subtract your liabilities from your assets. What remains is your net worth. Don't be despondent if the liabilities are significantly greater than the assets. Use it as a strong indication that you need to do something to control your financial life.

Buys Briefs

Question: When accounting for life insurance, do I use the cash value or the death benefit amount? **Answer:** Cash surrender value. The cash surrender value in the policy is the money available to you. The death benefit of the policy is what will be paid to your beneficiaries upon your death.

Cash Flow

Now that you have this snapshot of your financial situation, let's take a look at where we find most of our problems—cash flow. The idea here is not to achieve a balance, for the cash to flow out in the same amount as it flows in. With any luck at all, we'll be able to take a look at what is going on and have money at the end of the month to get you on the road to savings and investing. While you'll be able to find many complicated charts on calculating cash flow, I've tried to come up with something that's a little more user-friendly.

Income

Cash Flow is the difference between the money you have coming in and the money you have going out.

Let's start by taking a look at your monthly income from all sources.

Salary	_____
Alimony	_____
Rental Income	_____
Dividends/Income	_____
Other Income Sources	_____
Total Monthly Income	_____

Outflow

Outflow is debt payment plus expenses.

Next, let's take a look at what you have going out. You can do this by running through some of the following examples and filling in the blanks.

Mortgage/Rent	_____
Clothing	_____
Entertainment	_____
Travel	_____
Food	_____
Utilities, Phone, Cable TV	_____
Insurance Premiums	_____
Transportation	_____
Car Payment	_____
Daycare	_____
Medical/Dental	_____
Credit Card Payments	_____
Automobile Expenses	_____
Household Expenses	_____
Professional/Membership Fees	_____
Charitable Contributions	_____
Miscellaneous	_____
(dry cleaning, books and magazines, coffee breaks, etc.)	
Total Outflow	_____

You don't need an M.B.A. to understand that if your outflow is greater than your income you're in a world of hurt and you need to make some changes very quickly. Those changes can only come in two forms: you either *increase your income* **or** *decrease your spending.* If you make a sizable income and you have an equally sizable outflow, you also need to reexamine your spending habits. An important item we haven't even taken into account with your monthly expenses is an allowance for investing or saving.

If you're having trouble coming up with a realistic cash flow analysis, you might find it useful to go through your checkbook for the last three to six months and use that to chart your spending. Don't forget to also track cash advances from the ATM. Most people are shocked by the results of the checkbook review and use the information as a good starting point to target which expenses can be reduced. How many times do you eat out in a month? Did you visit the mall more times than you fed the dog last month? If you answered yes, that is a very bad sign for your finances—and your dog! Make sure you know the difference between needs and wants.

Your Own Financial Roadmap

I always stress the importance of *paying yourself first.* We religiously pay mortgages, car payments, and other expenses that we know we cannot avoid. If we don't put savings or investment as a monthly line item,

Buys Briefs

A **Systematic Investment Program**, also sometimes known as a Direct Investment Plan, is one that allows you to have a fixed dollar amount debited from your checking/savings account and invested directly into the stock or mutual fund of your choice. Amounts and frequencies vary by the rules of the company you're investing in.

we very often never see it happen. Pay yourself the day you get paid. Many people ask, "How much should I save?" While it may sound flip, the answer is "As much as you can." A good rule of thumb would be to earmark 10% of your gross income and be disciplined about saving. Remember: this percentage is for savings over and above any contribution you make to a retirement plan.

I don't want to be phony here, because I truly do hate a lot of tedious budgeting. But I will tell you that I believe in the importance of paying myself first so much that I participate in a systematic investment program where a certain amount is withdrawn from my checking account monthly. This is an excellent way to force you to pay yourself first and makes certain that investing is a part of your budget.

I do not believe in being investment poor and I am not urging you to a live a life of total austerity or be a slave to your investments. No one is more devoted to enjoying life than I am. I enjoy traveling, own my own boat, and love sales. On the other hand, I certainly don't want to outlive my retirement assets and I realize I must do something to ensure that doesn't happen. The moral of the story is that you need to strike a balance that will work for you. For most of us, that means spending less and saving more.

Don't Just Charge It!

One area that I frequently see that keeps us from being able to save is credit card debt. For whatever reason, people just don't understand how crippling this debt is, both now and in your financial future. We live in an age of immediate gratification, but it's extremely difficult to move ahead if you're paying 18½% interest on your credit card balance and pay only the minimum amount due. These cards should really be thought of as *convenience cards*—not *credit* cards. A credit card becomes a *convenience* card when you use it simply because it's convenient and you're able to pay the balance when you receive the bill. It becomes a *credit* card when you use it because you don't have the money to pay for a purchase and don't pay your total balances monthly.

You must set spending limits for yourself and those limits should be determined by your ability to pay that bill each month. It's very difficult to begin setting money aside if you have a large credit card debt on your back. Just think: you would need to have a return of 18½% on your investments just to *break even* with the cost of your credit card. If you currently have a sizable balance, at least shop for the credit card with the lowest interest rates. Make a vow to yourself not to add to the balance and make paying off this debt a top priority in your financial life. Many financial experts feel that it's a good idea to keep consumer debt payments less than 20% of your take-home pay.

Buys Briefs
Many major newspapers list the lowest credit card rates available on a weekly or monthly basis.

What You Need

An excellent way to build your investments is to take the money you have been using to pay off your car, credit cards, etc., and apply it to your investment account after you've paid off the debt. By doing this, you'll have a relatively painless way of converting debt dollars that you're accustomed to spending into investment or savings dollars.

Commonly financial goals fall into three major categories. These don't necessarily correspond to life stages, but are rather individualized and can overlap. For example, at the same time that we may be focusing on a short-term goal of saving for a car, we may very well be participating in our retirement plans, which may be longer-term, depending on your age.

Short-Term Goals

The first of these three categories of financial goals is short-term goals. These involve buying decisions that you anticipate making within the next few years. They may include buying a new car, purchasing a home, going on a major vacation, or remodeling your home.

These are perhaps the easiest goals to target. We can come up with a fairly specific dollar amount for the items we know we need and, by calculating the time to when we wish to make our purchase, we can determine what our monthly savings goal should be to accumulate the dollars needed by the target date.

> **Buys Briefs**
> Swapping a paid-off debt for savings is easy. If your monthly car payment is $329, when you've made the final payment, continue to write a check for $329 to savings or investments. That's another great way to pay yourself.

Intermediate Goals

The second category of goal is intermediate. These would be expenses that you might expect to incur over the next 5 to 15 years. Included may be college education for your children, buying a vacation home, starting a business, or buying a boat or recreational vehicle.

These goals are a little harder to target, because we view them as being well into the future so we have difficulty forecasting the amount of money we will need.

College Funding

For most of us, a priority is planning for our child's college education, so let's examine that goal in greater detail. As with all of our financial goals, the sooner you start the better off you are. An initial step in the process is to estimate the cost of your child's education. To help, I've included Table 2-1 on page 14. To use it, look at the table, and find the box showing your child's age and then find the years until he or she will enter college. Then check the next two columns to see the estimated costs for a four-year college education at public and private colleges.

Now that you have a rough idea of what the bill will be, you can go to the next step, which is estimating how much you'll need to invest to meet that goal. Table 2-2 on page 15 provides guidance on the amount that you need to invest monthly to accumulate enough to pay for your children's education. This information assumes a 7% fixed return on your investment.

Let's run through an example. If your child is 5 years old and you estimate college costs will approach $75,000.00, you would have to start making monthly investments of $296.06 now to accumulate that amount. Again, the chart reinforces the need to start early.

Long-Term Goals

The third category of goals, long-term goals are usually associated with retirement or something many years in the future. With a long-term goal comes many associated goals. For example, when we think of retirement, other planning issues are triggered, such as buying a second home, relocating, traveling, health care and life insurance needs, and frequently estate planning.

As I meet with individuals or speak with groups, this goal is becoming more immediate, because many people are planning for an early retirement. Add that to our increasing life span and the need for financial planning for retirement as early as possible becomes even more compelling. Studies show that our single greatest financial fear is outliving our retirement assets. Because of the importance of retirement planning, I intend to devote an entire chapter to it, so keep reading.

If your child is now age:	He or she will enter college in:	Public college (four years)	Private college (four years)
15	3 years	$40,513	$98,488
14	4 years	42,539	103,412
13	5 years	44,666	108,583
12	6 years	46,899	114,012
11	7 years	49,244	119,712
10	8 years	51,706	125,698
9	9 years	54,291	131,983
8	10 years	57,006	138,582
7	11 years	59,856	145,511
6	12 years	62,849	152,787
5	13 years	65,992	160,426
4	14 years	69,291	168,447
3	15 years	72,756	176,870
2	16 years	76,393	185,713
1	17 years	80,213	194,999
Under 1	18 years	84,224	204,749

Table 2-1. Projected costs of college education, based on a 5% average annual rate of inflation applied to average annual total expenses, reported by the College Board for the 1996-97 school year, of $7,733 for a four-year public college and $18,799 for a four-year private college. © Franklin Templeton. Used with permission.

Conclusion

Now that you've taken the time to assess your money habits through looking at budgeting, don't stop here. Many people have the tendency to give up and allow themselves to feel overwhelmed. DON'T FALL INTO THIS TRAP. It's crucial that you use this information to begin spending and saving more wisely. Set a goal, make a pact with a friend—do whatever it takes to make sure you're on the plus side at month's end and not the negative. It takes money to make money, yes, but it doesn't have to be a lot.

Monthly investment required to accumulate these amounts by age 18*

		$25,000	$35,000	$50,000	$75,000	$100,000	$125,000	$150,000	$175,000	$200,000	$225,000
	1	64.08	89.71	128.16	192.25	256.33	320.41	384.49	448.57	512.65	576.74
	2	70.97	99.36	141.94	212.91	283.87	354.84	425.81	496.78	567.75	638.72
	3	78.87	110.42	157.75	236.62	315.49	394.37	473.24	552.12	630.99	709.86
	4	88.02	123.22	176.03	264.05	352.07	440.08	528.10	616.12	704.13	792.15
	5	98.69	138.16	197.37	296.06	394.74	493.43	592.11	690.80	789.48	888.17
	6	111.26	155.77	222.52	333.79	445.05	556.31	667.57	778.83	890.10	1001.36
	7	126.27	176.78	252.54	378.81	505.08	631.35	757.62	883.88	1010.15	1136.42
Age of child now	8	144.44	202.21	288.88	433.31	577.75	722.19	866.63	1011.07	1155.50	1299.94
	9	166.82	233.55	333.65	500.47	667.29	834.12	1000.94	1167.77	1334.59	1501.41
	10	195.01	273.01	390.02	585.03	780.04	975.05	1170.06	1365.07	1560.08	1755.09
	11	231.48	324.08	462.97	694.45	925.93	1157.42	1338.90	1620.39	1851.87	2083.35
	12	280.39	392.55	560.78	841.18	1121.57	1401.96	1682.35	1962.74	2243.13	2523.53
	13	349.20	488.88	598.39	1047.59	1396.79	1745.98	2095.18	2444.38	2793.57	3142.77
	14	452.82	633.95	905.65	1358.47	1811.29	2264.11	2716.94	3169.76	3622.58	4075.41
	15	626.09	876.53	1252.19	1878.28	2504.38	3130.47	3756.56	4382.66	5008.75	5634.85

*Dollar cost averaging does not ensure a profit and does not protect against loss in a declining market. As an investor, you should also consider your ability to continue purchasing through periods of low price levels or changing economic conditions. Based on a fixed 7% interest rate, compounded monthly, and assuming no fluctuation in value of principal. The figures are not intended to be a projection of any investment results. No adjustment has been made for income taxes. Used with permission from Franklin Templeton Funds.

Table 2-2. Saving for college expenses.

Once you're on the "straight and narrow" and you've accumulated some money, you'll be able to apply the concepts I'm going to lay out for you in the following chapters. Sharpen your pencil, work out your budget, and alter your spending so that your money can work for you as hard as you work for your money.

3 Key Considerations

*B*efore we move forward and discuss conservative, moderate, and growth investors, there are some concepts that are very important in deciding where you are comfortable placing your assets. Unless we understand some of these considerations, we're apt to make some incorrect investment decisions. For example, you may find you'll change your mind about CDs after we look at the impact of inflation. Probably the two most important issues to consider before you begin any investment decisions are your time horizon and your risk tolerance. Let's take a closer look at these two issues.

Buys Briefs

Risk Tolerance describes your ability to tolerate market volatility. To make this more real, ask yourself how comfortable you'd be if your account value went down 30%. Now put a number on that. If your portfolio is worth $10,000.00 and a market decline reduces the value to $7,000.00, would you be able to tolerate that change?

Time Considerations

Time can be your friend if you have a long time or your enemy if you have a short-time horizon. The longer your time frame, the more aggressive your investments may be because time reduces risk in investing. If you look at the stock market on a year-

16

by-year basis, the rises and falls are enough to make you seasick. Yet if you look at the ups and downs over a 10- or 20-year timeline, the ride is much smoother and you don't need Dramamine.

Market Cycles are the normal up-and-down patterns of the market over a period of time.

Markets commonly move in cycles. Conventional wisdom has it that, if you don't have a 3- to 5-year timeline, you probably should not be in a market-related investment because of the timing of these market cycles. The worst thing you can do is have a short time frame and need to sell when the market is in a downdraft. If you have a longer time to let your money work, you're able to ride out these bumps in the market. So, first and foremost, if you're looking to place some money, remember: if the time is short until you need that money, you may not want to be in a stock-oriented investment.

Compounding is the interest paid on principal plus previously reinvested interest.

Time affects not only your selection of investments, but also their growth. Time works on your money through the process commonly called *compounding*. Essentially what happens is that, as your investment builds interest, that interest is added to your principal. It is then reinvested, so you generate earnings on both your original principal and the added interest. The significance of this over time can be seen in Figure 3-1.

Year	5%	6%	7%	8%	9%	10%	Year
1	1.050	1.060	1.070	1.080	1.090	1.100	1
2	1.102	1.124	1.145	1.166	1.188	1.210	2
3	1.158	1.191	1.225	1.260	1.295	1.331	3
4	1.215	1.262	1.311	1.360	1.412	1.464	4
5	1.276	1.338	1.403	1.469	1.539	1.610	5
6	1.340	1.418	1.501	1.587	1.677	1.772	6
7	1.407	1.504	1.606	1.714	1.828	1.949	7
8	1.477	1.594	1.718	1.851	1.993	2.144	8
9	1.551	1.689	1.838	1.999	2.172	2.358	9
10	1.629	1.791	1.967	2.159	2.367	2.594	10
11	1.710	1.898	2.105	2.332	2.580	2.853	11
12	1.796	2.012	2.252	2.518	2.813	3.138	12
13	1.886	2.133	2.410	2.720	3.066	3.452	13
14	1.980	2.261	2.578	2.937	3.342	3.797	14
15	2.079	2.397	2.759	3.172	3.642	4.177	15

Figure 3-1. Future value of $1 compounded annually

If you invested $1 at 8%, after 10 years that dollar would be worth $2.159. In year one you earn $.08, but by the end of the fifth year your invested dollar has grown to $1.469 through the power of compounding.

The Rule of 72

Another way to look at the relationship of time and money is by using a formula commonly called the *Rule of 72*. If you pick an annual return and divide it into 72, the number will be close to the number of years required for your money to double. So, for example, if your $100 investment is currently providing an annual return of 12%, you can figure out how long it will take to double your money by dividing 72 by 12. So in six years, your $100 will double at a compound annual rate of 12%.

Another way to use the Rule of 72 is in determining the rate of return you need to double your money. Simply divide 72 by the number of years you can invest to get the rate you need to double your money. For example, if you have $12,000 and you need it to double in 10 years, you divide 72 by 10. The answer tells you that you need to get an average annual return of 7.2% to double your $12,000 in 10 years.

You don't have to be a mathematical genius or an investment guru to see that the easiest and most effective way to get compounding to work for you is by investing early. The sooner you start investing, the sooner and the bigger the boost you get from the power of compounding. What Figure 3-2 on the next page is really showing us is that there is almost an $82,000 difference in starting your investments of $2,000 at age 22 versus starting your $2,000 investment at age 32. Notice the later you start you lose two ways. You end up contributing more and yet still have less in the end.

Financial Enemies

We've looked at the power of compounding over the years without the influence of our two biggest enemies: **taxes** and **inflation**. To make our scenarios more realistic, we need to take a closer look at these two forces because both take a big bite and substantially reduce your rate of return. Unless your money is in a retirement account or an annuity (which I'll cover later), all your dividends, interest, and capital gains are

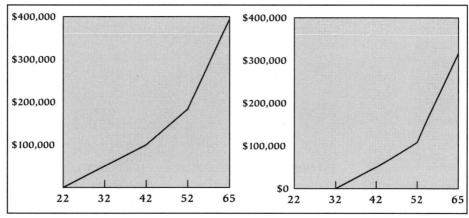

Figure 3-2. The chart on the left shows the results of investing $2000 per year for **10 years** starting at age 22. At age 65 this would yield $396,646. The chart on the right shows the result of investing $2000 per year for **33 years** starting at age 32. At age 65 this would yield $315,253. The difference between investor 1 and investor 2 is **$81,393**.

subject to taxes. A very important rule would be to delay or defer taxes on our investments as long as possible. Later in this book we'll look at some investments that allow you to do this. The longer your money is not taxed, the more of your earnings are free to compound.

> **Buys Briefs**
> A dollar is not always a dollar. If you earn a dollar's worth of interest on your investment and you are in the 28% tax bracket, your full dollar's worth of return won't go to work for you. You'll really be reinvesting only $.72. You can see that the impact of taxes is significant and seriously limits the compounding effect on your money.

Most people who make long-term investments do so with the idea of generating income in retirement. Those investments make more sense (and more dollars!) when they can defer taxes. There are two reasons for this. First, your tax bracket should be lower in retirement than it is while you're working and investing. Second, the longer you defer paying taxes on your interest, rather than paying them year after year, the more substantial the amount of capital will be that you will accumulate.

Let's take three scenarios. In each case, $2,000 is invested annually at an 8% annual compound rate of return for a 30-year period. Figure 3-3 on the next page shows the dramatic difference between the growth of

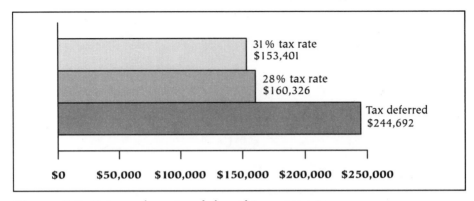

Figure 3-3. Returns from tax deferred investments

money in a taxable account (at two tax rates) and the growth of money in a tax-deferred account. Of course, taxes are due when you start withdrawing your money from a tax-deferred account, but your investments have grown much larger and your tax rate in retirement will be lower.

We'll say more about tax-deferred investments and the new IRA alternatives in our chapter on retirement. But for now remember: you want to do all you can to let your money grow tax-deferred.

Inflation

No chapter on the effect of time on money would be complete without talking about inflation. Inflation is the intangible enemy of wealth building. We know we lose money to taxes, but it's harder for most of us to understand the impact of inflation because we don't actually pay money to it. Rather, we lose *purchasing power* to it.

Inflation is an overall increase in the cost of living.

When we hear about inflation, we think that it's some economic principle that is hard to understand and doesn't really impact our daily lives. We are very mistaken in that belief.

Take a postage stamp, for example. It cost 8 cents 25 years ago; today that same postage stamp costs 32 cents—four times as much—and it's highly likely that price will go up in the near future. Do you get any more today for your 32 cents than you did for 8 cents 25 years ago? No, your letter still gets there in the same time frame as it used to, or longer. The difference in price is inflation. The postage stamp is not an isolated example. Think about the cost of housing, food, clothing, entertainment,

How Do I Know My Tax Bracket?
Use the following chart to figure out your tax bracket.

Federal Income Tax Rates
Tax Years Beginning in 1998

Married Filing Jointly

Taxable Income Over	To	Tax Equals	Plus %	Of Excess Over
0	42,350	0	15	0
42,350	102,300	6,352.50	28	42,350
102,300	155,950	23,138.50	31	102,300
155,950	278,450	39,770.00	36	155,950
278,450	—	83,870.00	39.6	278,450

The amount allowable as a deduction for personal exemptions is reduced by 2% for each $2,500 (or fraction of that amount) by which the taxpayer's adjusted gross income exceeds $186,800.

Single

Taxable Income Over	To	Tax Equals	Plus %	Of Excess Over
0	25,350	0	15	0
25,350	61,400	3,802.50	28	25,350
61,400	128,100	13,896.50	31	61,400
128,100	278,450	34,573.50	36	128,100
278,450	—	88,699.50	39.6	278,450

The amount allowable as a deduction for personal exemptions is reduced by 2% for each $2,500 (or fraction of that amount) by which the taxpayer's adjusted gross income exceeds $124,500.

cars, and almost anything else you purchase. A few more examples to show the power of inflation over the past 25 years. A Cadillac Sedan de Ville cost $6,500; now the cost is closer to $39,000. A Super Bowl ticket that cost $15 was up to $275 in 1998 (and worth every penny of it, since my team is the Denver Broncos).

Inflation isn't the problem today that it was during the late '70s and early '80s. But even a 3% inflation rate over time will make a considerable dent in your investment return. If you're currently living on $50,000 a year and inflation continues at 3%, 25 years from now you would need $90,500 to maintain your purchasing power.

For the past 50 years, inflation has averaged close to 4% a year. That sounds harmless enough, doesn't it? To put that into perspective, how-

Real Rate of Return is the percentage return remaining after subtracting taxes and inflation.

ever, during that same time period the purchasing power of $100 has fallen 86% to $14.50. This leads me to a very important concept called your real rate of return and allows us to look at the impact of inflation on investments.

Essentially the real rate of return is determined by subtracting the inflation rate from the gross return on your investment. If you have a Certificate of Deposit (CD) that earned 6% and inflation is 3%, your real rate of return is 3%. That doesn't sound nearly as good as the original 6%, does it? Remember: that's when we take only inflation into account. Let's take an example and look at the impact of both taxes and inflation.

Certificate of Deposit (CD) is a fixed income investment that pays a fixed rate of return over a specified period of time, insured by the Federal Deposit Insurance Corporation up to $100,000.

$1000 CD at 6% return
$1000 x 6% = $60.00
minus 28% taxes ($60 x 28% = $16.80) = $43.20
minus 3% inflation ($60 x 03% = $1.80) = $41.40

In this example, you've lost almost a third of your investment return after we calculate just federal tax and inflation. Your 6% return has become little more than a 4% return. Is this an important consideration over the long haul? You better believe it! Let's take a look at what taxes and inflation have done to CD rates over the last 10 years as shown in Figure 3-4.

Year	Six-Month CD Rate	Less Top Federal Tax Rate	Less Inflation	Real Return After Taxes and Inflation
1988	7.99	28.0	4.42	1.33
1989	8.11	28.0	4.65	1.19
1990	7.70	28.0	6.11	-0.57
1991	4.89	31.0	3.06	0.31
1992	3.24	31.0	2.90	-0.66
1993	2.86	39.6	2.75	-1.02
1994	5.40	39.6	2.67	0.59
1995	5.21	39.6	2.54	0.61
1996	5.21	39.6	3.32	-0.17
1997	5.71	39.6	1.83	1.62

Figure 3-4. A closer look at CD return rates

Now that you're aware of the perils of taxes and inflation, let's think about what all these concepts mean in our real world of investing. Your two major goals are to figure how to outsmart these two enemies. That means we've got to try our best to defer taxes and to outperform inflation so that we can come up with attractive real rates of return.

Buys Briefs

How much money should I have in savings? Experts recommend that you have anywhere from three to six months of your gross income in savings. I believe there's no cookie cutter answer. If you're a single mother with no outside sources of income and your job skills are not highly transferable, you should have a substantial amount of money liquid (up to 6 months). Conversely, if you're a young, single professional with transferable job skills, you need considerably less. In my experience, as women build assets they tend to have too much rather than too little in savings. Review your own situation.

As women, most of us tend to be conservative by nature and in love with the investments that are hit the hardest by inflation. If you've invested in a CD at 4% and inflation goes to 5%, can your CD keep up with inflation? Absolutely not. I will go so far as to say that if you keep all your money in savings accounts and CDs, it will be next to impossible for you to meet your long-term financial goals. Don't misunderstand me: savings accounts, money markets, and CDs can be a wonderful place to put money that you will need over the short-term or that you are saving for emergency situations. But they are not the place to put assets that you hope will build wealth. As we look at risk, you'll see that your money may not be nearly as "safe" in these investments as you thought.

Standard & Poor's 500 measures the aggregate value of 500 widely held common stocks. It consists of 400 industrial, 40 financial, and 60 transportation and utility stocks.

What do you think was the one investment category that consistently outpaced inflation over the last 20 years? If you guessed CDs, shame all over your body. The answer, of course, is stocks as shown in Figure 3-4 on page 24. Over the long haul, stocks have regularly provided double-digit returns. If you're looking to make long-term investments, you must have some of your assets in growth-oriented investments.

As you can see, over both 10- and 20-year timelines, stocks have significantly outpaced inflation. Subtract the rate of inflation from the return of the S&P 500 and notice what a nice piece of change you have left. Remember the importance of that real rate of return. Understand that what we're looking at here is the *average* annual return. (Averages can be deceptive. You can drown in a lake with an average depth of three feet if you happen to tumble into the part that is 20 feet deep.)

20-Year Historical Investment Returns

Year	S&P 500	Foreign Stocks	Long-Term Bonds	Treasury Bills	Inflation Rate
1978	6.4	28.9	1.2	9.4	9.0
1979	18.2	1.8	2.3	12.6	13.3
1980	32.3	19.0	3.1	16.4	12.5
1981	-5.0	-4.9	7.3	11.3	8.9
1982	21.9	-0.87	31.1	8.2	3.8
1983	22.4	20.9	8.0	9.3	3.8
1984	6.1	5.0	15.0	8.3	4.0
1985	31.1	53.6	21.3	7.3	3.8
1986	18.6	66.89	15.6	5.7	1.1
1987	5.1	23.2	2.3	5.9	4.4
1988	16.8	27.3	7.6	8.4	4.4
1989	31.4	9.2	14.2	7.9	4.7
1990	-3.3	-24.7	8.3	7.0	6.1
1991	15.97	12.5	12.79	5.85	3.7
1992	7.6	-11.85	8.53	3.44	3.1
1993	10.1	32.94	12.16	2.99	2.73
1994	1.29	8.06	1.34	5.02	2.81
1995	37.53	11.55	20.98	5.63	2.54
1996	22.92	6.05	3.28	5.25	3.25
1997	33.36	1.78	9.76	5.27	2.2

Past performance is no guarantee of future results

20-Year Average Return

	S&P 500	Foreign Stocks	Long-Term Bonds	Treasury Bills	Inflation Rate
	16.54	14.31	10.31	7.56	5.00

10-Year Average Return

	S&P 500	Foreign Stocks	Long-Term Bonds	Treasury Bills	Inflation Rate
	17.37	7.28	9.9	5.68	3.55

S&P 500 (Standard & Poor's) is a widely recognized unmanaged index of 500 publicly traded stocks that includes reinvestment of dividends.

Foreign stocks–Along with the special risks of international investing, such as currency fluctuations, the fund presents the added risks of political uncertainty and emerging market volatility.

Bond funds–Investors should be aware that the funds' share price generally moves in the opposite direction as interest rates. As interest rates rise, the share price will go down; the reverse is also true.

Treasury bills–Investors should be aware that the price of Treasuries usually moves in the opposite direction as interest rates. As interest rates rise, prices will go down; the reverse is also true.

Data are derived from Standard & Poor's 500-stock index, the Morgan Stanley, Europe, Australia, Far East stock market index (EAFE), the Lehman Brothers Government/Corporate Bond Index, Yields for 91-day Treasury Bills, Chase Investment Performance Digest, and Chase Global Data & Research.

The above figures have been obtained from sources believed reliable but are not necessarily complete and cannot be guaranteed. Errors and omissions excepted.

Figure 3-4. A comparison of returns on various types of investments

Unfortunately, the stock market isn't going to give you a nice, predictable return year in and year out. Some years you'll see positive returns; other years you may see negative returns. What's the magic formula that helps you deal with this and do well in the market? Plain and simple: it's long-term investing. Earlier in this chapter, we discussed the need to have a longer timeline for money that will be in a market-related investment (stocks or stock mutual funds). Remember how we saw that the longer your holding period, the less the effects of volatility.

Buys Briefs

Volatility is the characteristic of a security or market to rise or fall sharply in price within a short period of time.
Principal Loss is the decrease in value of the basic amount you initially invested.

As you start to digest these numbers and understand the importance of real rate of return, you start to see that the investment you thought was "safe" is not so safe from the effects of inflation. Yes, it is safe in terms of principal loss, but remember that inflation is chomping away at the returns on your investment.

Now that we've talked about the risk of the inflation rate, let's examine some of the other types of risks you face in the wonderful world of investments.

Types of Risk

I tell my classes very frequently that, before the session is over, they will come to understand that the greatest risk is not in investing but rather in *not* investing. I think you'll agree with this by the time you finish this book, so hang in there and you'll be a believer.

Risk of Principal Loss

Probably the greatest fear for most investors is the risk of loss of principal. Let's be perfectly clear about this: yes, the market goes up and down, and if you liquidate when the market is down, you may suffer loss of principal. A common mistake many people make when assessing loss is confusing market *fluctuation* with actual principal loss. One of the best ways to safeguard against loss of principal is through diversification. Many experts believe that asset allocation is the greatest key to risk management. Because of the importance of this concept, I've devoted an entire chapter to asset allocation.

Market Risk

The next kind of risk I want to look at is changes in market value. As the market fluctuates, so too does the account value you see on the statements you receive on your investments. If you have an account with a current value of $23,000 and then your next quarterly statement shows the value of your account as now $20,000, have you lost $3,000 during that quarter? Many people would say, "Yes, I have," but I would say, "No, you haven't. What you have seen is a market fluctuation in the value of your account. But remember: you don't realize a loss or gain until you sell your holding." If you liquidate your account when the value is down $3,000, then yes, you've lost $3,000, because you've taken action to "realize" that loss—you've made it real.

> **Buys Briefs**
>
> Remember that your statement reflects a snapshot of one day. If the closing date on your monthly statement is the 25th and the market goes down 400 points that day, your statement will reflect that decline. What you must bear in mind is that the next day, the 26th, the market may have recouped all the decline plus some. By the time you get your statement in the mail, it's highly unlikely that your account value would have changed.

Don't confuse market fluctuation with loss of principal. Think of it in the same way that you view equity in your home. If you see in a multi-list book that a home like yours has been listed for $20,000 more than you thought it was worth, does this mean that you've gained $20,000? Just as with stocks, gyrations in the real estate market don't mean anything until you buy or sell. If you keep this rule in mind, you'll be able to stick to your long-term strategy.

Interest Rate Risk

If you're a fixed income investor, another common type of risk is interest rate risk, sometimes called reinvestment risk. There are two ways that this risk may impact your portfolio.

The first is that when your bond or CD matures, interest rates may have fallen so that you're unable to obtain the higher level interest rate that you may have had up to this point. For example, if you held a 3-year CD at 6% and interest rates came down during that time, you may find that you're only able to renew your CD at 4%. If you renew at the current

4% rate, this significantly reduces the amount of return you'll receive.

The other type of impact could be on the current market value of any bonds in your portfolio. Next we're going to have a quick lesson on how the bond market works.

Most investors buy bonds for their income stream or for purposes of asset allocation and don't think much about them until they mature. If you hold a bond with a 20-year maturity, you'll receive the full face value of your bond when it matures, barring any disasters. It's important to know, however, that bonds are "liquid" investments. That means that you do not need to hold them until their maturity date. You can sell them any time prior to the maturity date at market value. We'll cover how this is determined in the chapter on bonds.

Credit Risk

This type of risk is associated with bonds. Credit risk means that you assume greater risk as you buy bonds with lower credit ratings. Remember: bonds are frequently rated. Two of the big independent rating services are Standard & Poor's and Moody's. I'll be talking a lot more about both of these later in Chapter 5.

> ### Buys Briefs
> **Fixed Income Investments** include bonds, certificates of deposit (CDs), and other instruments with fixed returns.
> **Mature** means to reach the predetermined date upon which you are owed the principal amount of your investment.
> **Current Market Value** is what your investment would be worth if you sold it now.
> **Liquid Investment** is an asset you can easily convert to cash without penalty.

We've seen that time can be either your friend or your enemy and we've identified our two biggest foes, taxes and inflation. From this point forward, our goal will be to minimize the effect of taxes and to outperform inflation in our investments. The most important calculation we make when evaluating performance is our real rate of return.

I've identified for you some of the types of risk we face when making investment choices. I hope by now it's obvious that losing principal isn't the only dragon out there we need to consider.

The information we've covered in this chapter will serve you well as we proceed. Armed with the knowledge you now possess, let's analyze some of the major investment categories, beginning with stocks.

4 Building Blocks: Stocks

At the most basic level, a stock represents an ownership interest in a business. As we discussed earlier, individual stocks and mutual funds have been the one investment category that significantly outperforms taxes and inflation over time. The moral of the story is that, like it or not, we'd better learn about stocks. Frequently when I make this point in class, people look back at me with fright in their eyes and I can see them envisioning a terrifying roller coaster ride.

You'll soon see that stocks are not all the same. You can pick from many different types so that you're buying stocks that are in line with your comfort level and investment goals.

When you buy the stock of any company, you own part of that business, so you have "equity" in the business just as you have equity in your home. For that reason, you frequently hear the stock market referred to as the *equity market* and stocks referred to as *equities*. As a shareholder, if

Buys Briefs

A **Mutual Fund** is an investment pool in which many people who have similar investment objectives entrust their money to professional money managers who invest it in securities such as stocks, bonds, or money markets. Each shareholder owns a proportionate share of the fund and each share represents ownership in all of the fund's underlying securities.

A **Proxy** is a written power of attorney authorizing another person to speak or act for the stockholder on her or his behalf at corporate meetings.

the business prospers, so do you. If the business falters, so do you. As an owner, your fortunes rise and fall with the success of "your business."

The more shares you own, the greater your interest in the business. Typically for each share of common stock you own you're entitled to one vote. These votes are usually cast at the annual meeting. Because many people can't actually attend these meetings, you may send a proxy, which allows you to vote by mail. Stockholders can vote on items ranging from hiring a new accounting firm to electing members to serve on the board of directors. Huge corporations have millions of shares on the market, so it's highly unlikely that you would have enough money to buy the number of shares that would be required to have controlling interest in McDonald's, for instance.

Classifications of Stock

There are literally thousands and thousands of stocks available for us to buy. Many of these stocks behave very differently from each other. You wouldn't expect the stock of Planet Hollywood to behave the same as that of a corporate giant like Ford Motor Company. Different types of stock have different levels of risks and rewards associated with them; what you buy should depend on your personal investment goals and risk tolerance.

A **Dividend** is a distribution of earnings to shareholders, paid in the form of money or stock. The amount is decided by the board of directors and is usually paid quarterly.

Stocks of newer, smaller companies are considered to be growth or aggressive growth. These companies typically don't pay dividends, may or may not have products currently available in the marketplace, and may very well not have any current earnings. These are stocks you're buying for their future potential. You've looked at the companies, liked what's in their product pipeline, think they have a good chance at success, and are willing to assume greater risk to reap greater rewards down the road. You hope you've located the next Microsoft or Intel! As you've probably guessed, many of these are risky because you have no assurance of success. If you understand that risk and you're willing to go with it, then these stocks are for you. If you are a Nervous Nellie and go into cardiac arrest with market volatility, you better be saying goodbye to this category.

International Stocks

One of the earliest studies conducted regarding asset allocation, which I'll discuss in detail in Chapter 8, clearly demonstrated the importance of adding international stocks to both enhance return and minimize risk. There are many ways for you to participate in this arena. One of the most prominent ways is to purchase foreign stocks on American exchanges by use of ADRs. These allow you to purchase some of the largest companies throughout the world as easily as you might purchase IBM. The investment opportunities that lie outside the U.S. are too attractive to ignore. I want you to take the following quiz and see how well you do. You may be surprised at some of the answers.

Buys Briefs

What is an ADR? An American Depositary Receipt (ADR) is a certificate that represents the ownership of foreign shares that are usually held abroad by a big U.S. bank with foreign operations. These ADRs are traded on the New York Stock Exchange. These usually represent big companies such as Toyota or Nestle.

Test Your Global Investing I.Q.

1. How much of the world's investment opportunities are outside the U.S.?
   A. One-third
   B. One-half
   C. Two-thirds

2. How many of the world's largest 100 companies are not American-owned (as of the end of 1996)?
   A. Fewer than 50
   B. 50 to 75
   C. More than 75

3. Identify which of these products or brand names is foreign-owned:
   A. Baskin Robbins
   B. Lean Cuisine
   C. Panasonic
   D. All of the above

4. Foreign investing involves greater political, economic, and currency risks than investing in the U.S.
   True
   False

5. Adding foreign securities to a U.S. portfolio can potentially:
   A. Increase risk
   B. Reduce risk
   C. Improve returns
   D. Both B and C

6. How many times has the U.S. stock market ranked number one among the world's top performing markets over the past 15 years (through 1996)?
   A. 0
   B. 3
   C. 5

7. A global mutual fund contains:
   A. U.S. securities as well as foreign securities
   B. A broad spectrum of non-U.S. securities
   C. A greater number of securities than any other type of fund

8. Investing your retirement savings in something as risky as foreign securities is unwise.
   True
   False

9. How much of your portfolio should you invest overseas?
   A. Less than 5%
   B. 5% to 15%
   C. 20% to 40%

Answers:

1. **C** Approximately two-thirds of the world's securities are traded on stock exchanges outside the U.S. (Source: Morgan Stanley Capital International.)

2. **B** 60 of the world's largest 100 companies (in market capitalization) are located outside the U.S., as of December 31, 1996.

3. **D** Baskin Robbins – Allied Lyons (England), Lean Cuisine – Nestle (Switzerland), Panasonic – Matsushita (Japan).

4. **True** International investing can pose greater risks, as well as rewards, compared with U.S. investments. These include, for instance, risks relating to fluctuations in the value of the U.S. dollar relative to the value of other currencies, the custody arrangements made for the funds' foreign holdings, differences in accounting, political risks, and the lesser degree of public information required to be provided by non-U.S. companies.

5. **D** Over the past ten years ending December 31, 1996, a portfolio with 70% in U.S. equities and 30% in overseas stocks would have earned higher returns with lower risk than a portfolio invested only within the U.S. (Source: Morgan Stanley Capital International.) The reason: not all markets move in the same direction, so poor performance in one market can be offset by better performance in another market.

6. **A** The U.S. stock market never ranked #1 among foreign stock markets over the past 15 years ending December 31, 1996. It's been in the top five only four times. (Source: Morgan Stanley Capital International.)

7. **A** Global mutual funds include U.S. securities as well as foreign securities. International funds contain no U.S. securities in their portfolio. A third group of funds focuses on a specific region of the world, like the Pacific Rim or Western Europe. These funds are more volatile than international and global funds.

8. **False** It's important to include growth in your retirement investment program to gain the potential to outpace inflation. Foreign stocks have historically been an effective way to add growth to your portfolio. (Source: Morgan Stanley Capital International.)

9. **C** Asset allocation experts recommend that 20% to 40% of your portfolio should be in foreign investments.

(Quiz provided courtesy of the Aim Family of Funds.)

In addition to being able to purchase international stocks through ADRs, you can also buy them in mutual funds, which I'll discuss in greater detail in Chapter 6.

Growth and Income

Growth and Income Stocks are those stocks with potential for appreciation in the price of the stock as well as dividend income.

The average investor is more comfortable with stock that is commonly referred to as growth and income. These companies are generally the backbone of corporate America and are household names that you would tend to recognize very quickly (e.g., Johnson & Johnson, Pepsi, and IBM). You should expect moderate growth as these established companies continue to do well. You can frequently expect these companies to pay you dividends.

Many of the companies that make up the Standard & Poor's 500 (S&P 500) are good examples of growth and income stocks. Just in case some of you are thinking that, because these stocks are more moderate, you can't make much of a return in this category, think again. Take a look again at the chart showing the returns of the S&P 500 over the last 10 years on page 24. I don't think anybody would sneer at an average annual return of over 17%.

Income

Income Stocks are low-volatility stocks that pay high dividends.

There's yet another classification of stock that allows you to be more moderate in your portfolio and still provide you nice returns. These are referred to as income stocks. The first type of stocks we discussed were stocks you buy when growth is your goal. Next were the growth and income stocks. They have some elements of each—appreciation (growth) in the price and a dividend (income). Income stocks are primarily, as the name implies, those that kick off a hefty dividend, which translates to income. You would never expect the price of these to triple in value or plummet over two days as an aggressive growth stock could. These tend to be the more conservative, less volatile stocks.

The best example of this category would be stocks of utilities companies. They typically pay you a nice dividend and you can expect to see appreciation in the stock over a period of time. If you look at a utility index over a long period of time, you will find that utilities do not experience the kind of volatility associated with other stocks. These stocks were formerly called "widow and orphan" stocks because of their more conservative nature. These are not for the get-rich gambler in you because these are primarily income-oriented. Again, don't assume that because these stocks are more conservative you can't experience good

The Dow Jones Utility Average (DJUA) is a price-weighted average of 15 utility companies that are listed on the New York Stock Exchange and are involved in the production of electrical energy.

returns. A chart of the last 10 years of the performance of the Dow Jones Utility Average shows that utilities have enjoyed good price appreciation without a great deal of volatility.

A word of caution: utility stocks can be very sensitive to changes in the interest rate environment. I'll discuss this more later. Historically, rising interest rates haven't been very good news for utility companies, so keep that in mind as interest rates change. Don't lose sight of the idea that utility stocks are most commonly purchased for income, not growth potential.

Preferred Stock

Some investment books actually put this type of stock in the bond section, because in many ways preferred stocks (preferreds) act more like bonds than stock. While preferreds don't have a fixed maturity date, they do pay a fixed dividend. These stocks are purchased when your goal is safety or income more than growth. If the company goes bankrupt, a preferred stock shareholder has a claim on the company's assets prior to those of the common shareholder. (Bond holders are in the claims line ahead of preferred stock holders.) Because of the high dividend yield, preferred stocks don't appreciate nearly as fast as the common stock of the same company. The good news is that they usually don't lose value as fast in a downswing either.

Buys Briefs
How do I calculate the yield on my investment? You divide the amount you receive annually in interest or dividends by the amount you originally invested.

Selecting Stocks

We've just seen that there are lots of different types of stocks. Now let's look at some general considerations when picking your stocks.

P/E Ratio

Many of you may have heard the term price-earnings ratio (P/E) or multiple. This is one of the most commonly used tools when assessing a stock. The P/E ratio is the price of a company's stock divided by its annual earnings. For example, a $80 share of stock in a company that earned

$8 a share in the previous year would have a P/E ratio of 10. Obviously a company without earnings has no P/E. Generally speaking, a high P/E stock carries a higher risk. If the company's earnings don't grow quickly enough to justify its high multiple, the share price can fall quickly.

The higher the P/E, the more investors are paying for a company's earning power and, therefore, the more earnings growth is expected. Low P/E stocks tend to be in low-growth or mature industries. In general, low P/E stocks have higher yields (i.e., pay higher percentage dividends) than high P/E stocks.

> ## Buys Briefs
> **Price-Earnings Ratio (P/E Ratio)** is the price of a company's stock divided by its annual earnings. Also known as a stock's multiple.
>
> A **Bull Market** is when the prices of stocks, bonds, or commodities rise for a long time. A **Bear Market** is when prices decline over a long period.

Is it always a bad sign if the company doesn't have earnings? Not necessarily. As we discussed earlier, stocks of smaller or new companies may take a while to become established and to have an earnings stream. You're betting on future, not present, earnings.

This measure is widely publicized—and frequently misused. The only way this ratio makes sense is by comparing apples to apples. If you're looking at a large utility company, it would not make sense to compare its P/E ratio with that of an Internet stock. When using this tool, bear in mind the type of stock you're purchasing and compare it with the stocks of similar companies.

Sometimes a P/E ratio is used to evaluate the condition of the overall market. A P/E ratio in the range of 13% to 15% is normal during a bull market for the S&P 500. During a bear market, it drops 8% to 10%. Before the crash of '87, the S&P 500 had a P/E ratio of 22, clearly indicating the overpriced state of the market.

Any of you involved in investment clubs know that there are many sources of information. You can get annual reports directly from the company, as well as information and recommended lists from many stock brokerage firms. Many of the financial magazines feature a "sure-fire" list of stocks to buy. All in all, the difficulty isn't in obtaining information but rather in choosing what information to use in making your decisions.

Two of the most widely used and respected sources of information on stocks are Value Line and Standard & Poor's. Both of these are independent rating services that have been around for quite some time. Many people routinely use both in evaluating stocks. Since investment clubs use Value Line, let's take a look at that first.

Value Line

The *Value Line Investment Survey* provides an incredible amount of information on one page. The information includes the current stock price, P/E ratio, and the target price range. The real guts of a Value Line report are the ratings about company timeliness and safety. Timeliness relates to the anticipated relative performance of the stock in the next 12 months. Safety refers to the creditworthiness of the company. Both factors are rated from 1 (highest) to 5 (lowest).

At the bottom of each Value Line page, you'll see what is designed to be a user-friendly report on recent developments and prospects for the company. These reports are typically issued once every three months.

Major libraries have Value Lines available for your use. The book looks like an overgrown phone book and is organized by industry. In the front of the book you'll find a guide that will help you walk through the page in even greater detail. The book is updated with weekly supplements on certain companies. The *Value Line Investment Survey*, like almost all sources of financial information, is also available on the Internet.

Standard & Poor's

This widely used rating service is as famous for its bond ratings as its stock ratings. This report also gives you a variety of information about a company, including earnings, dividends, market action, and price history. The highlight of the Standard & Poor's report is the opinion located near the top of the page. Ratings are reflected by stars, with a five-star being the highest rating carrying a buy recommendation. This reflects Standard & Poor's belief that a five-star stock is expected to be among the best performers over the next 12 months. A one-star stock carries a sell rating and reflects the expectation that it will be well below average in performance and will fall in price. To help you gauge how a stock has performed, it's measured against the S&P 500 Index.

Initial Public Offerings (IPOs)

An **Initial Public Offering** is the first public trading of a company's stock; also known as a new issue.

When a company has progressed to a stage when it needs additional funds to grow, it contacts an investment banking firm. This firm prepares the necessary documents and attempts to determine what investors would be willing to pay for the stock of this company. If the price is agreeable to the company, a prospectus is written and the investment bankers try to drum up interest in the stock. Prior to the stock being sold to the public, the investment banker, usually in concert with other investment bankers, sets the price for the stock and buys the stock directly from the company. The bankers then sell these shares to the investing public. This represents the initial public offering (IPO) of stock from this company.

Many people eagerly snatch up IPOs because the price of these stocks often goes up in the early stages. The price swings are often dramatic, both up and down. These new issues are highly volatile and often represent new companies with unproven product lines. As you've no doubt guessed by now, these stocks can be very aggressive and you do need to do your homework carefully before leaping into IPOs.

Trading Stocks

We've looked at sources of information and some factors to consider when deciding which stocks to buy. Now, let's see how you trade stocks.

You can buy stocks in round lots or odd lots. A round lot is buying stock in multiples of 100 shares. An odd lot represents numbers less than 100. In an ideal world you would buy all of your stocks in round lots, since most firms handle transactions in 100-share multiples. You may even pay a higher price to buy or sell an odd lot, because the normal way of doing business is in 100-share lots. If you own fewer than 100 shares, the company may ask you to either liquidate your small number of shares or buy additional shares to bring your holding up to 100 shares. This is because companies find it expensive to handle the administration for fewer than 100 shares and don't like these small accounts.

Now you're ready to buy your 100 shares of "Buys Boats." What's next? Typically, you would call your financial advisor and ask about the current market price of the stock you're interested in buying. Your advisor may tell you that "Buys Boats" is trading at 15¾ by 16¼. This means that the current market price to buy the stock is 16 ¼ and the current market price to sell is 15¾.

15¾ ($15.75/share): price you would get if you sold "Buys Boats"
16¼ ($16.25/share): price you would pay to buy "Buys Boats"

You're probably wondering what becomes of that $.50 in price difference between these two quotes. That number is frequently called the "spread" and represents profit for the traders. This spread narrows or widens according to the supply and demand for the stock being traded. This figure does not include the commission you'd pay on this transaction.

Buys Briefs

A **Commission** is the fee paid to a broker for executing a trade, based on the dollar amount of the trade and the number of shares traded. Commission charges are not regulated and can vary significantly from firm to firm for the same transaction.

A **Market Order** is an order to buy or sell a security at the best available price at the time the order is entered.

A **Limit Order** is an order to buy or sell a security at a specific price or better.

If you decide "Buys Boats" is an attractive investment at this price, you tell your advisor to go ahead and buy 100 shares. When purchasing at the *market price*, you may end up paying a little more or less than the amount quoted to you because prices can change quickly. This is called a *market order*. Most people buy stock in this manner. The trade is entered immediately and, if the stock is widely traded, you will know within seconds the exact amount of your purchase price.

While buying at the market price is most common, there are other ways to enter trades to buy and sell stock. Suppose you feel "Buys Boats" is overpriced at 16¼ and you want to buy it at 15. You may instruct your advisor to put in an order for you to buy the stock at that price. What your broker would be placing is called a *limit order*. This order may be good for one day only or may be marked "GTC" (good 'til canceled), which is usually good for six months. This trade will fill once the stock hits that 15 price or better.

There are other types of orders that you can instruct your advisor to enter that are more sophisticated and are designed to cover a variety of situations, such as limiting the downside of a loss and locking in profit on the upside. You need to work with your advisor to be certain you're trading stocks in the manner that meets your specific situation.

When you buy or sell your stock through an advisor or broker, you're going to pay a commission. The amount of commission you pay varies from firm to firm, as does the amount of service the firm offers you. We all know you don't get something for nothing. If you're dealing with a full-service firm, you can expect to pay higher commissions than if you're dealing with a low-service trading firm. You'll likely pay considerably less if you trade on the Internet, because the amount of service provided is minimal. Only you can determine which route is best for you. If you would like to have an ongoing relationship with an advisor, mutually working toward meeting your investment goals and want ongoing investment advice, you're better off paying a little more to get this level of service. If, on the other hand, you want to do your own research, know exactly what stock you want to buy and at what price you want to buy or sell it, you're better off going with a cheaper, no-relationship scenario. Sometimes these are called deep-discount brokers.

A general rule with commissions is the larger the number of shares you trade and the higher the price of the shares you're trading, the lower your commission will be as a percentage of your trade. Every time I discuss this in class, my students ask me to repeat this because it sounds confusing. I think the use of a simple example will clarify this point.

Example of Commission Cost from a Full-Service Brokerage Firm

100 shares @ $5/share = $500

$45 commission and trading cost

Total Cost $545

Note that $45 represents 9% of $500

100 shares @ $50/share = $5000

$105 commission and trading cost

Total Cost $5,105

Note that $105 represents just 2% of $5000

As the numbers indicate, it's very expensive to buy or sell a few shares of stock or to trade a very cheap stock. Commissions add to the cost of the transactions and subtract from your profits, so don't trade without a good reason to do so or without considering the costs.

How Stock Is Priced

We all know that the market determines the price of stock; what we don't know is what that really means. With stocks, as with many items, the law of supply and demand determines value. If investors like a company and feel it will have good future earnings, they are active buyers of the stock and the price goes up according to the demand. If, on the other hand, people lose confidence in a company and wish to sell their stock, the fact that there are more sellers than buyers drives the price down. Sometimes the factors that change the price of stock are objective. These include earnings forecasts, market share growth, new product development, pending litigation, etc. Other times the market may react to subjective data, such as selling a particular company stock merely because other companies in the industry are not doing well or overestimating negative news about the company or the economy.

Generally speaking, older companies with a long history and proven products are less likely to be highly volatile than newer companies. Start-up firms may not have the financial assets or product history, so investors are not as confident. They're more willing to dump these companies if the going gets rough. The more you know about a company, the more likely you are to understand price swings in the stock and whether they represent an opportunity to buy or a signal to sell. Later in this chapter, I'll point you in some directions to help you get the information you need about the stocks you're considering purchasing.

Things to Like About Stock

We are euphoric, of course, when our stock doubles in price. But just in case that doesn't happen, there are some other positive aspects to owning stock. Don't neglect the importance of these other factors in adding value to your stocks.

Stock Dividends

Most of us are familiar with interest from our CDs, savings accounts, etc. Instead of paying us interest, stocks of large, well-established, successful companies frequently pay dividends. The board of directors decides whether or not the company will pay a dividend by looking at the money left over after the company has paid all its debts. This dividend paid to the shareholders of the company can be a certain dollar or stock amount. Dividends are a way not only to reward shareholders but also to enhance the value of their stocks, since many people like to buy stock in companies that pay big dividends.

Total Return is the amount of appreciation you get on your investment plus the dividends it pays.

A dividend does not necessarily remain a fixed amount. Boards of directors typically make this decision quarterly and they may go up or down as the fortunes of the company go up or down. Dividends are always paid on a per-share basis to common stockholders. This means that if a company declares a $.06 dividend per share and you own 200 shares, you're entitled to a dividend of $12 for that quarter. If the company has a terrible quarter, there may be no dividend at all. Companies do not suspend or lower a dividend readily because many people would sell that stock if they did so. Lowering a dividend is not a positive sign and suspending a dividend is downright problematic.

Dividends play a very important part in the performance of your portfolio. A commonly used phrase when referring to stocks is "the total return." The total return represents the increase in the value of your share of stock (growth) and the amount of the dividend you receive (income).

People assume that if their stock does not pay a dividend, that's bad news and something must be wrong. That's not necessarily the case. Here's why. Suppose your goal is to get in on the next Microsoft or Intel, so you buy into a company in its early stages of development without a proven track record or financial resources. Your goal when buying into this company is to see the price of your shares go up as the company succeeds. As your company's products hit the market, they start to do decently and begin to show a profit. Would it be reasonable to expect the company to pay you anything from that early profit? Would you even want that? The obvious answer is no. You would want that money to go back into the business for new product development, additional research, or marketing until the company is well-established. With any luck at all, this will allow your stock to go up as the company and its products mature in the market place.

Dividend Reinvestment Plans (DRIPs)

Many brokerage accounts provide a mechanism for you to reinvest your dividends in additional shares of stock. These purchases are made with your quarterly dividend, so you don't know in advance what the purchase price will be or how much stock you'll be buying. Reinvesting dividends is always very important and will contribute significantly to your asset build-up. Dividend reinvestment plans are wonderful ways to painlessly and often inexpensively purchase additional shares with your dividends. It's very important that you keep track of the prices of all of these purchases, just as with other investments, so you'll be able to calculate your capital gain or loss when you decide to sell.

In addition, some companies have a plan that allows you to purchase stock directly from them. You normally have to own at least one share of stock first before you can participate in these plans. The amount of stock you're allowed to purchase varies from company to company, but usually there's a certain maximum in a 12-month period. These are usually inexpensive purchases and can be set up on a systematic investment basis. For example, you may wish to have McDonald's take $250 a month from your checking account to buy its shares.

One problem with these purchases is that you never know what your purchase price will be. Plus, they don't allow you to seize opportunities as they arise. For example, if you're a big fan of AT&T and the stock price drops dramatically on an earnings surprise, you may wish to make a purchase that day. That sudden decision doesn't fit with systematic investment plans or DRIPs. Depending on your investment strategies and knowledge of the market and of the particular company, this drawback may be minor or major.

All in all, DRIPs warrant your attention because of their convenience and because they save you money. You may obtain information by contacting the company directly or researching books on this topic.

Stock Splits

Stock Split is the term used when a company divides each share of its stock into two or more shares.

Most people get very excited about the prospect of a stock split, although they're not exactly sure why. Here's what happens when a stock splits. If you have 100 shares of "Buys Boats" worth $100 per share, your account value is $10,000. If that world-famous company announces a 2-for-1 stock split, you would then have twice as many shares (200) but the same account value ($10,000). For example, 100 shares @ $100 valued at $10,000 after a 2 for 1 split would be 200 shares @ $50 valued at $10,000.

The obvious question is, if the account value is the same, why are we so happy about the stock split? The answer is that it is common for the price of the stock to rise again after the split.

You're probably wondering who decides if a stock split is to occur and why it happens. Remember that earlier in this chapter we said that it's best if you buy stock in round lots (100-share multiples). As stocks get more and more expensive, it becomes difficult for potential investors to come up with the money to buy. To make the stock more attractive to new investors, the board of directors may decide to split the stock so the price will be more affordable. Theoretically, this will attract more buyers and drive the price of the stock to higher levels. This doesn't always happen, of course, but you now understand why a stock split is good news.

The Trend Is Your Friend

This is an expression commonly heard in stock market circles. It means that if the market is going up, it's good news for your portfolio. By and large, individual stocks tend to move up and down with the direction of the market. We've all come to know and love the term "bull market," a period in which stock prices tend to rise. The one we don't like to hear so much is a "bear market," when stocks generally decline. All stock markets experience periods of volatility, when prices go up and down. Some of the volatility may be related to economic conditions, global conditions, political issues, corporate earnings, or not much of anything at all. If the market is looking for an excuse to pull back, that is, if investors generally feel that a decline in stock values is likely, sometimes one small event will be enough to trigger a severe downward motion.

Markets generally move in cycles, advancing over a period of time and then contracting over a period of time. I know that most of you won't believe me, since over the last three years the market has generally expanded and contractions have lasted only a day or two. Believe me when I say that has not been the historical behavior of the markets.

A "routine market decline" is a drop of 5% or more. Since 1900 we've had 322 of these, as of last count, and over time the average length of a decline has been 40 days. It's not uncommon to have several throughout the course of a year.

A "moderate correction" involves a decline of 10% to 15%. There have been over 100 of these, they've lasted on average slightly more than 100 days, and we've averaged one a year.

A "severe decline" involves a market pullback of 15% or more. Since 1900 we've had 50, with the last one quite some time ago. These declines can last several months and the market has historically experienced these about every two years.

The worst stock market event is a bear market, a prolonged period of falling prices in stocks, bonds, or commodities, for a decline of 20% or more. The chart below gives you a little more perspective.

History of Bear Markets

Number of times since 1900	29
Historical frequency	1 per 3 years
Last bear market	October 1990
Average Dow Jones Industrial Average loss	35%
Average duration	364 days

I tell you these numbers not to frighten you but to help you understand that market declines are *natural* occurrences. Over time the positives have outweighed the negatives, so don't let the bumps in the road become the focus of your investment philosophy. Many wise investors welcome these pullbacks, because they offer an opportunity to add to their holdings or start new investments at cheaper prices.

Defensive and Cyclical Stocks

Since we understand that the market moves differently in different economic situations, we now need to look at a couple of classes of stock that respond directly to changes in the business cycle.

Defensive Stocks are stocks that are less susceptible to price drops in changing market conditions.

Defensive Stocks

The first of these is called *defensive stocks*. We call them defensive because they're "well defended" against changes in the economy. What this means in plain English is that these stocks are in products or services that you would buy regardless of interest rates and economic conditions. Once you understand that, all you need to do is ask yourself, what products would you buy no matter what the economy was doing? If the first thing that comes to your mind is food, you go to the head of the class. Beverage stocks frequently move in concert with food stocks, so they too have generally been considered as defensive. Other types of stocks that might belong in this category are drug companies and health care generally. If you're taking prescription medicine, the ability to pay for these pills is high on your priority list.

Another example of a defensive stock is utilities. They are defensive for a couple of reasons. First, utilities frequently pay a nice fat dividend, which investors like. Also, no matter what the economic conditions, people use heat in winter and air conditioning in summer and lights when it's dark. What could be more defensive than that?

Cyclical Stocks

Cyclical Stocks are stocks that tend to rise quickly when the economy turns up and fall quickly when the economy turns down.

The other category of stock we need to know is *cyclical stocks*. The technical reason for this name is that, unlike defensive stocks, cyclical stocks *do* react to changes in the business cycle. An easy way to understand what these are is that they are frequently the opposite of the defensive. A cyclical stock represents a product or service you would delay purchasing in difficult economic times. These are things you don't buy when interest rates are really high or economic conditions are tough (a recession or depression). Cyclical stocks would be investments in the housing industry, heavy equipment, automobiles, the steel industry, appliances, boats, etc. You would hardly go buy a new car if you were worried about losing your job. It's also unlikely you'd buy a new home if mortgage rates were 13%. People tend to delay all these types of purchases until the economy improves, so the stock price suffers with the economy.

What you see with cyclical companies is that their fortunes change dramatically as the economy changes. If you need that new washer and dryer, your need doesn't go away; it just becomes pent-up. When interest rates drop, people go out and make these purchases that they've delayed and the value of the stocks of these companies usually goes up correspondingly.

Managing Expectations

One of my personal single, biggest fears as an investment advisor is that investors have come to expect 20%-plus returns as the norm, with only brief interruptions in the upward motion of the market. If we look at the performance of the market over time, we see that, yes, it has performed very well lately, but we can't expect the abnormally high returns we have seen over the last few years without a market correction. I don't mean to be a prophet of doom. But I wish to make people more realistic in their expectations so they'll be more reasonable in forecasting returns and sticking with their long-term investment objectives when things aren't as rosy. Remember those corrections we discussed earlier. This leads me cleverly to my next topic.

Thinking Long-Term

I can't stress to you how important it is to think long-term. It's probably the single best way to succeed with market-related investments. Earlier, when we looked at inflation, I included a chart that showed you how well stocks have done over time and how they've outperformed other investment categories. While we saw nice hefty average annual returns, it's so important to understand that those returns were an *average*, not a guarantee. The very term average should remind us that some years are higher and some years are lower.

Markets move in up and down cycles. If you don't allow yourself a long enough time horizon, you may find yourself liquidating in a down cycle. If you've made a commitment to market-related investments, remember the three- to five-year time horizon we discussed earlier. There's no question that you'll experience ups and downs as the market goes through its gyrations. But if you can remember the significance of those returns over time and stick with your investment strategy, you'll thank yourself down the road. The huge mistake that investors make is panic selling into a down market. The more informed you are, the less likely you are to make that mistake.

Buying on Sale

In my Investment Basics for Women classes and seminars, I ask the participants how many of them like sales. Rare is the hand that doesn't go up. I myself love sales and tell them that when I see a "sale" sign, I immediately head for the item. My friends kid me that I buy it and then ask, "What is it?" I know it must be good because it's on sale!

Seriously, though, we all like to get a bargain. And when are buys a bargain? Things are on sale when they're priced below what we believe to be their true value. This also is frequently the case with stocks and stock mutual funds. If you have been eyeing a quality stock, believe that the company is well-positioned for future growth, and see the price go down, what then? If you don't see this as a potential buying opportunity, I'll send you back to the beginning of the book.

If you're committed to your long-term horizon and the market goes down and the stock goes on sale, we need to see this as the same type of value that we place on other items as they go on sale. It's interesting that the market is frequently one area in which we refuse to buy on "sale." Instead, we wait until it goes back up and then we'll buy.

Put yourself in this scenario. Suppose that I had called you the night of the crash in 1987 and said, "This is Kathy Buys and I think there are some wonderful values out there. Look at how Disney pulled back and McDonald's looks attractive. How many shares are you interested in buying tomorrow?" What do you honestly think you would have said? You would have been watching television or hearing the radio blaring the news that the market was down 508 points, the largest one-day fall ever. It truly sounded like the end of the civilized world as we know it. Were most of you reaching for the phone to place buy orders? I think not. Consider what would have happened if you would have invested trades at that time. Within six months you'd have looked like a champ and you'd certainly be happy campers today. Let's take this thought a step further.

Recently the markets have been at record highs no matter what index you look at—the Dow, the S&P 500, or the NASDAQ. (We'll discuss these indexes a little later.) This situation tells us that every time historically the market has pulled back, it has gone on to higher highs. Don't misunderstand me: I'm not saying that the market will recover overnight. During the mid–'70s, you needed the patience of a saint to have lasted through the prolonged bear market. The key is to buy quality and stick to your long-term discipline and use pullbacks as opportunities to buy when you feel it's appropriate, not signals to sell. Remember the adage: *don't try to time the market; give the market time.*

So When Do I Sell?

Thinking long-term, buying stocks on sale, and sticking to your investment discipline doesn't mean you have to hold onto any "dogs" in your portfolio. At some point in time, there's no question that you'll come up with the occasional loser and have to do something about it. The hardest thing for most of us is cutting our losses. If we buy a stock at 50 and it goes down to 30, most of us will want to wait until it at least gets back to 50 to get our money back. Guess what? It may never make it and you may be losing out on another opportunity in the meantime.

It's never an easy decision to sell a stock, whether it's up or down. One of the considerations I use when deciding to sell is comparing the stock that is down in price with similar stocks. If you own the stock of a pharmaceutical company, for example, and it's steadily dying while others are rapidly rising, you need to look long and hard at what's going on with the company that you own. If, on the other hand, the whole sector is declining, your stock may not be such a "dog" after all.

As I said, it's difficult to cut your losses and run. It's also difficult to take your gains and run. The single biggest reason for this phenomenon is called *greed*. If your stock has gone from 25 to 50 per share, you're holding a 100% gain. Let's say your target for this stock was 50; now that it has hit 50, you think it will go to 60 and so on and so on and so on. You may find yourself still hanging on for more upside as the stock starts to slip into reverse.

One way to overcome this natural reaction is to have what's called a "sell discipline." This involves determining what percentage gain or loss you're willing to accept and executing a sell if the stock reaches those limits. You may decide that you're willing to sell when a stock gains 25% and you wish to limit your losses to 25% on the downside. After you've made your decision, don't look back.

I recently sold Dell Computers after making a 30% profit. Of course the stock continued upward after I sold. I need to be sure to focus on my 30% gain and not the "what ifs" of holding on.

If you follow a sell discipline, you bring a more objective approach to your stock trading and avoid some of the emotions that get us in trouble. Don't be greedy. I like to tell people that bears can make money in the market, bulls can make money in the market, but pigs just stink!

How Do You Follow Stocks?

Any of you who've purchased a stock and anxiously gone to your paper to see how you've done have been faced with a very unfriendly, confused mass of indecipherable codes and tables. And you need a magnifying glass to even see all of those numbers and letters. The unfortunate truth is that you must be able to understand this information to know how your stock is doing. Let's try to wade through some of this data so that you'll find it useful rather than a difficult foreign language.

Let me start by saying you don't want to live and die by the daily fluctuations of your stocks. If it will put you in cardiac arrest to see that your stock is down .50 on the day, don't track it on a daily basis! Remember: you've probably purchased these stocks for the long term. Don't get caught up in daily price swings.

Let's take a look at what the information on the stock page is telling you. Below is a listing for June 24, 1998 from *The Wall Street Journal* for Merck Pharmaceuticals, the largest pharmaceutical company in the world and one of the 30 stocks included in the Dow Jones Industrial Average (DJIA).

52 Week					Yld		Vol				
Hi	Low	Stock	Sym	Div	%	PE	100s	Hi	Low	Close	Change
133	82	Merck	MRK	1.80	1.4	34	29760	132 5/16	126 5/8	131 1/4	+ 3 5/16

- **52 Week Hi and Lo**
  These numbers reflect the highest and lowest this particular stock has traded within the last 52 weeks.
- **Symbol (Sym)**
  Although each stock is listed alphabetically by name, every stock has an abbreviation called its symbol that's used for trading. This is what you see flashing across your screen if you watch CNBC or CNN. You'll find this symbol in Value Line and Standard & Poor's as well. The symbol may or may not be easily identifiable with the name of the stock.
- **Div and Yld %**
  The current dividend and yield percentage give you information about the stock at a glance. Shareholders can easily see what their last div-

idend was under "Div" and the "Yld %" reflects the percentage of the distribution (dividend or other distributions) relative to the price of the stock (divide the dividend by the price of the stock at the time the dividend was declared).

- **PE**

  The price-earnings ratio is figured by dividing the closing price of the stock by the current per share earnings over the last four quarters. It's very important when comparing PE ratios to compare similar stocks.

- **Vol 100s**

  This reflects the activity of trading for the stock during that trading day. Take the number listed under this heading and multiply it by 100. In our Merck example, we would take 29760 times 100, which tells us that 2,976,000 shares were traded on 6/24/98.

- **Hi, Low, and Close**

  These headings give you the information that you're usually most interested in. The "Hi" and "Low" represent the highest and lowest prices for the stock during that trading day. The "Close" states the price of the stock at the end of trading and the "Change" tells you the difference between the prior day's close and today's close. In our example, we can calculate from the "Change" that the stock closed at 127 5/16 the day before by subtracting the "Change" from the "Close."

Buys Briefs

Stock prices are quoted in terms of points, rather than dollars, and increments of sixteenths (1/16 = 6.25 cents). This practice seems to date back to the early years of our country, when trading was done in Spanish dollars, which were divided into "pieces of eight."

If you don't have access to *The Wall Street Journal*, almost every major newspaper has a stock page in its business section. Unfortunately, they may all list the stock name a little differently, so you may have to do some searching. Most of the rest of the information will remain consistent with what we've looked at here. Once you get the hang of these tables, it isn't nearly as difficult as it seems at first.

Market Indices

There are several indices that track how stocks are doing. Let's review some of them.

Dow

Now that you know how to follow your own stock, let's take a look at how you follow the market generally. Most of you have heard about the Dow. We turn on the TV and are told about the Dow in very somber tones. Our lives seem to revolve around this index and it seems as if our entire financial future rides on the performance of the Dow. In fact, the Dow Jones Industrial Average tracks only 30 of the thousands of stocks traded and these 30 are blue chip companies that are listed on the New York Stock Exchange (NYSE). This index has become so prominent because it's the oldest and most famous measure of stock market performance. But if you own a small, aggressive growth company, don't expect the Dow to reflect the performance of your stock.

> **Buys Briefs**
>
> The **Dow Jones Industrial Average (Dow)** is the price-weighted average of 30 actively traded blue chip stocks. It is prepared and published by Dow Jones & Company and is the most widely quoted of all the market indicators.
>
> The term **Blue Chip** stock comes from the colored chips issued to gamblers in casinos, with the blue chip being the most valuable. Blue chip stocks tend to be the biggest companies.
>
> The **NYSE** is the oldest and largest stock exchange in the United States. It's also called The Big Board.

Below are the companies included in the Dow Jones Industrial Average (DJIA):

AT&T	Allied Signal
Alcoa	American Express
Boeing	Caterpillar
Chevron	Coca-Cola
Disney	DuPont
Eastman Kodak	Exxon
General Electric	General Motors
Goodyear	Hewlett-Packard
IBM	International Paper
Johnson & Johnson	McDonald's
Merck	3M
J.P. Morgan	Philip Morris
Procter & Gamble	Sears
Travelers	Union Carbide
United Technologies	Wal-Mart

S&P 500

A much broader index than the Dow is the S&P 500. This index represents about 80% of the market value of all the stocks traded on the NYSE. Since this index consists of 500 companies, versus 30 in the Dow, most people believe it's a much better representation of the market as a whole. Very commonly, growth and income mutual fund managers measure their performance against the S&P 500 to prove the value of their management skills.

NASDAQ

This is the National Association of Securities Dealers Automated Quotations, an automated information network that provides brokers and dealers with price quotations on OTC (over-the-counter) stocks. Once NASDAQ was the least respected of the indexes. Many companies that could not qualify for listing on the NYSE went public (started trading) on the NASDAQ. Typically these were small, start-up companies, many of which were considered highly speculative. Once companies became successful and were able to meet the requirements of the NYSE, they left NASDAQ and went to the "prestigious" exchange.

The NASDAQ price index represents all domestic over-the-counter stocks except those traded on exchanges. NASDAQ, or the over-the-counter market (OTC), is not in a physical location on an organized exchange. Many of you may have visited the NYSE or a regional stock exchange, where stocks are traded in arenas. But you will never visit NASDAQ, because it's a market in which security transactions are conducted through a network of dealers connected by telephones and computers rather than on the floor of an exchange.

NASDAQ has thrived beyond its humble origins. In recent years, many companies that could qualify for listing on a major exchange have chosen to remain with OTC trading, believing that the system of multiple trading by many dealers is preferable to the centralized trading of the NYSE. Since the NASDAQ exchange functions through technology, it makes sense that many of the high-tech companies have chosen to remain

> **Buys Briefs**
> **Regional Stock Exchanges** are organized national securities exchanges located outside New York City and registered with the Securities and Exchange Commission (SEC). Included would be Boston, Chicago, Philadelphia, and Pacific stock exchanges.

with the NASDAQ. You will find companies such as Intel, Microsoft, Dell Computers, and other highly successful companies trading here. NASDAQ has now become a major player and bills itself as "the market for the 21st century."

This market, as with all of the exchanges, is heavily regulated. Prices of OTC stocks are published in daily newspapers in much the same manner as stocks on the NYSE and regional exchanges.

Morgan Stanley Capital International Europe Australia Far East Index

Since this is quite a mouthful, this index is usually referred to as "EAFE." It's the most popular index for measuring the performance of foreign stocks. It includes stock market returns from 20 countries, with results expressed in U.S. dollars. This is an important index to use if you invest in international stocks or mutual funds.

Other Indexes

There are many other indexes that measure various asset classes. These include the Russell 2000 (small company stocks), the Wilshire 5000 (stocks from companies of various sizes), and the IFCI Emerging Markets (emerging market stocks).

Consumer Price Index

A discussion of indexes wouldn't be complete without mentioning one that should be very important to you. The Consumer Price Index is the generally accepted measure of consumer price inflation. This index is compiled by the U.S. Department of Labor to measure prices paid for selected goods and services. It has a great deal to do in determining the direction of interest rates and tells us if inflation appears to be under control.

> ### Buys Briefs
> The **Wilshire 5000** is the broadest of all the indexes, representing the value in billions of dollars of all New York Stock Exchange, American Stock Exchange, and OTC issues for which quotes are available.
>
> **The Consumer Price Index (CPI)** is the measure of change in consumer prices as determined by a monthly survey by the U.S. Bureau of Labor Statistics. CPI components include housing, food, and transportation. This is also referred to as the cost of living index.

Now that you've conquered the growth side of investing (stocks), let's take a look at the income side (bonds).

5 Building Blocks: Bonds

When you buy a stock, you have an ownership interest in the business. When you own a bond, you do not have ownership; what you have

instead is an IOU. When you buy a bond, you're loaning money to a business or government in exchange for a promise of repayment and a guarantee of interest.

When you purchase a bond, you'll know the specific interest rate you're going to receive and the length of time until you get back your principal. The time to the maturity date can range from less than a year to 30 years. (Note: The terms *short*, *intermediate*, and *long* are used to categorize bond maturities. Short = less than 1 year; Intermediate = 1–10 years; Long = more than 10 years.)

Although bonds have maturity dates, that doesn't mean that if you buy a 20-year bond you must hold that bond for the full 20 years. Bonds are liquid and can be sold at any time at current market prices. They are generally considered less risky than stocks and consequently have not provided the returns that stocks have over a period of time. Bonds are primarily used for income or to diversify your portfolio.

The Bond Market

One of the most important things to understand about bonds is that they commonly have two values associated with them. The first is the *maturity value*. If you have a $10,000 bond that matures on 6/15/00, you would expect to receive your full $10,000 at that time. Since bonds are liquid and can be traded before that maturity date, the other value is the *current market value*. This value is determined in large measure by the direction of interest rates since you purchased your bond. Remember our discussion in Chapter 3. If interest rates have gone down, the value of your bond will have gone up; if interest rates have gone up, the value of your bond will have gone down.

> **Buys Briefs**
>
> The **Maturity Value** is the value as of the pre-established date upon which the issuer of the bond refunds your principal.
>
> The **Current Market Value** is the price you would obtain if your sold your bond prior to maturity, based on current market conditions.

To understand what happens to the price of bonds, look at Figure 5-1. Let's say you bought a bond due to mature 2/15/10 with an interest rate of 8%. You decide you want to sell that bond before that date and the current interest rate is 5%. It's easy to see that your bond (at 8%) is

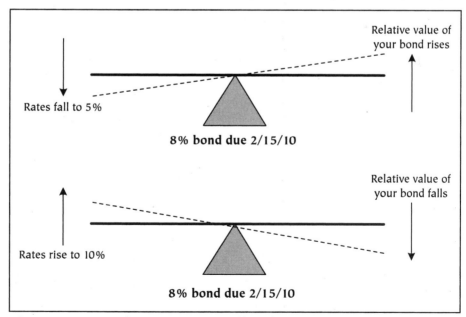

Figure 5-1. How the interest rates affect the value of bonds

worth more than bonds being issued now (at 5%), since your rate of return is higher. Because of this, you would be paid more for your bond because of the higher return it would offer potential investors. The reverse would be true if you sold your 8% bond when the prevailing interest rates were at 10%. Obviously your bond would be worth less.

Bond Ratings

Bond Rating
refers to the method of evaluating the possibility of default by a bond issuer.

Another very important factor in evaluating the value of bonds is the bond's rating. U.S. government bonds are considered to be the highest credit quality available and are backed by the full faith and credit of the U.S. government. We'd like to believe that our government will stand behind its obligations. Bonds are also issued by municipalities and corporations. These vary in quality according to the creditworthiness of the issuer. Because of the differences in security, bonds are frequently rated so the investor can make an informed decision about how much risk may be associated with the bonds. Two of the largest rating services are Standard & Poor's and Moody's. The lists below show how these services rate bonds.

Standard & Poor's Bond Ratings

AAA	Highest quality
AA	High quality
A	Good quality
BB	Questionable
B	Speculative
CCC	Risky
D	In default, dead in the water

Moody's

Aaa	Highest quality
Aa	High quality, marginally higher long-term risk than Aaa
A	Good quality
Baa	Medium grade
Ba	Poor quality, speculative
B	
Caa	
Ca	
C	Lowest rating possible

The higher the quality of the bond, the lower the interest rate is likely to be. This is because you're not assuming as much risk so you won't get as much "reward."

If you buy a U.S. treasury bill or note or bond, you can feel very comfortable in the safety of that investment and you're willing to give up some return for that peace of mind.

If you buy a low-rated "junk" bond, on the other hand, you expect it to pay higher interest for the greater risk. Otherwise you'd just buy more U.S. Treasury bonds. It's all a matter of the risk/reward relationship. The greater the risk, the greater the potential reward. The smaller the risk, the smaller the potential reward.

In real life here's how it works. If you were offered a bond rated AAA paying 7% or a bond rated BBB paying 7%, which would you pick? This isn't rocket science stuff: the choice would be pretty clear. In the real world, however, the AAA bond is always going to pay less than the BBB bond because it offers greater security. You as the investor make a choice, weighing the risks and returns involved. The choice isn't quite so clear when you're looking at the difference between a AAA bond at 7% and a BBB bond at 9%. The difference between the returns reflects a different degree of risk. Do you want the safety of the AAA bond or take a little more risk for the higher return of the BBB bond?

Municipal Bonds

As I've said, the three major flavors of bonds are government, corporate, and municipal. Municipal bonds are different from bonds issued by the federal government or by corporations, so we need to look at these a little more closely.

These bonds are typically issued by local municipalities, school districts, states, or counties, to fund projects at the local level. What sets these bonds apart is that the interest they yield is exempt from federal tax. In addition, if you purchase the bonds in your state of residence, Puerto Rico, or other trust territories, the interest from these bonds is said to be double tax-free, meaning that they are free from state tax *and* federal tax. If you purchase a bond that originates in another state, the interest from that bond will be free from federal tax but will be subject to tax imposed by your state of residence. For example, if I live in Colorado and purchase a Peoria, Illinois Public School bond (hard to tell where I'm from, isn't it?), the interest from that bond will be free from federal tax but subject to Colorado tax.

> ### Buys Briefs
> **Double Tax-Free** refers to the interest that's exempt from federal and state income taxes. Also called double tax-exempt.
> A **General Obligation Bond** is a municipal bond backed by the full faith and credit of a municipality, issued for schools and libraries, for example.
> A **Revenue Bond** is a municipal bond paid off with revenues from the project built with the proceeds, such as from toll roads, stadiums, and airports.

The two major types of municipal bonds are General Obligation and Revenue. General Obligation bonds are issued by municipal agencies such as cities or school districts that have taxing authority. Payments of principal and interest on these bonds are backed by the full faith, credit, and taxing power of the issuing agency. Revenue bonds are payable from a source of income generated by use of a facility. Common sources are tolls, rents, or charges from facilities like airports, water treatment plants, and hospitals.

It's easy to see why these bonds are very attractive to investors in certain tax brackets. For example, if you're in the 34% combined tax bracket (state and federal tax) and you obtain a 5½% tax-free return, that's equal to an 8.4% taxable return. Figure 5-2 shows you why these bonds

		Illinois Tax-Equivalent Yields					
Federal Tax Bracket	State and Federal Tax Bracket			Equivalent Taxable Yields			
28.0%	30.2%	5.73	6.45	7.16	7.88	8.60	9.31
31.0%	33.1%	5.98	6.73	7.47	8.22	8.97	9.72
36.0%	37.9%	6.44	7.25	8.05	8.86	9.6	10.47
39.6%	41.4%	6.83	7.68	8.53	9.39	10.24	11.09
		Assumed Tax-Free Rates of Return					
		4.0%	4.5%	5.0%	5.5%	6.0%	6.5%

Figure 5-2. The payoff of municipal bonds for different tax brackets

appeal to a number of investors. I've used the state of Illinois as my example. The numbers will vary from state to state, so it may be worth your while to see what the numbers would be in your state.

Call Risks

Bonds may involve a particular risk—a call provision. That means that the issuer may decide to issue new bonds at a lower interest rate; the issuer then "calls" in all bonds issued earlier and pays them off.

Let's take a closer look at how a call can affect your bond investment. Suppose you have an IBM bond that has paid you 8% over the last 10 years and isn't due to mature for another 10 years. You think you're a pretty smart investor, because current interest rates are around 5%. The folks at IBM are pretty smart too and figured out 10 years ago that interest rates might go down over the term of their bond. So they put in a call provision that allows them to redeem your bond early. Now that interest rates have dropped, they've realized that they could save a lot of money by refinancing their bond debt at 5% instead of paying you 8%. So they call your bond, pay you off, and refinance their debt at better interest rates—much the same as you would do with a mortgage on your home.

You now face the reality of losing that very attractive 8% return and trying to find another bond to invest in at a time when interest rates are lower. You were expecting your $50,000 investment at 8% to return $40,000 after 10 more years. Now, if you can get only 5% bonds, your return in 10 years will be only $25,000. That difference is significant. You've been counting on that interest and now, because of the 3% drop in interest rates, you will see a big drop in your return. That's the effect of a call risk.

You can see that when you buy bonds, you need to pay attention to what the call provisions allow the issuer to do. Not all bonds have call provisions and not all bonds are called. However, it's an important consideration in purchasing bonds, since callability can make a significant difference in the actual returns of your bonds over time. Bonds can be a very important part of your investment portfolio, but you want to do your homework before buying a bond.

Zero Coupon Bonds

A **Zero Coupon Bond** is a security purchased at a discount that does not pay you current interest. Rather, the interest accumulates within the bond so that the amount you collect at maturity is the full face value of the bond.

All of the bonds I've talked about so far (treasury, corporate, and municipal) are available in something called a *zero coupon bond*. As you know, regular bonds (coupon bonds) generate a steady stream of income to you through interest payments. A zero coupon bonds works differently. You purchase this bond below the face value of the bond (also known as buying at a discount); the longer the term until maturity, the lower the amount that you pay. Why? Because the bond pays no current income directly to you. Instead, it pays the income back into itself, so at maturity the bond is worth more than you paid for it. There is no coupon; that's why they're called zero coupon. When the bond reaches its maturity date, it will be worth the full face value.

I know this is confusing, so let's look at an example. You might buy a zero coupon U.S. treasury with a face value of $1,000. The price at which you'll purchase the bond will depend on how much time there is until the bond matures. For example, you may be able to purchase a zero coupon U.S. treasury bond on 7/1/98 that matures on 7/1/08 for $500. At maturity (7/1/08) this bond will be worth $1,000.

The longer the bond has to build and mature, the cheaper it will be to buy. The shorter the timeline, the more expensive it will be, since it doesn't have as long to build up interest.

One way to understand the distinction between zero coupon bonds and other bonds is that *coupon bonds* are designed to provide you *current income*, while *zero coupon bonds*, because they pay you no current income, are best used to meet a *future need*. As with other bonds, zero's may be sold prior to their maturity date at their current market value.

You probably think that, because the bonds don't pay you any income directly, you don't have an annual tax consequence. If so, then bad news—you're wrong. The IRS says you owe tax on the amount of interest you would have earned if your zero had been a regular bond. This means you're really paying taxes on income you haven't received in your hot little hands. Obviously you wouldn't incur this annual tax if these bonds were in a tax-deferred account, such as an IRA.

How to Buy Bonds

With the exception of treasuries, you usually need to purchase bonds through some type of intermediary. You can't, for instance, call Disney and say you'd like to buy a corporate bond. You can call your financial advisor and direct her or him to purchase that Disney bond for you. This is equally true of municipal bonds. Bonds are generally sold in a minimum of five-bond "lots." If the face value of each of the bonds is $1,000, that means you would be expected to invest $5,000 in these bonds.

The alternative, if you don't want to buy a specific bond or you don't want to spend a minimum of $5,000, is a bond mutual fund. You can buy mutual funds that purchase only municipal bonds, corporate bonds, government bonds, foreign bonds, or a combination of these. While individual bonds pay interest every six months, many bond funds pay monthly. You may either receive this money in the form of cash or reinvest these dividends. You'll learn more about mutual funds in the next chapter.

If you want to buy treasury bills, notes, or bonds without paying brokerage fees, you may purchase them directly from the treasury. You set up an account called Treasury Direct by completing the forms you can get at your local bank or from the federal reserve bank in your area. You can obtain additional information about enrolling on the Internet at www.publicdebt.treas.gov. You send a check to invest and the interest and principal are paid directly into your bank account. The one disadvantage of Treasury Direct accounts is that, if you decide to sell prior to the maturity date, you have to transfer your bond to a brokerage account and pay a commission.

Savings Bonds

I'd be remiss if I didn't include these old standbys in this chapter. These bonds are purchased at half of their face value and then redeemed at maturity for their face value. Many employers sponsor participation to buy savings bonds through payroll deduction. It's no secret that these bonds frequently underperform the rate of a CD and are considered a very conservative investment.

Because of widespread criticism and declining sales, the U.S. Treasury recently revamped these securities. The rate paid on savings bonds will be higher and easier to calculate and the interest will be paid more frequently. Prior to this time, interest rates on savings bonds were nearly impossible to figure. Investors who held the bonds for less than five years got 85% of the average yield on six- month treasury bills, while those who them held for five years or more got 85% of the average rate of five-year treasuries. Both rates would be quite different and very confusing for purchasers to figure. The interest rate now is guaranteed to be 90% of the rate paid on five-year treasury notes.

There are tax advantages associated with savings bonds. The interest paid on your bonds is not subject to federal tax until you redeem them. You never pay state or local income taxes on savings bond earnings. An added bonus is that, if you cash in your bonds to pay for educational expenses for college, you can be exempt from paying any income taxes on all the interest earned. To enjoy this benefit, bonds must have been purchased after 1990 in the name of the parent or guardian, not the child. For 1998, the maximum income limit to qualify for the full deduction is $78,350 on a joint return and $53,250 on a single return.

If you own old savings bonds and are trying to figure what they're worth, there's help at hand. The treasury has a Web site at www.publicdebt.treas.gov where you can download the "Savings Bond Wizard." You can fill in your serial numbers and get a value for your bonds.

As with stocks, you can see there are bonds to meet a wide variety of needs. Your selection can factor in items such as your tax situation, how much risk you're willing to take, and whether or not you're looking for current income. The risk/reward relationship is very important in the bond world. The greater the risk, the greater the reward will be in interest. Weigh the risks in selecting your bond. Remember: don't chase *yield*; chase *quality* if your goal is to have a "safer" bond.

6 Building Blocks: Mutual Funds

*I*n the last few years, billions of dollars poured into open-end mutual funds. Americans have generally decided that mutual funds offer them a marvelous investment vehicle that has allowed them to benefit from the incredibly strong bull market—and I agree. It's estimated that three trillion dollars are currently invested in mutual funds. Mutual funds are clearly the most popular investment choice—yet most people don't really understand how they work.

If you think they're a recent invention, you're mistaken. Mutual funds actually began in the 1920s. In its simplest form, as we mentioned in Chapter 4, a mutual fund raises money through shareholders and is a diversified portfolio managed by professionals.

Mutual fund companies offer a variety of funds, each having different goals and objectives. All of these different funds together are referred to as a "family of funds." For example, the Aim Family of Funds includes offerings such as the Aim Aggressive Growth Fund, the Aim Weingarten Fund, Aim Global Utilities, Aim Municipal Bond Fund, etc. If you look up Aim in the mutual fund section of the paper, you will see all of the Aim family's fund choices listed under that heading. The same would be true for Janus, Fidelity, Alliance, and all other major fund families.

Open-End Mutual Funds are funds that do not have a limit set on the total number of shares that they can issue and can create new shares on demand, in contrast with closed-end funds.

Let's say I'm managing the Best of Buys Growth and Income Fund. I collect $10,000 from Sue, $100 from Carol, $100,000 from Jane, and $250,000 from Heidi. I combine all these dollars with the dollars from other purchasers of my fund and I decide what to buy and sell, when, and at what price, in line with the goals of my fund as spelled out in the prospectus. If I buy the stocks of 150 companies, each of your shares represents ownership in all of those companies. At the end of a business day, my fund adds up the value of all of the shares of all the stocks I own and totals the value. After subtracting expenses, I then divide this value by the number of the shares outstanding in my fund to come up with the value of each individual mutual fund share. This value is referred to as the Net Asset Value (NAV).

> ### Buys Briefs
> A **Prospectus** is a formal written offer to sell securities that sets forth the facts so investors can make an informed decision. A mutual fund prospectus contains financial information, the background of the managers, and other essential data.
> **Net Asset Value (NAV)** is the price of each share of a mutual fund. It is calculated by dividing the value of the fund's assets by the number of shares outstanding.

From the example of my fund, you can see that you have automatic diversification because you own part of all of the 150 holdings in my portfolio. You can also see that you're enjoying the value of professional management since I, as the manager of this imaginary fund, am making all of the investment decisions.

Mutual Fund Fees

If you think that all of this comes to you at no cost whatsoever, I'd like to move to your magical world. Obviously you pay for mutual funds one way or another. Let's take a look at some of the most common mutual fund expenses.

Sales Charge

Mutual funds come in a variety of different fee structures and are starting to resemble alphabet soup, with A, B, C, M, Z, I, II, and no-load types of shares. Three of these are the most common, so we'll examine them in greater detail.

The first pricing structure we'll cover is called a front-end load. "Load" in a mutual fund means "sales charge." So obviously with this type of fund you pay the sales charge at the "front end," when you buy it. These mutual funds are commonly called class A. If you own Oppenheimer Global Class A, for example, you paid the sales charge when you made the purchase.

Class B shares have a deferred sales charge and are designed to reward you for holding the shares over a certain period of time. You pay no initial sales charge, but you will pay a sales charge if you liquidate your holdings before a specified period of time, commonly six years. The following chart is an example of Oppenheimer Global Class B shares and the corresponding sales charge if you redeem your shares within the first seven years.

Oppenheimer Global Class B Shares							
If you liquidate in year:	1	2	3	4	5	6	7
You'll pay a sales charge of:	5%	4%	3%	3%	2%	1%	0

With a no-load fund, you don't pay when you purchase them nor do you pay upon liquidation. Many students in my classes have told me that they owned "free" mutual funds. It took me a while to understand that they were equating "no-load" with "free." Let's be realistic here: that would make them charitable organizations run entirely by volunteers who get all their research for free, trade for nothing, and have toll-free numbers donated by the local phone companies. Guess again!

How Do Mutual Fund Companies Make Money?

The **Annual Expense Ratio** is the annual expenses of operating a fund, expressed as a percentage of assets.

It seems as if there's a new mutual fund company coming into existence every other minute—and in fact, that perception would be close to reality. Your mutual fund choices are now over 10,000 and continuing to grow. More than 15% of these have begun operations since 1997.

When you see a business sector growing like that, you know it's a profitable venture. How do mutual fund companies make their profit? The answer is, all mutual funds have something called an annual expense ratio. Most investors don't have a clue what the annual expense ratio is. Why not? Because, as you've probably guessed, the companies disclose the annual expense ratio in the prospectus—which usually lands in the circular file because it's so painfully tedious to read. These expense ratios vary dramatically among funds and average approximately 1.4% for funds investing in U.S. stocks. That may not sound like a lot, but let's look at some numbers. If your mutual fund managed $16 billion (which is not uncommon) and your expenses were 1.25%, that amounts to $200 million dollars for that fund alone. Most mutual fund companies run many funds, so, while there are expenses involved, you can see there's room for a tidy profit. The largest expense item is the "management fee" that goes to the company running the fund.

There's nothing wrong with an annual expense ratio; it's just that most investors are unaware of it. In addition, funds may charge what are called 12b-1 fees. These fees are used to cover sales and marketing costs. In reality, if your fund is providing good performance over the long haul, all this information and 50 cents will buy you a cup of coffee—you don't care. It's important, however, to know some of the details and to research what you're planning to buy. These expenses can add up to a lot of money over time.

You can get specific information about a fund's fees and expenses by looking at the fee table in the front of every mutual fund prospectus. This table will disclose shareholder transaction expenses as well as annual fund operating expenses. These will include all the costs we've been discussing, such as 12b-1 fees and management fees.

Fund Prospectus

If you're interested in buying a mutual fund, you have a lot of sources of information available to you. Initially, your advisor or the mutual fund company will provide you with a prospectus and sales material. I know that they're painful reading, but the one place to find all of the information is the prospectus. These are "full-disclosure" documents: the fund is required to reveal all relevant facts.

Efforts are currently under way to make these more readable because they can put you to sleep faster than a lullaby! Effective June 1, 1998, the Securities and Exchange Commission implemented updated rules for mutual fund prospectuses, intended to make them more user-friendly and help investors better understand the funds. The new format calls for less technical information and mandates the use of plain English. A particularly helpful aspect will be the required brief summary. This summary will contain a lot of basic information about the fund, such as the investment objective, the investment strategy, a narrative risk summary, and a bar chart showing annual returns over 10 years. Other changes have been incorporated that should streamline and simplify these documents. Meanwhile, if you're looking at an older-model prospectus, try to suffer through it and get as much information as you can about the fund you're considering purchasing. Information is power—and sometimes you have to work for it.

Sales Material

You'll be able to tell the difference between this and a prospectus at a glance, because the sales material will be visually exciting and easy to read—these are not full-disclosure documents. This is where the fund managers put their best foot forward, but they're not free to do whatever they like to make the sale. All of the information they tell you must be true. They must be able to document the performance numbers, size of the fund, ratings, etc.

Types of Mutual Funds

Mutual funds are classified according to investment objective. The following are some of the major classifications.

Aggressive Growth Funds These funds generally feature high risks and returns. They frequently purchase newer, rapidly growing companies. These funds typically don't produce dividends.

Balanced Funds As the name implies, these funds feature a balance, primarily by investing in both stocks and bonds. They provide current income and long-term growth.

Bond Funds These funds invest in bonds and can vary widely according to the type and the credit quality. Common types of bond funds include U.S. Government Bond Funds, Corporate Bond Funds, Tax-Free Bond Funds, International Bond Funds, and frequently combinations called Strategic Bond Funds.

Emerging Markets Funds These funds purchase securities from areas of the world in early developmental economic cycles. They are considered risky and are frequently highly volatile.

Global Funds These funds purchase securities from throughout the world, including the U.S.

Growth Funds Less risky than global funds, these funds pursue long-term growth by focusing on stocks believed to have the potential to increase in value. If the companies are profitable, they are reinvesting the monies into themselves rather than paying dividends.

Growth and Income Funds Much more moderate than their growth-oriented cousins, these funds have as their goal both appreciation in the price of the stock and an income stream from the dividends paid. For this reason, many of these funds are called equity income funds.

Index Funds Essentially, these funds replicate a variety of market indices and mirror the performance of that particular index. For example, one may invest in the stocks listed in an index such as the S&P 500.

International Funds These funds purchase securities from throughout the world, excluding the U.S.

Money Market Funds These funds invest in short-term instruments that are considered the safest, most stable type of securities available. Shareholders in such funds can earn current money market interest rates and maintain liquidity. The fund's net asset value remains a constant $1 per share. Only the interest rate fluctuates. Tax-exempt money market funds are also available.

> **Buys Briefs**
> Is there a sales charge for a money market fund? No, typically not. Many money markets are a part of mutual fund families and offer check-writing privileges. Most funds are not federally insured.

Sector Funds These funds frequently invest in a single industry, such as utilities or technology. They are considered somewhat aggressive, simply because they're not diversified.

Small Company Stock Funds These funds also feature high risks and returns. They frequently invest in small, young companies that trade over the counter and do not pay dividends.

Socially Responsible Funds A unique category, these funds may invest in stocks, bonds, or indices, but only if the policies of the companies meet a specific set of social standards. These funds typically would exclude companies that have poor environmental records, have a history of discrimination against women and minorities, or do animal testing. They also generally exclude those that specialize in products such as tobacco and alcohol.

Fund Rating Services

With the growth of the mutual fund industry, an accompanying growth has occurred in mutual fund rating services. If you're interested in mutual funds, you should be familiar with these services.

Probably the best known of these services is Morningstar, which tracks approximately 1700 funds. Morningstar uses stars to rate funds. The stars represent risk-adjusted performance, so a five-star fund must have a return high enough to justify the risks it assumes. This service provides user-friendly information and gives a brief analysis report talking about fund strategies and analyzing performance. Most major libraries have Morningstar reports available, and it is also available on disk and over the Internet.

Value Line is another well-respected service, tracking approximately 2000 mutual funds. Value Line covers much of the same information as Morningstar and uses a star rating system as well—only in reverse: one star is the highest rating and five is the lowest.

Lipper Analytical covers the broadest range (over 10,000 mutual funds) and is one of the most widely used services. This company provides information to companies such as *The Wall Street Journal* and many brokerage research departments. Rather than rate an individual fund, it provides analytical data on that fund's performance within a larger universe of funds. There is no qualitative analysis added to the numbers.

In addition to these independent rating services, it's hard to pick up a financial magazine that doesn't rate its top ten best funds in the world or something equally sweeping. The best advice is to look at several different sources in combination so that you get an assessment from a variety of sources about the mutual fund you're investigating.

Convenience of Mutual Funds

Mutual funds are very easy to buy. If you wish to manage your own investments, mutual funds can be as handy as your telephone. You simply call the fund you're interested in and they'll happily send you information and an application. Return the application with a check and you're in business. Mutual funds are purchased in dollar amounts, as opposed to numbers of shares. (Some funds have low minimums—$100 or less—so you don't need a lot of money to start.)

The more you invest in a load fund, the more likely you are to receive the benefits of *breakpoints*. The following table illustrates how breakpoints are applied.

The **Breakpoint** is the dollar amount at which the sales charge is discounted when you make a large mutual fund investment.

Franklin® Templeton® Equity Funds Breakpoints

Account/Purchase Size	Sales Charge
Less than $50,000	5.75%
$50,000–$100,000	4.50%
$100,000–$250,000	3.50%
$250,000–$500,000	2.50%
$500,000–$1,000,000	2.00%
$1,000,000 or more	0.00%

If you wish to work with an advisor or desire help in choosing a fund, you can seek out a financial professional. I'll help you with that later in the book.

A commonly heard term when discussing the purchase of mutual funds is *dollar cost averaging*. This involves purchasing a fixed dollar amount on a regular basis regardless of price. Since share prices move up and down with the market, some months you'll be buying more shares at a lower price while in other months you'll be buying fewer shares at a higher price. This process eliminates the possibility that you will place all of your money at the time when share prices are at their highest. For many years this has been recommended as the best way to invest. In recent years, with an ever-rising stock market, this method of investment would have cost you higher prices with most purchases. You need to understand the tradeoffs. One major advantage of dollar cost averaging is that it forces you to invest regularly.

Choices

Just as we discussed the wide variety of stocks, so too is there an incredible assortment of mutual funds—aggressive growth, growth, growth and income, international, sector-specific, index. Bond funds vary as greatly, consisting of government bonds, low-quality corporate bonds, high-quality corporate bonds, foreign bonds, municipal bonds, and a variety of combinations.

Selecting Your Mutual Funds

One of the most crucial factors in determining a fund's success is the expertise of the management team. Let's face it: when you're buying a mutual fund, you're buying management.

Some funds are managed by one person. This is commonly referred to as the "star system." This one person is responsible for the overall management of the fund and decides what to buy or sell and when. Other funds use a team approach, in the belief that the gigantic size of some of the funds makes it impossible for any one person to effectively manage all aspects of the portfolio. You can find successful examples of each. My personal preference is a team approach. It just makes sense to me. As complicated as the market is and as many sectors as there are to analyze, I'd rather have a team working for me. If you have all of your hopes pinned to one star, what happens if he or she leaves?

Performance

What I believe to be a key criterion for selecting funds is long-term performance. Five years is good; ten years is better. While past performance is no guarantee of future performance, it sure gives you a good idea of how the fund has performed in various market and economic conditions. (Of course, you'd want to be sure that the management team that achieved this performance is still in place.)

It is somewhere between rare and never that I would buy a brand new fund. Stick with the long-term, proven performers.

Following Your Mutual Funds

The first thing I want to say here is don't do this too often. Yes, I know the temptation is great to check daily to see how you are doing and I guess that's all right as long as you keep it in perspective. It's very important to understand that mutual funds should be considered long-term investments. You should review performance perhaps every six months or every year and not be concerned by the daily fluctuations you see in your local newspaper.

With that warning in mind, let's now look at how you can track your funds. I've chosen the Alliance Premier Growth Fund Class A for our example, from *The Wall Street Journal* on July 24, 1998.

	NAV	Net Chg	YTD % Chg
Alliance Cap A:			
PrGrth A	26.40	-.15	+ 27.5

Probably the first thing you notice from this example is that the name seems to be in a foreign language. As printing space is limited, each fund name is abbreviated. (Note that, even though I haven't shown any in my example, there would be several funds listed in alphabetical order above and below PrGrth A.) The first number to the right of the fund is the net asset value (NAV), the per-share value in the portfolio as of the close of the last business day. Next is the Net Chg, the change in price (+ or –) from the prior business day. The last column, YTD % Chg, states the performance of the fund year-to-date in terms of a percentage.

Although I've chosen my example from *The Wall Street Journal*, most major newspapers have a financial section that reports mutual fund quotes. The format may vary slightly, but the basic information will be the same. You may even find that on Fridays or in the weekend edition, some papers have extended quote information. Follow the handy table they provide for your convenience to explain any notes, abbreviations, or format.

If your fund consistently performs poorly, it may be time to look a little deeper. If you own a small cap growth fund, for example, and your return numbers are consistently negative, be sure to compare it against other funds in the small cap growth category. If you notice that other aggressive growth funds have positive numbers and yours does not, you probably should investigate further.

Another time changes may be appropriate is if your investment goals and objectives change. Most mutual fund companies will allow you to do free or very inexpensive exchanges among their funds, so you can adapt your portfolio as your needs change. For example, if you are near or entering retirement, you may wish to have more income funds in your portfolio and change your focus from growth. Exchanges allow you to do so at little or no cost. (But remember to look out for the tax consequence before you make any changes.)

The Mutual Fund Universe

Any of you who've picked up a paper or read a magazine know that it seems there are more mutual funds than Carter has little liver pills. I recently read that we will soon have 12,000 mutual funds from which to choose. That means there are substantially more mutual funds than all of the stocks traded on the New York Stock Exchange and the American Stock Exchange combined.

I remember when, earlier in my career, someone gave me one page, 8½ by 11, from *The Wall Street Journal*, that listed all of the mutual funds trading at that time. How times have changed! Now you need a magnifying glass to wade through the page after page of tiny print listing all the funds. Most people are totally overwhelmed by the sheer number of funds.

Here's a thought that's really alarming: in 1990, there were only about 3100 mutual funds in existence. Why is this alarming? If you believe in using long-term performance as a yardstick in selecting your funds, you're going to have trouble, since only 3 in 10 on that huge list were in existence in 1990. This says to us that a lot of them are a long way from having a 10-year track record.

You'll notice that many of the financial magazines have headlines that read "The Seven Best Mutual Funds in Existence," "The Eight Most Dependable Funds," "The Top Ten Best Funds for Your Portfolio," and so on and so forth. Such articles may be a great way to sell a magazine, but they're not such a great way to select your mutual funds. If you believe in what we've been talking about in this chapter, you know it's critical to buy mutual funds that will fit the objective or goal you're targeting. That may sound easy—but a recent study analyzed a sampling of funds and found that 56% of them were misclassified. Simply put, more than half of the funds claiming to have one type of goal consisted of investments that would have been more appropriate for other goals.

While it may be difficult and you'll have to do a little work and research, it's well worth your effort to spend time selecting the funds for your portfolio. As you begin your selection process, remember to ask yourself what your investment objective is, how long you have to get there, and how much risk you can tolerate. In the next chapter I'll help you by looking at how these mutual funds might fit into the portfolios of three types of investors—conservative, moderate, or growth.

7 Investor Profiles

N ow that we've covered the basics and you have a foundation in the broad types of investments, let's move forward to help you identify which investment types fit different investor profiles. In this chapter we'll look at three categories—conservative, moderate, and growth-oriented—and examine some specific classes of investments that might be appropriate for each category. While we're at it, we'll look at the pros and cons of each. Be warned: there's no rubber stamp and you'll probably find you don't fit neatly into any of these categories. While I'll name the specific holdings, such as lower-rated bonds or aggressive growth stocks, remember that this includes mutual funds that hold these types of investments as well. If you own mutual funds, plug them in according to what they buy when you look at the risk pyramid.

The Conservative Investor

By definition this person does not like risk (not that anybody really does!) and really hates volatility. Unfortunately, low risk also generally means low reward, but this type of investor is willing to accept the trade-off. The primary goal here is return *of* principal not return *on* principal.

At the lowest level of risk, we find such places for our money as savings accounts, money market accounts, certificates of deposit, savings bonds, and treasury bills. Notice that each of these provides safety of principal, no growth, and relatively low yields. It's important to remember what we discussed in Chapter 3. While you may not run the risk of losing your principal in conservative investments, you certainly have the risk of inflation. If, for example, your three-year CD is at 5% and inflation jumps to 6%, your real rate of return looks grim. That's one of the tradeoffs for the closest you'll ever get to absolute safety of principal.

The Moderate Investor

This investor is willing to accept some volatility in her or his portfolio in exchange for higher returns. Most of the people in this category should have a long-term commitment to their market-related investments and be willing to ride out the tough times. It would not be uncommon to be in the range of half stocks and half bonds, with flexibility on either side, in a moderate portfolio.

In this category, you would find investments in such things as U.S. government securities, high-quality taxable and tax-free bonds, preferred stocks, and common stocks of high-quality companies. The characteristics of these investments are that they provide moderate returns and growth potential and are not highly volatile. This investor is better protected against inflation because of the growth holdings. The tradeoff is that you need to be prepared to accept some bumps along the way.

The Growth Investor

If you have the large majority of your assets invested in growth, you need to be very comfortable with volatility, because true growth investors will have many higher-risk holdings in their portfolios. The focus will be on growth, so they won't have many fixed income holdings. Growth investors are willing to live and die as the market dictates. They feel it's worth assuming the additional risk for the greater potential rewards.

Notice how we've gone from the purely conservative investor with little risk of principal loss but significant inflation rate risk to a category where those risks would be reversed. Investments in this category include lower-rated bonds, aggressive growth stocks, emerging market stocks and bonds, and many options and futures strategies.

Figure 7-1 is an investment pyramid showing various investments and their levels of risk and reward.

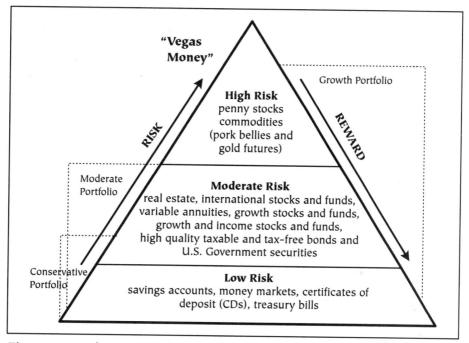

Figure 7-1. This pyramid illustrates various investments and their levels of risk

Understanding the level of risk associated with each type of investment allows you to pick the investments appropriate for you, based on the amount and type of risk you're willing to tolerate. The two most important things in deciding your personal risk profile are the number of years you have until you need the money and your ability to tolerate risk. Generally, the more time you have and the more risk you can tolerate, the more growth-oriented investments you would want to include in your holdings, because you have more time to recover from any short-term losses associated with market volatility. The shorter your time horizon and the worse your nervous condition, the more conservative you need to be.

I've presented three investor profiles and investment categories here. In the real world, most of us are blends of these profiles. In the next chapter I'll demonstrate that, by adding some of the moderate investments to a conservative portfolio, we actually reduce the risk in the portfolio. Every investor needs to decide what's right for her. To help guide you, let's look at a couple of examples.

Investor A Sally is 30 years old and single. She makes $35,000 a year as a research assistant and participates in her retirement plan at work. She currently contributes $100 a month to a mutual fund and has $1,500 in her savings account.

Given Sally's length of time to retirement, her young age, and no immediate need for the money, she should be primarily invested in growth-oriented investments such as stocks or stock mutual funds. These types of investments could make up 80%-100% of her portfolio, depending on how aggressive she wants to be. Remember: the greater your exposure to the market, the more aggressive your portfolio.

Investor B Lisa is 45 and divorced. She makes $50,000 a year as a human resource manager. She plans to retire at age 60, is purchasing a home, and is currently paying half the expenses for her son's college education. Up to this point, she has contributed only minimally to her retirement plan at work, but now wants to make that her focus. She has $5,000 in the bank and is comfortable with some volatility, but would not want to see swings of more than 20% in her portfolio value.

Being a little closer to retirement, Lisa is getting more cautious about major pullbacks in the market. A balanced moderate portfolio may fit better in a situation like this. For example, she may wish to have 60% of her portfolio in growth-oriented investments and 40% in fixed income. She is willing to give up some of the potential returns in exchange for a smoother ride with her account value.

Investor C Peggy and her husband want to retire in five years. She is 57 and makes $40,000 a year as a nurse. Her husband Joe is 60 and earns $35,000 a year as a mechanic for the local school district. They have both contributed moderately to their retirement plans at work, have paid off their mortgage, and have $10,000 in savings. Outside of their retirement plans, the bulk of their $50,000 nest egg is in growth-oriented mutual funds.

As a rule of thumb, the closer you are to needing your retirement investments, the more moderate to conservative your investments should be. Many people at this stage of the game are trying to minimize risk and are beginning to focus on income-oriented investments. Because we know how dangerous inflation can be to a portfolio that is only fixed income, Peggy and Joe should continue to have exposure to growth, perhaps in the 30% range. After they retire at age 62, they're likely to live at least another 20 years. That means that they'd better be investing to ensure that their nest egg continues to grow, rather than shifting their entire focus of their portfolio to fixed income investments.

In the above examples, I've tried to demonstrate portfolio mixes using the number of years until retirement as the focus. Obviously that's not the only factor that would determine your portfolio mix and asset choices. Other considerations that may influence your decisions about investing include your age, career stage, job skills, and health.

If you are young, you have a lot of time ahead of you to let your investments grow. If you are in an early career stage, you know you have your peak earning years ahead of you, so you can afford to be more aggressive, especially in your retirement accounts. If, on the other hand, you are older and approaching retirement, a significant setback in your portfolio could be catastrophic.

Another determinant of portfolio mix would be the size of your portfolio. If you have a small amount of money, you could not achieve market diversification by buying a single stock. Therefore, mutual funds would be your best investment choice. As you continue to fund your portfolio, you can become more diversified over time. A larger portfolio allows you to buy a wider range of assets, such as stocks and bonds, and achieve broader diversification immediately. Although the approach may vary based on how much money you have to start with, the ultimate goal is still the same—diversification.

As you build your portfolio, consider your income tax bracket. The higher your tax bracket, the greater the appeal of tax-favored investments. If your bracket is lower, you're probably better off with taxable investments where you'll achieve a greater after-tax return.

Another important consideration would be the rate of return you want. If you'd like your portfolio to achieve an inflation-adjusted return of 8%, you know you need to look toward growth-oriented investments. If you decide you'd be satisfied with an overall return of 5%, you can go toward the conservative range of the investment pyramid.

You also need to bear in mind personal factors in your life. Is your marriage solvent? How is your health? Is there stability in your job? Are your job skills easily transferable? Do you have a great need for liquidity? Do you plan to provide for your children's education? If so, how near is that need? Since the answers to these and other questions vary, it's easy to see that there is no "one size fits all" portfolio.

Using the information in this chapter, let's now see what happens when we mix different levels of risk and reward from the investment pyramid. Onward to asset allocation!

8 | Asset Allocation

One of the most commonly heard financial terms today is *asset allocation*. You see the term in the newspaper, mutual funds mention it in their literature, and it's currently one of the most "in vogue" investment themes. The plain fact is that most people don't understand what asset allocation is or what it means to them. In this chapter, we're going to make sure that you aren't one of those people. We'll look at asset allocation, define some key concepts, clarify many of the terms, and demonstrate exactly how you can use it effectively.

If you think you can skip this chapter because you're just starting out, you're wrong. What we're about to discuss applies to investment novices as well as to those who have a substantial portfolio. No chapter skipping for any of you!

Your Key to Successful Investing

Asset allocation can be monumentally important in determining your overall investment returns. As a matter of fact, I think you'll be shocked to learn that it's the single most important thing to consider in developing your portfolio. I can't emphasize this enough.

Wouldn't it be heavenly to come up with an investment strategy that allows you to focus on your long-term goals, create a portfolio designed to meet those goals, and at the same time reduce your risk? Absolutely—and asset allocation allows you to do that in a calm, rational, directed manner.

What's the hot stock of the day? Did the market go up or down today? If you are properly asset allocated, these questions won't throw you into anxiety attacks. Now that I've caught your attention, we'll examine more closely what's involved in this process.

What Is Asset Allocation?

Let's begin by defining asset allocation. In its simplest form, it means diversifying your investment portfolio among different asset classes, such as stocks, bonds, and cash. As we continue in this chapter, we'll discover that this division is just the tip of the iceberg. It's a good start, but we're going to see that we need to look below the surface of these assets and begin to further refine and categorize them more specifically.

The basic idea of asset allocation is that, by spreading your money out in different types of investments, you benefit from those that are doing well and limit your exposure to those that aren't doing so well. For example, suppose you own a variety of stock mutual funds and the one that buys large company stocks is doing very well but the one that owns small company stocks is lagging. You're gaining because you have some exposure to the better performer and you're minimizing your exposure to the lesser performer by not having all of your money in that category. Now I know you're wondering, "Why not just put all my money in the one that's doing well?" Hang in there and, as we look further at asset allocation, you'll see very clearly why you don't want to do that. For now, take it on faith.

Some of the founding principles of asset allocation were developed by Harry Markowitz, whose discovery earned him a Nobel Prize in Economics in 1990. It's based on research that began in the 1950s that shows how investors who combine assets with different characteristics can achieve optimal long-term growth. In the early years, this investment strategy was used only by sophisticated pension plans and institutional money managers. I don't mean to scare you and make it sound too complex, because you're going to see that asset allocation is widely used today in managing assets for individual investors like all of us.

More Than Diversification

The common adage, "Don't put all your eggs in one basket," fits nicely when we start to think about asset allocation. The ultimate goal of this strategy is to smooth out the ups and downs of the financial markets by reducing the volatility, or the risk, in your portfolio. Remember: the mortal sin for the average investor is to panic and sell when your account value goes down. Let's face it: we all get a pain in the pit of our stomach when we get our account statements and see a significant decline in the value of the account. There's no way to eliminate all of the volatility, but the more asset-allocated you are, the less dramatic those peaks and valleys may be.

This is not a strategy of going for the home run and chasing the hot stock of the day. Rather, it involves creating a diversified portfolio and sticking to your investment plan over time. Women don't like risk or volatility. This strategy helps us to be more comfortable, because we know that we're well-diversified. Many believe asset allocation helps them sleep at night no matter what the market is doing during the day.

Key Principles

A major principle behind this theory is that asset allocation determines most of the performance in your investment portfolio. This is really important to think about, so let's look at this more closely.

A very famous study that's often cited concludes that 91.5% of the investment return among a sample of pension plans was determined simply by the portfolio mix of asset classes. This study further showed that market timing accounted for less than 2% of the return and stock selection for less than 5%.

Let's think about what these results are telling us. The business pages of most newspapers focus almost entirely on the daily swings and events in the market. Investors constantly search for the hot stock of the day. What we see in the media is short-term thinking. But this study tells us that, in spite of what the media may lead us to believe, the short-term focus has little effect on our long-term portfolio performance. The good news is that we don't have to spend our time trying to decide if the market is too high or too low or if we should buy this stock or that stock. Isn't it a relief to understand that you don't have to be a market guru or polish your crystal ball to obtain good results from your investments? That sounds fairly reasonable so far, doesn't it? It is.

Diversification

A second major principle of asset allocation is that broad diversification substantially reduces risk. In fact, many experts would contend that broad diversification is the greatest key to risk management. This is not rocket science stuff. If you have all your money in one thing, it's feast or famine depending on the performance of that one investment. Why would you knowingly expose yourself to that level of risk?

Adding Asset Classes Reduces Risk

It's not the risk level of each asset class that's important; it's how the classes work together. I know that goes against a lot of our thinking, but I'm going to tell you something that will help convince you.

Finally, we need to understand that carefully adding some "risky" assets to a portfolio can actually reduce the overall risk in that portfolio. To understand why adding asset classes actually lowers the risks in a portfolio, you need to learn more about an important term called *standard deviation*.

While that sounds like a big deal, it's simply a term used to measure risk in a portfolio. For example, you may have a standard deviation of 35% if all of your money is invested in small cap stocks over a long period of time. This means your risk factor is 35%. By adding just a few more asset classes, such as large cap stocks and government bonds, studies have shown that you may cut that risk factor almost in half. I don't want to get too complicated with all of this, but you could if you wanted. You math geniuses can dig up the studies and run the calculations! The bottom line is there's a great deal of research to demonstrate the benefit of using this process.

What you see in Figure 8-1 on the next page is a portfolio we'll call Portfolio A. This portfolio consists 100% of intermediate- to long-term

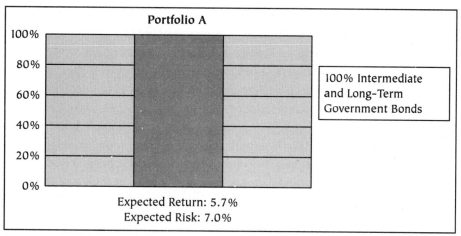

Figure 8-1. One type of investor portfolio

government bonds. To most of us, that sounds about as safe and risk-free as it could be, something for a very conservative investor who hates volatility. If you look at the bottom of the figure, you'll see the expected return for this portfolio would be 5.7%. The expected risk for volatility is 7%. Now let's look at Portfolio B (Figure 8-2).

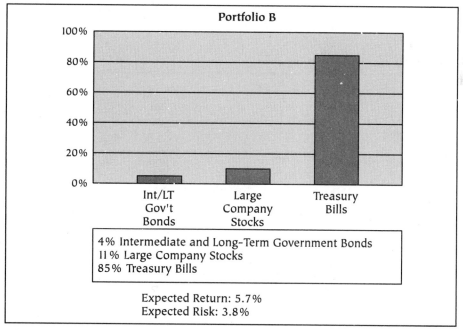

Figure 8-2. A second type of investor portfolio

Notice that, by adding a few other asset classes, namely treasury bills and—yes—some stocks, we keep our expected return the same (5.7%) while cutting the expected risk in half. I know that some of you are wondering, "How could that be, since everybody knows that stocks are riskier than bonds?" The reason for this is that asset classes behave differently in response to different economic, political, and financial conditions. The whole idea is to own some asset classes that zig when others zag.

To better understand why Portfolio A has a higher expected risk factor than Portfolio B, we need to review a concept we discussed in Chapter 3. As interest rates go up, the value of bonds goes down and vice versa. (See page 55 for a review.) If we have 100% of our portfolio in bonds, even U.S. government bonds, we can expect to see that higher level of volatility simply because we're not dealing with a more diversified portfolio. Remember: different asset classes behave distinctly, so interest rate changes will not affect all investments in the same manner.

What Is Risk?

It may be helpful for you to go back to Chapter 3 and review the section on risk. You've now graduated from the stage where you thought the only kind of risk is loss of principal. Keep these concepts in mind as we move forward and assess the risk of having all your eggs in one basket.

A Look at Asset Classes

Now that we've discussed the overall framework and set some general concepts in place, let's plunge into the substance of asset allocation. There are about 120 asset classes that have been identified. These range from categories of stocks and bonds to real estate and gold. Studies show that if we pick 10-15 of these, we'll capture most of the advantage of asset allocation. Can you imagine having the money to invest in all different 120 classes? Just in case that's a little outside your budget, let's focus on the 10-15 that may be most helpful and see what benefits we can get. While these are the most common ones you are most apt to use, I'll cover a few more in Chapter 13, "Financial Potpourri."

Initially we need to examine what it means to properly diversify a stock portfolio. We all know that a stock is not a stock is not a stock. Of the thousands of stocks in the universe, we certainly don't expect all of them to behave the same. Large companies frequently do well in times of uncertainty and small company stocks are often considered the riskier of the two. Over time, however, small companies may provide a higher rate of return. Not only are there differences between small and large companies, but also between foreign and domestic companies. Again, it wouldn't be reasonable to expect IBM to behave in the same manner as Mitsubishi because of the economic and political differences that exist globally.

Diversifying a Stock Portfolio

To illustrate some of these differences, let's look at Figure 8-3.

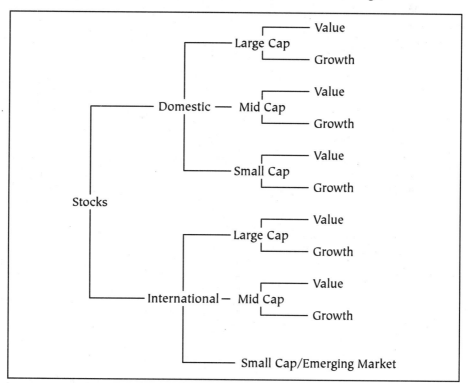

Figure 8-3. Diversifying a stock portfolio

Notice that I first divide stocks into two broad categories: domestic and international. I then further divide them into large cap, mid cap, and small cap, so we cover companies of various sizes.

Buys Briefs

Market Capitalization (Cap) is the total value of a company's securities on the market, calculated by multiplying the number of outstanding shares by the current market price per share. Large cap: companies with a market capitalization of $5 billion or more. Mid cap: companies with a market capitalization between $1 billion and $5 billion. Small cap: companies with a market capitalization of less than $1 billion.

I think it's important here to understand that, when most asset allocators talk about a small company, believe me, they aren't talking your idea of small or my idea. They're usually talking about companies that have a capitalization of $1 billion or so. (Yes, that's *billion*.) It's fairly clear that when we're looking at this category we're not talking about a mom-and-pop store.

In our chart, on the international side, we have not only large cap and mid cap again, but also a new category, called small cap/emerging markets. Emerging markets might be areas such as Southeast Asia and Eastern Europe—markets that are just opening up. The risks in investing in foreign securities are intensified in emerging markets. They have smaller, less developed trading markets and exchanges, which may result in less liquidity and greater volatility.

Emerging Markets are areas with developing or emerging economies and markets, such as parts of Latin America, Africa, Asia, and Eastern Europe.

The final diversification we see is whether a company is oriented toward growth or toward value. This division demands a fuller explanation, so I'll come back to this shortly. It's clear from this example that from the general heading "stock" we've come a long way in diversifying our portfolio. Now let's take a look at how we can do the same thing with bonds.

Diversifying a Bond Portfolio

A **Short/Intermediate Bond** has a one- to ten-year maturity.

Figure 8-4 shows us the possible diversification of a bond portfolio. The first diversification of a bond portfolio is by maturity. Is it a short to intermediate bond? Or is it an intermediate to long bond? We then further diversify across borders. Is the bond foreign or domestic? Lastly, we diversify by the credit quality of the bond. Is it high-quality, such as a treasury, or a high-yield, lower-rated corporate bond?

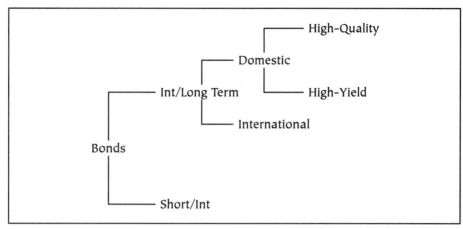

Figure 8-4. A possible way to diversify a bond portfolio

A **Long Bond**
is one with a
maturity of 10
years or more.

Advantages of Diversification

We've now seen that a great deal of diversification is possible in just the stock and bond arena. Now I'd like to show you a chart that will let you see what you're gaining by all of this diversification.

Alternating Stars			
1980		**1990**	
Stocks	+ 32.3%	Stocks	-3.3%
Bonds	+ 3.1%	**Bonds**	+ 8.3%

As we look at diversifying among even the basic asset classes, you can see that in some years stocks are lead performers and in other years bonds are the winners. Notice that in 1980 stocks significantly outperformed bonds, while in 1990 stocks were essentially underwater and bonds were returning nicely for us. In the next chart we see the same is true for diversifying across borders.

Domestic and International Stock Returns			
1980		**1990**	
Domestic	+ 21.9%	Domestic	+ 5.1%
International	-0.87%	**International**	+ 23.2%

In 1982 domestic stocks were very strong, significantly outperforming international. The exact opposite was true in 1987, the year we all remember fondly for the correction in our market. We see that not only are we lowering our risks by being diversified, but we are also helping our chances of capturing the better-performing asset class without chasing it.

Growth and Value Investing

As we've just noted, the final step in the diversification in the stock portfolio deals with diversifying across styles that we labeled "Growth" and "Value." It's very important to understand these two concepts, because once you do you'll not only be able to asset allocate properly but also have a better understanding of the mutual funds, stocks, or bonds that you own or are considering buying.

Growth

A growth company is one that typically has an annual increase in sales, earnings, and market share. Examples of this kind of company would include Coca-Cola, Merck, or Microsoft. These stocks are usually expensive, since investors are willing to pay a higher price because they think these companies will continue their record of growth and earnings and the stock prices will go up accordingly. A growth mutual fund manager is perfectly willing to pay the higher prices for these stocks. The growth philosophy is that there's a good reason why these stocks are expensive, that they will continue to perform, and that paying a high price is a wise investment.

> **Buys Briefs**
>
> **Growth Stocks** are stocks of companies with above-average growth potential relative to the market. They frequently have higher P/E ratios and lower dividend yields than the rest of the market.
>
> **Value Stocks** are securities whose valuations are below the market average or their historical average. Value stocks often sell cheaply because investors feel they have certain characteristics that make their future earnings prospects questionable.

Value

A manager of a value mutual fund is the "bargain hunter" of the market. She or he is doing what is near and dear to most of us women, trying to buy stocks that they think are "on sale," selling for less than their true worth. Value stocks may be companies in an industry that is currently out of favor. Some value stocks are those companies that are hard hit by changes in the economic cycle such as recessions, high interest rates, etc. Because of this, their earnings are more cyclical and less predictable than those of growth companies. Other companies in this "value" category would be those that may be currently out of favor with the market generally.

Do you remember the savings and loans crisis? It was a time when you couldn't give away bank stocks. Value enthusiasts were madly buying these stocks while other investors were selling. Their belief was that it was just a matter of time until bank stocks came back into favor. You didn't have to read the financial pages every day in 1996 and 1997 to know that those two years were gigantic for mergers in the banking sector and those stocks have been soaring. It took time and patience, but value investors were clearly right in their call.

An interesting thing to note about this style of investing is that value stocks and mutual funds are considered more defensive in the event of a market correction, which is easy to understand. Remember: these stocks are more cheaply priced and out of favor. They've already been beaten up by the market and, theoretically, don't have as far to drop when the market goes down. Growth managers, on the other hand, are out there paying premium prices for the stocks they're buying, so if there's a market pullback their stocks may quickly lose more since their prices were high.

Why You Need Both

Given the definitions of value and growth investment orientations, it's easy to see that a large company growth manager and a large company value manager would be buying very different stocks for their portfolios. At different times, different styles lead the pack. Growth styles are favored to perform in periods of economic contraction, while the value style is favored in periods of market expansion. In 1986 the growth style of investing underperformed the value style. By 1988 those positions and returns flip-flopped. The moral of the story? In an ideal world, you should own both growth and value stocks or mutual funds.

Earlier I briefly covered adding asset classes to your portfolio. Now that you're aware of how stocks and bonds can be broken out into a wide range of asset classes, let's delve into this further to see how adding asset classes can benefit your portfolio.

More About Adding Asset Classes to Your Portfolio

As we look at the asset class small cap, for instance, we find it has a significant amount of risk as measured by standard deviation. If we simply add two more asset classes to our portfolio—large companies and government bonds—studies show that we can cut the risk in that portfolio in half. Think of how significant this reduction is—and yet we're still in only *three* asset classes. If we add additional asset classes—such as real estate, corporate bonds, treasury bonds, foreign bonds and international stocks—we can reduce that risk again by half. Simply by going from one asset class to eight, we've essentially cut the risk factor in our portfolio by 75%! Now I bet you're beginning to see what I meant when I earlier talked about being able to sleep better at night if you're asset allocated.

Performance of Different Asset Classes: Lessons to Be Learned

Look at Figure 8-5 on page 93. It shows a few of the asset classes and how they perform on a yearly basis over a 20-year period.

While this may look like a mad jumble of numbers, you'll see it really does yield some valuable information. If you remember nothing else about the book except what we're about to discuss, that alone will make the book worth the price you paid for it and the time you spent reading it.

Although this chart may look diseased, the idea here is to show you that the top performing asset class shifts from year to year. If you didn't have exposure to all of the asset classes, you would miss out on the best performers. We can learn another lesson about being invested in just one asset class by looking at a couple of return numbers from the emerging market stocks category, which was not included in the chart, in the interest of space. In 1988 the total return was a whopping 58.2%. Defying the odds, 1989 was almost as impressive, coming in at 54.7%. As is normally the case following such a stellar year, the next year showed a downward correction, with a total return of –29.9%. This is true for almost all of the asset classes: if a class leads the pack one year, it frequently falls in performance the next year.

It's important to think about what we've just learned here. When we look to invest our money, what do we tend to do? We look for last year's

Year	Foreign Stocks	U.S. Stocks	Foreign Bonds	U.S. Bonds
1978	32.62	6.58	N/A	1.39
1979	4.75	18.60	N/A	1.93
1980	22.58	32.50	N/A	2.71
1981	-2.28	-4.92	N/A	6.25
1982	-1.86	21.55	N/A	32.62
1983	23.69	22.56	N/A	8.36
1984	7.38	6.27	N/A	15.15
1985	56.16	31.73	35.01	22.10
1986	69.44	18.66	31.36	15.26
1987	24.63	5.25	35.15	2.76
1988	28.27	16.56	2.34	7.89
1989	10.54	31.63	-3.41	14.53
1990	-23.45	-3.11	15.29	8.96
1991	12.13	30.40	16.22	16.00
1992	-12.17	7.61	4.77	7.40
1993	32.56	10.06	15.12	9.75
1994	7.78	1.31	5.99	-2.92
1995	11.21	37.53	19.55	18.47
1996	6.05	22.95	4.08	3.63
1997	1.78	33.35	-4.26	9.65

Past performance cannot guarantee comparable future results. Domestic stocks are represented by the Standard & Poor's 500 Stock Index, a group of unmanaged securities widely regarded by investors to be representative of the U.S. stock market in general. Domestic bonds are represented by the Lehman Brothers Aggregate Bond Index. Foreign stocks are represented by Europe, Australia, Far East (EAFE) Index, a group of unmanaged securities compiled by Morgan Stanley Capital International. Foreign bonds are represented by the Salomon Brothers non-U.S. World Government Bond Index. An investment cannot be made directly in an index. Performance results assume the reinvestment of dividends, if any. There is no guarantee that any AIM fund will be able to achieve the results of any foreign market.

Figure 8-5. Year-by-year results on four major asset classes. Chart shows average annual returns in U.S. dollars, December 31, 1977 to December 31, 1997. The shaded boxes indicate the best performing asset class for that year. (Provided courtesy of The AIM Family of Funds®)

top performer. The chart we're now reviewing gives us evidence that last year's top performer usually won't be the top performer this year. In fact, it may actually underperform. Chasing returns is usually a good way to guarantee that our portfolio won't provide the returns we're looking for. The smart thing may very well be to fill in gaps in our asset classes by picking the group that didn't do quite so well last year and starting to build our positions in that area.

Understanding How Asset Classes Behave

One of the elements frequently used in asset allocation is a sophisticated mathematical formula that looks at the relationship between asset classes called the *correlation*. OK, so what does that mean?

A key to reducing risk is identifying which types of assets perform in the same manner at the same time and which act in opposite ways. Let's think about what that means. If you're committed to asset allocation as we've been discussing it, being broadly diversified in a variety of asset classes, would you chose two asset classes for your portfolio that move in exactly the same direction? If you didn't say, "No, no, no!" go back to the beginning of this chapter and start all over again. (Do not pass Go. Do not collect $200.)

Here's why. How much diversification and benefit do you really gain if you buy two asset classes that both go up at the same time and go down at the same time?

The idea here is to find a way to be adequately diversified so that our portfolio doesn't go up or down on the strength or weakness of a single asset class. The more highly correlated asset classes are, the more likely they'll behave the same. The lower the correlation, the less likely they'll behave the same. The ideal would be to have asset classes that are negatively correlated, meaning that one goes up when the other goes down: they don't move in the same direction. For example, while small stocks and treasury bills are not negatively correlated, the correlation between the two is very low, so you would expect that there would not be much similarity in the way they perform in the same market environment.

As we began our study of asset allocation, the first categories were *stocks* and *bonds*. What we now see is that these two classes are *not* closely correlated. Frequently they move in opposite directions in their performance. Interestingly, between 1926 and 1993, there were 20 negative years for stocks, 18 negative years for bonds, but *only* five bad years for both. This is quite an endorsement for the concept of asset allocation.

Is This Diversification?

Now that you're becoming absolutely brilliant about asset allocation, let's start to apply some of this to our portfolios and walk through a real-life example. Suppose someone came to me, "I have some General Electric, Merck, McDonald's and Caterpillar stock. I also own some great mutual funds, including the Janus Fund and Oppenheimer Growth. What do you think of my portfolio?" Obviously these are quality companies, excellent mutual funds, and this individual is probably very proud of their portfolio. She has probably done some reading about these funds and stocks and is confident of the quality of her holdings.

But what about diversification? Based on what you know now, what about this portfolio? Is it really diversified? No it's not. If we examine each holding, every single position in this portfolio relates to one asset class—large company growth stocks. The same is true for the mutual funds. This portfolio will live and die by the performance of that one class.

I once had an individual come in for a consultation confidently displaying his 22 mutual funds. He had selected these from lists he'd reviewed in *Money Magazine*, *Kiplinger's Personal Finance Magazine*, and similar publications. He was quite proud of his effort and was almost smug when asking me for an analysis. He owned several high-quality mutual funds, but incredibly, of his 22 mutual funds, 16 fell into the large cap growth asset class. It was highly likely that he may very well own the same stock in all 16 of these funds, since they would all be buying many of the same holdings. He was stunned to find that, although he had a rather sizable portfolio and owned 22 funds, he had very little diversification.

Long-Term Horizon

Once you've come up with your asset allocation blend, it is imperative that you be committed to it for a long time frame. Many people would say five years at a minimum. You've got to stick to your strategy, even if you see one asset class booming. Your urge will be to sell all and jump completely into that asset class. What was great last year may be just that—last year's news. Remember the difference in the performance of asset classes over a long timeline.

The volatility of an investment is substantially reduced when you move from a one-year horizon to a five-year horizon. While I always preach the gospel of long-term investing no matter what, it's particularly critical in your commitment to asset allocation.

Determining Your Investment Objective

Now that we have a handle on all this, let's see how you go about determining your investment objectives. A common rule of thumb: the higher your level of exposure to the stock market, the more aggressive your portfolio, and the more bonds you add, the more conservative your portfolio becomes. Since we all know you don't get something for nothing, it would be reasonable to expect returns to go down as more and more bonds are added to the portfolio. The good news is that volatility should go down as well. An investor who would be very aggressive could have 100% of her portfolio exposed to the stock market via either stocks or stock mutual funds. An investor who is much more conservative, on the other hand, may have only 30% of her portfolio exposed to the market.

Let's explore a middle-of-the-road investor who may have 60% of her portfolio exposed to stocks and 40% in bonds. We've gone far enough into asset allocation to understand that, while we say 60% in stocks and 40% in bonds, we know that within those two categories we'll further diversify and cover a number of asset classes. So, while 60/40 is the overall breakdown, it's likely that within the 60% that is market-related you may have a portion of your portfolio in small cap U.S. growth, small cap U.S. value, large cap U.S. growth, large cap U.S. value, and large company foreign and emerging markets. Within the 40% that would be targeted to bonds, you would own some intermediate to long-term high-quality bonds and international long-term foreign bonds, and it's likely you may even have a pinch of high-yield bonds as well. Notice how we have gone from the big picture, deciding how aggressive you want to be as measured by your exposure to stocks, and moved into a variety of asset classes in line with your investment goals.

At this point we've covered a lot of material about asset allocation. We've looked at a variety of asset classes, we've seen the benefit of being broadly diversified, and we understand we don't have to chase the hot performers to do well. It's now obvious that being in a number of asset classes can greatly help us reduce risk in our portfolios.

The Next Step for You

Let's move on now to some of the steps you need to take to actually implement what we've learned. To begin, look at your current holdings and examine your portfolio's asset allocation. Most people own fewer asset classes than they think. Examine your portfolio to see how much large cap and small cap you have, how much is domestic and how much is foreign, what is growth, what is value, etc. Use the definitions of the asset classes that I've provided for you. They'll help you plug in your current assets under the different asset classes. If you're like most people, you'll find you've got a whole lot in one and very little or none in another.

The next step is to decide on your investment goals. How much risk do you want to assume and what are your timelines? Ask yourself how much exposure you want to the market, understanding that the more exposure you have, the more volatility you can expect.

If you wish to be like our example, middle-of-the-road investor, you should be somewhere in the area of 60% stock or stock mutual funds and 40% bonds or bond mutual funds. Use that as a yardstick when looking at where you are currently positioned. If you consider yourself a moderate investor and you find that your portfolio is 100% invested in stocks, trust me, that's not in line with what you had in mind and you probably want to refocus your portfolio.

Make sure you know what kind of assets you have, what your goals are, and the timeline associated with them. If your portfolio is out of balance, you may need to reallocate it, plugging some of those holes you've discovered and making it more in line with what you've decided are your investment objectives and goals. (Note: some changes may have tax consequences associated with them in the form of capital gains. Make sure you consider that when making changes.)

Mutual Fund Style

Given that we are now committed to asset allocation, one of the most important factors in determining whether a mutual fund is right for your portfolio is adherence to style. Remember our breakdown of stocks and bonds. Adherence to style refers to the extent to which the manager stays true to the asset classes that have been indicated as the fund's investment targets. For example, if you find a mutual fund with its goal stated as large cap domestic growth and you see that the portfolio is becoming more and more internationally focused, you want to reexamine the use of the fund and find one that's committed to adhering to that stated investment style. A fund that bounces all over chasing what the manager thinks is the hot asset class is going to undermine the whole idea of asset allocation.

Where to Turn for Help

As I mentioned in Chapter 6, there are two documents closely associated with mutual funds.

The first source of information that everybody tells you to look at is the prospectus. While this is theoretically very good advice, it has been my experience over the years that investors usually take one look at the fine print, complicated numbers, and intimidating look of a prospectus and place it in the circular file. The information that you're seeking is there, yes, but unfortunately not in an appealing package.

The other document that you receive when you buy or request information on a mutual fund is a sales piece. This piece is a lot more user-friendly, because its purpose is to get you to buy that particular mutual fund. In spite of the sales pitch, however, much of the information in these pieces can be very helpful and many times they highlight the style of the fund.

Monitoring Your Portfolio

There are really two elements to monitoring. The first and most obvious is seeing how well your portfolio is performing. Don't do this on a daily, weekly, or even monthly basis. Semi-annually to annually would be a good time frame for examining your portfolio.

Let me throw up a big red flag here. Suppose you have 60% of your money in stock-oriented investments and 40% in bonds and then you pick up the newspaper and it says the Dow is up 20%. Should you be disappointed if your total portfolio isn't up 20%? If you think it through, it wouldn't be reasonable to make that assumption. After all, you don't have 100% of your portfolio in Dow-oriented stocks. You need to be realistic when you're looking at the performance of your portfolio. You need to be certain you are comparing apples with apples. Compare your large cap growth with other large cap growth funds, your intermediate bond fund with other intermediate bond funds. Only by comparing like portfolios can you come up with a realistic evaluation of how well your portfolio is performing in line with what other mutual funds are doing.

The second step to monitoring your portfolio is one that's very easily overlooked. That is periodically rebalancing your portfolio. What does this mean?

Let's take an example. If you decided at the beginning of the year that you want 20% of your portfolio in large cap foreign and that particular segment of the market had a terrific year, you'd be substantially up in that position. When you reviewed your portfolio, you'd probably find you'd have significantly more in that mutual fund than you'd originally targeted. You would then want to "take some chips off the table" in that asset class and place those chips in an asset class that will keep you in line with your initial targeted percentages. Rebalancing your portfolio really forces you to do the right thing: you'll be selling some of your winners and sticking to your investment discipline.

We have now covered much of what you need to know on this topic. I've thrown a lot of information at you in this chapter and I hope you can see it's well worth your time to learn about asset allocation. As we discussed, this strategy has been demonstrated to be the single most important determinant in the performance of your portfolio. You should feel relieved that you don't need to spend time chasing hot stocks and timing the market. You simply have to be serious about placing your money in a variety of asset classes and making certain it's doing for you what you had in mind. When you make a commitment to asset allocation, you're making a commitment to long-term, serious management of your portfolio.

9 Making Your Retirement Years Golden

I know it's hard for many of you "Thirty-Somethings" and younger to believe this, but even you should be planning for retirement. It's never too early to start this process, and the earlier you start the easier it is. However, I've dealt with enough people to know that it's hard for many younger people to believe they will ever age, let alone retire. It's just too far off to be real. The rest of us know it comes all too quickly!

People routinely talk to me about their desires to retire comfortably and perhaps to retire early. When you picture retirement, what comes to your mind? Trips to Europe, a home in a sunny climate, golf on a regular basis, or driving around the country going everywhere you've ever wanted to visit at a leisurely pace? If you plan far enough ahead and stick to your plan, this can become a reality. If you don't, your reality will become something else entirely.

I see many people who have little or no hope of retiring at any time. Their concern is for the most basic of life's necessities—food, shelter, and personal needs. If you think it's too early to start planning for your retirement, guess again. Look at the cost of waiting as shown in Figure 9-1.

What it takes to save $100,000 by Age 65, assuming 6% interest

Current Age	Monthly Deposit	Total Deposits	Penalty for Waiting 1 Year	Penalty for Waiting 5 Years
21	40.42	21,342	877	4,707
22	43.06	22,219	905	4,867
23	45.88	23,124	945	5,043
24	48.92	24,069	973	5,208
25	52.17	25,042	1,007	5,387
26	55.66	26,049	1,037	5,567
27	59.40	27,086	1,081	5,758
28	63.44	28,167	1,110	5,944
29	67.77	29,277	1,152	6,137
30	72.45	30,429	1,187	6,334
31	77.49	31,616	1,228	6,535
32	82.94	32,844	1,267	6,740
33	88.83	34,111	1,303	6,950
34	95.20	35,414	1,349	7,168
35	102.12	36,763	1,388	7,382
36	109.63	38,151	1,433	7,604
37	117.81	39,584	1,477	7,830
38	126.73	41,061	1,521	8,059
39	136.48	42,582	1,563	8,289
40	147.15	44,145	1,610	8,528
41	158.87	45,755	1,659	8,769
42	171.79	47,414	1,706	9,010
43	186.06	49,120	1,751	9,257
44	201.87	50,871	1,802	9,507
45	219.47	52,637	1,851	9,760
46	239.14	54,524	1,900	10,017
47	261.22	56,424	1,953	10,277
48	286.16	58,377	2,001	10,536
49	314.47	60,378	2,055	10,800
50	346.85	62,433	2,108	11,067
51	384.17	64,541	2,160	11,338
52	427.57	66,701	2,212	11,610
53	478.56	68,913	2,265	11,878
54	539.23	71,178	2,322	12,160
55	612.50	73,500	2,379	12,433
56	702.58	78,879	2,432	12,697
57	815.74	78,311	2,480	12,971
58	961.80	80,791	2,547	13,268
59	1,157.47	83,338	2,595	13,542
60	1,431.21	85,933	2,643	14,067

Figure 9-1. The penalty for waiting increases as you get older

Explanation of Figure: Figure 9-1 shows the amount of money that must be deposited at the beginning of each month in order to accumulate $100,000 by age 65. Interest is credited at a 6% net annual rate and compounded monthly (i.e., it is credited at the end of each month assuming a 6% annual after-tax or untaxed growth). The penalty for waiting one year is calculated by subtracting total deposits at the current age from total deposits one year later (e.g., at age 45 the penalty for waiting one year is $54,524 − $52,673 = $1,851). The penalty for waiting five years is calculated by subtracting total deposits at the current age from total deposits five years later (e.g., at age 45 the penalty for waiting five years is $62,433 − $52,673 = $9,760).

We haven't had a great history of planning to meet our retirement needs. There are some good reasons for this that we'll look at later. It's more important now than ever that we take charge of this critical area, for several reasons.

Life Expectancies

By and large, Americans are living longer than ever. That's the good news. The bad news is that you may end up broke in your later years. If we're planning to retire at age 65 and we're expecting to live to be age 85, there's an obvious need for a pot of money to keep us going for those 20 years. We're not only living longer, we're living healthier, and that means many people want to maintain a youthful, active lifestyle. This lifestyle may dictate the need for money for activities such as travel and entertainment and all those fun things we look forward to in retirement.

Sources of Retirement Income

In the past there were three main sources that most people looked at to provide their retirement income: company retirement plans, Social Security, and personal savings. As times change, it's clear that the major contributor to our retirement nest egg has shifted. Let's take a look at these sources and how they may or may not benefit you.

Company Pensions

Many of us remember, and even see our parents enjoy, the benefits of company pension plans. With this type of retirement plan, you receive money from your company based on your salary and the length of time you worked for the company. In earlier times, everyone felt assured that if they stayed with the same firm for many years, they would retire with a nice pension benefit that would be adequate to meet their needs for income in retirement until they died. Those days are rapidly disappearing. Most companies are minimizing or eliminating these plans and instead are offering 401(k)s or similar choices that require you to fund your own retirement. We'll look more at these plans a little later.

Social Security

The second traditional source for retirement income has been Social Security. When I ask those attending my classes how many of them expect Social Security to meet their income needs, nary a hand goes up. People are beginning to realize that Social Security will only provide a small percentage of their retirement income—and it's good to understand that fact of life.

It should come as no surprise to you that the system is projected to be broke about the time the youngest of the baby boomers (those born in 1964) can receive any benefits. From its inception, Social Security was not meant to be a complete source of funds for everyone's retirement. It was designed to be a financial safety net for those who had no retirement plan whatsoever. When this program was enacted in the early 1930s, 65 was targeted as the benefit age because life expectancies were not as great and the government never intended to have to continue payments until the age of 85 or longer. Very frankly, they thought you'd be dead by then.

The debate rages about what to do about Social Security to make the system more solvent. The question is not *if* something must be done, but rather *what* must be done. No one questions that the system is in trouble. Don't count on it as your sole source of income or you'll be in a world of hurt.

There's a final depressing thought on Social Security—on average, retired men receive approximately $3,000 a year more in Social Security benefits than retired women. This is because women frequently leave the work force to have and raise their children. The problem is further exacerbated by the fact that, while women are in the work force, they earn significantly less than their male counterparts. All in all, it's safe to say that if Social Security is your Plan A, you'd better be developing a Plan B.

Personal Savings

With the demise of traditional company pension plans and the depressing state of Social Security, that leaves one resource responsible for planning your retirement—you!

In this chapter, we're going to look at the positive things you can do to ensure that your retirement years are golden. No matter what your age or income, there are some things you can do to prepare for your retirement years.

How Much Do I Need?

One of the most common questions I get asked about retirement is "How much will I need to retire?" My answer: "Nobody has ever complained to me about having too much." While that answer may initially appear flip, it's true that it's far better to err on the side of too much than too little.

Experts commonly advise that you'll need a retirement income equal to 70% of your pre-retirement income. Like all rules of thumb, this one needs to be taken with a grain of salt. If you plan to retire in a rural area, play golf at the local public course, and not travel extensively, you're obviously going to need less than your friend who intends to retire at a deluxe villa in Palm Springs and spend much of the time cruising around in style. When you estimate your retirement needs, it's very important to determine what kind of lifestyle you hope to have and where you're likely to be living.

As you begin to calculate your monthly retirement needs, here are some of the major expenses that you need to project.

Actual Retirement Costs

Housing	$_____
Medical	$_____
Food	$_____
Recreation	$_____
Travel	$_____
Taxes	$_____
Personal Items	$_____
Insurance	$_____
Transportation/Auto	$_____
Household Expenses	$_____
(maintenance, utilities, phone)	
Special Purchases	$_____
(computer, furniture, gifts)	
Hobbies	$_____
Other	$_____
Total	$_____

After you've totaled the amount on this side of the equation, on the other side you need to list and total your expected sources of income.

Social Security	$_____
Employer-Sponsored Pension Plans	$_____
Personal Savings	$_____
IRAs, SEPs, and Roth IRAs	$_____
Employer-Sponsored	
Retirement Plans (401(k),	
403(b), ESOP)	$_____
Other	$_____
Total	$_____

After you've gotten the total of your projected approximate annual income, subtract the total of your estimated annual expenses and you come up with either an income surplus or a shortfall. Remember: many projections you make today are based on assumptions about tomorrow which may or may not prove valid. This manner of rough calculation will give you a starting point in assessing your retirement situation.

The nonprofit American Savings Education Council has a simplified worksheet for estimating retirement needs. This is available on the Internet at www.asec.org. Another useful retirement site is www.pathfinder.com/money. This site has an interactive calculator that allows you to analyze your retirement savings. If you're over age 50, whether or not you're retired, you may want to view www.aarp.org. This is the site for the American Association of Retired Persons and can provide a great deal of information.

If you project a shortfall, don't despair; there are some things you can do. The most obvious action is to increase your level of savings to compensate for the difference. Another alternative would be to position your money in slightly more aggressive assets with higher return expectations. You may also need to delay retirement or plan to work part-time after retirement. Downsizing your home and your lifestyle is yet another alternative.

Please, please, please be realistic about your retirement income! People have approached me wondering if they could get an income of $20,000 a year from a $100,000 investment with the safety of a U.S. government bond. Only in their dreams, unfortunately! Without making this overly complicated, think about this. If you're buying a bond, a CD, or an interest-generating investment and the current interest rates are 6% on that $100,000, you can figure closer to $6,000 than $20,000. Think about the sum of the assets you're considering for income and simply apply a variety of interest rates, considering your risk tolerance, and calculate a realistic return. When was the last time you heard of a U.S. government bond giving you that 20% interest rate?

Now That You Know What You Need, How Do You Get There?

I'll give you a moment to pull yourself together after running your retirement needs calculations. I'd be willing to bet that most of you are not on target to meet your ultimate goals. Now let's turn that knowledge into action. Following are different types of retirement plans. You'll be able to take advantage of one or more of these to prepare more appropriately for your retirement.

Company Retirement Plans

Probably the most common retirement plan in corporate America today is the 401(k). This plan allows you to contribute a percentage of your gross income (up to 15% or $10,000, adjusted yearly for increases in the cost of living) to invest toward retirement. This contribution is considered pre-tax dollars, so you lower your taxable income by the amount of your contribution.

Let's look at an example. If you make $30,000 a year and put $3,000 into your 401(k), your taxable income for that year would be $27,000. That sounds good so far, doesn't it? Just wait; it gets even better. All of the money in your 401(k) grows tax-deferred. This means you don't have a tax bill until you begin withdrawing this money. One of the rules of a 401(k) is that you generally can't begin to take your money until you are 59½ or you pay a 10% early withdrawal penalty. When you take the money out, it's taxed as ordinary income.

> **Buys Briefs**
>
> A **401(k) plan** is an employer-sponsored retirement plan that allows employees to set aside a percentage of their income on a pre-tax basis. This money is typically invested in stock and bond mutual funds and grows tax-deferred.
>
> **Top-Heavy** describes a plan in which the assets of the key employees exceed 60% of the total assets.

There are exceptions to this rule, which we'll discuss in a minute.

In addition to the funds that you contribute to your 401(k), many times your employer will provide a match up to a certain percentage or dollar amount as an incentive to get you into the plan. This match may be in dollars or in the form of company stock. It is in the company's interest to do this because, if there is not broad employee participation in the plan, it may be considered "top-heavy" and that would limit the contributions that the more highly compensated employees can make.

The match, if any, is totally at the discretion of the company and should be considered pure gravy. If your employer provides a 50% match on all your contributions, that means that you're getting a 50% return on your money before it's even placed in your investment option: it's basically free money. Your contribution to the plan is immediately vested; that means that it belongs to you immediately. The employer's match portion may have a vesting schedule, which means that the funds don't belong to you until you meet certain time requirements. The length of time it takes to become fully vested varies among employers. Typically a company may have a five-year vesting schedule.

This would mean, for example, that if you quit after year one, all of your contributions and 20% of the employer match would be yours to keep. If you stayed through year two, you would keep all of your contributions and would receive 40% of the employer match. This percentage would continue to rise through year five, after which you would be entitled to 100% of the employer match. Each plan may be slightly different in this regard, so you should contact your human resources department to make sure you understand the features of your particular plan.

Buys Briefs

Vesting is the right an employee gradually acquires by length of service with a company to receive employer-contributed benefits such as payments from pension, profit sharing, stock purchase, employer match in 401(k), etc.

Investment Options in a 401(k)

Mutual funds are the investment vehicles most commonly offered in 401(k)s. Some plans may offer company stock as well. Employers will typically offer a menu of eight to 10 different funds that represent a variety of asset classes and risk levels. Your employer should provide detailed information about these funds and an adequate education so that you can make an informed decision about how to place your money. Your employer is responsible for providing this to you, so insist that you receive it.

This would be a good time to review Chapter 8, because you can apply all of what I said there about asset allocation when making your investment selections. The longer you have until you will need this money, the more aggressive you may wish to be.

Hint: no matter how well your company stock has performed over the last several years, it's not a good idea to have all of your retirement assets in that one area. That lack of diversification could leave you at great risk.

After you make your investment selections, they are not cast in concrete. You can and should monitor the performance of these funds and make sure your asset allocation stays in line with your wishes. You are typically allowed to make several changes throughout the year. In monitoring these funds, as with all funds, don't get caught up in daily tracking or constantly changing your funds. When you're considering a change, look at performance, of course, but make sure you're measuring it against similar funds and indexes, as I emphasized earlier.

The Danger of Loans

Many 401(k) plans have loan provisions associated with them. These allow you to withdraw a portion of your funds and then pay them back to your own account with interest. In my opinion, loan provisions should generally be left alone. It's simply not a good idea to borrow from your retirement account unless you are absolutely sure that you'll be returning that money. This is not money that you want to withdraw for a trip to Disneyland or a new car, for example. We've seen how important it is to build your retirement assets, so I would urge you not to take a loan lightly.

Opportunity Cost is the cost of losing an "opportunity" to obtain a higher rate of return in an alternative investment.

Over the years I've worked with many people who've changed jobs, not repaid their loans, and ultimately suffered a 10% early withdrawal penalty and had to pay taxes on the money as ordinary income. In that case, this is some of the most expensive money you'll ever borrow in your life. If you pay a 10% penalty and you are taxed at a 28% rate, the loan is effectively costing you 38%. That's worse than the greatest rip-off you can find in the credit card industry, not to mention the opportunity cost, because you do not have that money compounding and growing tax-deferred in your retirement account.

If you think you're brilliant by paying yourself 5½% interest, you need to calculate what your return would have been on that money you borrowed if you'd left it invested in a mutual fund in your 401(k). Over the last three years, the average annual return on the S&P 500 was over 30%—and that doesn't even include the effect of compounding. How is your 5½% looking now? The bottom line: always think long and hard before withdrawing money from any retirement account.

403(b) Retirement Accounts

While we've been discussing 401(k)s, those of you who work for non-profit organizations are probably thinking that the rules are strikingly similar to the rules for your 403(b). You are correct. The one distinction is that 403(b)s very commonly use annuities as their funding

403(b) is a retirement plan much the same as a 401(k) but for non-profit organizations. An insurance company frequently provides the investments.

vehicles. The insurance chapter (Chapter 11) discusses annuities in greater detail.

Within these annuities you'll also find a variety of mutual fund choices and much of the discussion about 401(k)s applies to these programs as well. Two of the differences with a 403(b) are that you have 100% immediate vesting and the plan contribution limits generally allow up to 25% of your gross compensation or $10,000, whichever is less.

These programs offer you a great deal and I would urge you to participate in your company plan. If you're unable to contribute the maximum, at least contribute up to the matching contribution. This match is a wonderful and painless way to increase your retirement assets. It's very easy to contribute to these plans, because the contributions are automatically deducted from your paycheck. This forces you to be disciplined and to pay yourself first. These accounts are frequently win-win situations. You're funding your retirement, lowering your taxes, and enjoying the benefits of tax-deferred growth. All in all, these plans should be at the top of your list in retirement planning if they're available to you.

What if You Are Self-Employed or Work for a Small Company?

Simplified Employee Pension Plan (SEP) is a type of retirement plan that allows your employer to contribute a fixed percentage of your income on a pre-tax basis into a self-directed retirement plan.

Have I got a deal for you! One of my favorite retirement plans is a Simplified Employee Pension (SEP) Plan. The plans are available for self-employed individuals, small businesses, or independent contractors. This plan allows your employer to set aside up to 15% of the income of participating employees for retirement. Your employer must put the same percentage in for you as they put in for themselves. The plan also must include all employees who are at least 21 and have earned at least $400 in three of the preceding five years.

Another benefit of a SEP is that most offer a wide range of investment options including stocks, bonds, and mutual funds. Each individual is typically able to control the investment decisions in her or his own accounts and all monies grow tax-deferred. The money in your account is always fully vested, so it's yours right away. Withdrawals must follow the same rules as for an IRA. If you are in a SEP at work, you may still contribute that $2,000 to an IRA, but it may or may not be deductible. In addition, there are no big fancy IRS reporting requirements for the company, so the plans are inexpensive to administer. All in all, these plans are winners, so if your company doesn't have a plan, go tap your boss on the shoulder and show her or him this section of the book.

SIMPLE IRAs

This is one of the newer kids on the block in the retirement plan arena. The acronym SIMPLE stands for Savings Incentive Match Plan for Employees. This IRA was designed for businesses with 100 or fewer employees as an alternative to the more expensive and harder to administer 401(k). This plan has a $6,000 deferral limit and mandates that your employer must match your salary deferrals dollar for dollar up to 3% of your pay. This amount can be lowered to 1% in two out of five years or the employer can contribute a match of 2% of pay for every eligible employee. The plan must include all employees who have earned at least $5,000 during two preceding years and can reasonably be expected to earn as least as much in the current year. Your contributions will reduce your current taxable income and all the earnings grow tax-deferred. The program has 100% immediate vesting and is easy to establish and maintain.

The Taxpayer Relief Act

The 1997 Taxpayer Relief Act introduced a number of changes affecting most taxpayers and their retirement plans. Unfortunately, taxpayers are not feeling very relieved by this act and are finding the new options very confusing. I'm going to try to cut through that confusion and help you understand these changes so you can decide what's best for you.

The Traditional IRA

Familiar to many of us, this is the IRA that has been in place for a number of years. It is available to all investors with earned income at least equal to the amount of money they wish to contribute. That means that, if you want to contribute the maximum of $2,000, you must have earned at least that much money in that tax year. Many investors who contributed to the traditional IRA were able to deduct all or part of their contributions from their current taxes. The ability to deduct your contribution from your taxes depended on whether or not you were covered by an employer's retirement plan.

If you were not covered by any retirement plan at work, you are allowed to deduct $2,000 ($4,000 per couple) from your income taxes, regardless of your income. If, on the other hand, you or your spouse participate in an employer's plan, you still may be able to get a full or partial deduction as long as your income falls within certain ranges, as shown below. Even if you're not eligible for a tax deduction, you're still allowed to make a non-deductible contribution to a traditional IRA.

Active Participant in an Employer's Retirement Plan	Adjusted Gross Income in 1998	Maximum Deductible Contributions
Single		
No	Any amount	$2,000
Yes	$30,000 or less	$2,000
Yes	$30,001 - $39,999	$200 - $1,999
Yes	$40,000 and over	No deduction
Married (filing a joint return)		
No	Any amount	$2,000 per person
Both	$50,000 or less	$2,000 per person
Both	$50,001 - $59,999	$200 - $1,999 per person
Both	$60,000 and over	No deduction

Within this IRA, you're able to begin withdrawals after age 59½ without penalty and you must begin withdrawals shortly after you reach age 70½. Since these earnings have been growing tax-deferred, that means that you'll begin paying the taxes as you make withdrawals. If you withdraw money from a traditional IRA prior to age 59½, you will be hit with a 10% penalty for early withdrawal. There's a way to avoid that penalty using substantially equal periodic payments, which I'll describe in more detail later.

What's New in '98 and What Does It Mean to You?

Here are the most important changes in 1998 and their significance to you in doing your financial planning:

- The amount of income you're allowed to make has been raised in '98, so if you've earned too much in the past to be able to deduct all or part of your contribution, you may now be able to do so. In '98, if you make $30,000 or less, you're able to deduct your full contribution.

- For the first time in '98, if your spouse has a retirement plan at work but you don't work or don't participate in a plan at work, you can take a full deduction of up to $2,000 per year if your joint adjusted income is less than $150,000.

- You now have penalty-free access to your IRA funds for the purchase of a first-time home (up to $10,000 over a lifetime) and for higher education expenses.

- In the past, if you were a big saver you were penalized. A 15% excise tax was assessed to individuals and estates with large retirement plan balances. This 15% tax has now been totally eliminated.

Why Contribute to a Traditional IRA?

Never lose sight of the fact that you don't pay taxes on investment earnings in your IRA until you begin withdrawals, so your money is growing free from the bite of taxes on an annual basis. This means that your money is compounding tax-deferred and should well outpace the growth in taxable accounts. Probably the biggest distinction between this and other types of IRAs, like the Roth IRA, is that contributions may be partly or fully deductible, depending on where you fall within the prescribed guidelines. If you're not eligible to fund a Roth IRA, due to its income restrictions, then you would certainly want to contribute to a traditional IRA to benefit from the tax-deferred growth.

Roth IRA

This is the IRA that's new in 1998. It's named after the senator who introduced the idea. What makes this a truly unique IRA is that your money grows *tax-free* as opposed to *tax-deferred*. To make this perfectly

A **Roth IRA** is an IRA for after-tax investments; the earnings and withdrawals for retirement are tax-free.

clear, you will not pay any federal taxes as your IRA grows or when you begin withdrawals.

The contributions to these accounts are made with after-tax dollars so they are *never* deductible on the front end. Remember that with a traditional IRA you may have a partial or total deduction on your contribution, your money grows tax-deferred, and you pay taxes on the back end as you withdraw. The Roth flips this concept and allows no deduction up front, lets your money grow tax-free, and incurs no federal tax on the back end. A major condition with the Roth is that it will be tax-free and penalty-free only if your account has been open at least five years and you are 59½ or older.

Can You Contribute to a Roth IRA?

Adjusted Gross Income in 1998	Annual Contributions Limit
Single	
$95,000 or less	$2,000
$95,001 - $109,999	$200 - $1,990
$110,000 and over	No contribution
Married filing a joint return	
$150,000 or less	$2,000 each
$150,001 - $159,999	$200 - $1,990
$160,000 and over	No contribution

You may avoid the 10% early withdrawal penalty, although not the income tax penalty, if you meet certain other conditions. For example, if you take the money because you've reached 59½ or you've become disabled, there's no penalty. In addition, if you use the money for higher education expenses or for a first-time home purchase (up to $10,000 maximum, just as with the traditional IRA), the 10% withdrawal penalty will not be applied. Always keep in mind the importance of the five-year timeline with the Roth IRA, because that's the minimum requirement for earnings to be withdrawn tax-free under any condition.

Did I stump you? Notice that I said for the *earnings* to be withdrawn tax-free and I didn't say anything about the original contributions. What does that tell you? An amazing twist with the Roth IRA lets you draw down your contribution dollars first. Since you've made those contributions with after-tax dollars, you've already paid taxes on that money, so withdrawals of that money are not subject to *either* income tax *or* early withdrawal penalties.

Another advantage of the Roth IRA is that you can continue to contribute after age 70½, as long as you've earned as much in income as the amount of your contribution. Traditional IRAs do not allow this. In addition, the Roth IRA does not require you to begin making minimum withdrawals from your IRA at age 70½, as is mandated for the traditional IRA.

Is a Roth IRA Right for You?

- You may contribute to a Roth IRA if your modified gross income is less than $95,000 if you are single and below $150,000 for married individuals filing jointly. If you exceed these income levels, you're automatically eliminated from establishing a Roth IRA, although Congress is reexamining some of the income provisions.
- If you are young and have many years for your account to grow tax-free, a Roth IRA may be the right choice for you.
- For those in lower tax brackets or those who expect to be in higher tax brackets in retirement, it may make a lot of sense to bite the tax bullet now rather than pay a higher rate when you begin withdrawing.
- If you're unable to qualify for the tax deduction available with a traditional IRA, that factor may make the Roth IRA the IRA of choice. The worksheets on pages 116-118 prepared by Franklin® Templeton® can help you analyze your situation and figure out which IRA is best for you.

To Convert or Not to Convert: That Is the Question

The Taxpayer Relief Act of 1997 allows you to convert all or part of your existing IRA to a Roth IRA if your adjusted gross income is under $100,000. In 1998 you're given a "special introductory offer." If you converted to a Roth IRA prior to January 1, 1999, the tax consequences of

Which IRA Is Right for You?
–the Regular IRA or Roth IRA?

The Taxpayer Relief Act of 1997 created some exciting new investment opportunities, one of which is t
IRA. However, deciding whether the regular IRA or the Roth IRA offers you the best mileage for your retirement
dollars can be challenging. This worksheet is designed to help you determine which IRA may provide you with
greater retirement income. Please keep in mind, your adjusted gross income (AGI) must be less than $110,000
(single) or $160,000 (married filing jointly) to be eligible for a Roth IRA.[1]

Step 1: Assumptions

1. The amount you plan to contribute annually to your IRA. Single individuals may
    contribute up to $2,000; married couples filing jointly may contribute up to $_____
    $4,000.

2. The total amount of your armual IRA contributions that will be nondeductible. If
    you expect all of your contributions to be deductible, enter "0." $_____

3. The annual rate of return (between 4% and 12 %) you expect to earn on your
    investments prior to retirement.   _____%

4. The annual rate of return (between 4% and 12%) you expect to earn during
    retirement.   _____%

5. The number of years (between 5 and 30 in increments of 5) you have to save for
    retirement. (Please use a number that would result in your retiring no sooner
    than age 59½.)   _____years

6. The number of years (between 5 and 30 in increments of 5) you plan on taking
    distributions from your IRA after you retire.   _____years

7. Your federal income tax rate prior to retirement (15%, 28%, 31%, 36% or
    39.6%).   _____%

8. Your anticipated federal income tax rate during retirement (15%, 28%, 31%,
    36% or 39.6%).   _____%

9. Subtract your tax rate prior to retirement (line 7) from 1.00
    (for example, 1.00 - 0.28 tax bracket = 0.72). Multiply the result by line 3.   _____%

10. Subtract your tax rate during retirement (line 8) from 1.00. Multiply the result
    by line 4.   _____%

1. A partial Roth IRA contribution can be made if your AGI is between $95,000 and $110,000 (single)
or $150,000 and $160,000 (married filing jointly).

FranklinTempleton

Step 2: Factors

Future Value Factor

11. In the table below, find the number of years to retirement (from line 5) in the left-hand column and your expected rate of return while working (from line 3) across the top. The intersection is your future value factor. (For example, if you have 20 years until retirement, and expect an 8% rate of return whjile working, 49.42 is your future value factor.)   _____

12. In the table below, find the number of years to retirement (from line 5) in the left-hand column and your expected after-tax rate of return while working (from line 9) across the top. The intersection is your after-tax future value factor.   _____

	Rate of Return										
	2%	**3%**	**4%**	**5%**	**6%**	**7%**	**8%**	**9%**	**10%**	**11%**	**12%**
5	5.31	5.47	5.63	5.80	5.98	6.15	6.34	6.52	6.72	6.91	7.12
10	11.17	11.81	12.49	13.21	13.97	14.78	15.65	16.56	17.53	18.56	19.65
15	17.64	19.16	20.82	22.66	24.67	26.89	29.32	32.00	34.95	38.19	41.75
20	24.78	27.68	30.97	34.72	38.99	43.87	49.42	55.76	63.00	71.27	80.70
25	32.67	37.55	43.31	50.11	58.16	67.68	78.95	92.32	108.18	127.00	149.33
30	41.38	49.00	58.33	69.76	83.80	101.07	122.35	148.58	180.94	220.91	270.29

Years to Retirement (left-hand column labels)

Income Factor

13. In the table below, find the number of years you plan to take distributions (from line 6) in the left-hand column and your expected rate of return during retirement (from line 4) across the top. The intersection is the factor that will determine your annual retirement income.   _____

14. In the table below, find the number of years you plan to take distributions (from line 6) in the left-hand column and your expected after-tax rate of return during retirement (from line 10) across the top. The intersection is the factor that will determine your after-tax annual retirement income.   _____

	Rate of Return										
	2%	**3%**	**4%**	**5%**	**6%**	**7%**	**8%**	**9%**	**10%**	**11%**	**12%**
5	4.81	4.72	4.63	4.55	4.47	4.39	4.31	4.24	4.17	4.10	4.04
10	9.16	8.79	8.44	8.11	7.80	7.52	7.25	7.00	6.76	6.54	6.33
15	13.11	12.30	11.56	10.90	10.29	9.75	9.24	8.79	8.37	7.98	7.63
20	16.68	15.32	14.13	13.09	12.16	11.34	10.60	9.95	9.36	8.84	8.37
25	19.91	17.94	16.25	14.80	13.55	12.47	11.53	10.71	9.98	9.35	8.78
30	22.84	20.19	17.98	16.14	14.59	13.28	12.16	11.20	10.37	9.65	9.02

Years to Retirement (left-hand column labels)

Step 3: Calculations

IRA Value at Retirement

15. Multiply line 1 by the future value factor on line 11. $_____

Determine Your Annual Retirement Income

16. Divide line 15 by the income factor on line 13. $_____

Total Income from a Roth IRA

17. Multiply line 16 by the number of years you plan on taking distributions
     (line 6). $_____

Total Income from a Regular IRA

18. Multiply the amount of nondeductible contributions (line 2) by the number
     of years you have to save for retirement (line 5). Divide the result by the
     number of years you plan on taking distributions (line 6). $_____

19. Subtract line 18 from line 16. $_____

20. Subtract your tax rate during retirement (line 8) from 1.00
     (for example, 1.00 - 0.28 tax rate = 0.72). Multiply the result by line 19. $_____

21. Add line 18 to line 20. Then multiply the result by the number of years you
     plan on taking distributions (line 6). $_____

22. Subtract the amount of nondeductible contributions (line 2) from the total
     amount you plan to contribute annually (line 1). Then multiply the result by
     line 7. If you don't plan on investing the tax savings you receive by making
     deductible contributions, then enter zero on lines 22 and 23. $_____

23. Multiply line 22 by line 12. Divide the result by the after-tax income factor on
     line 14. $_____

24. Multiply line 23 by the number of years you plan on taking distributions
     (line 6). Add the result to line 21. $_____

Result

25. Enter the amounts from lines 17 and line 24 below. The greater of the two indicates which option
     may provide the highest total amount of retirement income.

Roth IRA *(line 17)*	Regular IRA *(line 24)*
$_____	$_____

This is not a complete analysis and does not factor in any applicable state or local taxes. Therefore, we
suggest you contact your investment representative and tax advisor for more specific information
relating to your individual circumstances. For more information on your regular and Roth IRAs, call a
Franklin Templeton Retirement Plan Specialist at **1-800/527-2020**

the conversion will be included in your income on a pro rata basis over a four-year tax period beginning in 1998.

If this is starting to sound confusing, that's because it is. Many people do not seem to understand that the government never gives us something for nothing. The way to understand the tax picture is that the government is essentially saying, "Pay me now or pay me later." If you opt to convert, you will have a tax event on deductible contributions and earnings in your traditional IRA.

The question of whether or not to convert is very complex and you should spend a lot of time and energy deciding whether this decision is right for you, especially if you have a sizable account. One important consideration is your tax bill. If you convert a large amount of money, you could trigger a very large tax event. Taking money from your IRA to pay the taxes due on the conversion is not a good idea and it will actually work against the goal of building your retirement account. If you don't have assets outside of the retirement account to pay the tax bill, that alone makes the conversion significantly less attractive.

Next you'll see a worksheet provided by Franklin® Templeton® that can help you determine if you should convert your regular IRA to a Roth IRA (pages 120-126). I urge you to take the time to fill in the blanks and, then, after completing this worksheet, to talk with your tax advisor to make certain the decision is right for you.

Like so many things in life, this decision is not nearly as simple as it may appear on the surface. Many people are fearful that down the road the government may change its mind about the tax-free provision or in some other way, such as adopting a flat income tax, that will make this IRA unattractive. Conversion is a serious, and sometimes expensive, financial planning decision and you should not make it lightly.

IRA Rollovers

By now you're probably starting to understand why I said people are not very relieved by the Taxpayer Relief Act of 1997. It's all a little confusing. One of the areas of confusion is the difference between conversions, as we discussed above, and IRA rollovers.

Should You Convert Your Regular IRA to a Roth Conversion IRA?

The Taxpayer Relief Act of 1997 created some exciting new investment opportunities, one of which is the Roth IRA. The new IRA allows all contributions to accumulate and, if certain conditions are met, be withdrawn tax free. This is different from your regular IRA because all distributions (excluding nondeductible contribution amounts) are taxed upon withdrawal. Considering the choices now available, you may need to tune-up your IRA investment by deciding if you should convert your regular IRA to a Roth Conversion IRA.

Please keep in mind, if your adjusted gross income is over $100,000, or you are married but file separately, you are not eligible to convert your regular IRA. Any amounts converted (excluding any nondeductible contributions) will be included as taxable income during the year you convert. However, if you make a conversion prior to January 1, 1999, you may take advantage of a special tax provision, which allows you to pay one-fourth of the taxable amount in the year of conversion and each of the following three years. The 10% federal tax penalty on premature distributions does not apply to conversions.*

Mutual funds, annuities, and other investment products:
• are not FDIC insured;
• are not deposits or obligations of, or guaranteed by, any financial institution;
• are subject to investment risks, including possible loss of the principal amount invested.

---

*As of the date of this brochure, legislation was pending that, if passed, could result in taxes and penalties on certain distributions from a Roth Conversion IRA within five years of conversion. This legislation may also prohibit conversions from SEP-IRAs and SIMPLE-IRAs.

FranklinTempleton

Deciding whether to convert your regular IRA to a Roth Conversion IRA can be challenging. To help, we have designed the following hypothetical scenarios to illustrate who may benefit from a conversion and who may not. Of course, your own investment results will differ so we suggest you contact your investment representative and tax advisor to help determine the better option for you.

Scenario #1

Jim Blair, age 30, is currently in the 15% tax bracket. He plans to take a lump-sum distribution from his IRA at age 60, when he expects to be in the 28% tax bracket. Currently, Jim makes deductible contributions to his IRA, which is now worth $10,000. Should he convert his regular IRA to a Roth Conversion IRA?

Regular IRA (no conversion)		
Current IRA account value	$10,000	
Account value at retirement, assuming 8% annual return	$100,627	
Total retirement income before taxes, assuming 8% annual return		$100,627
Tax on distribution: 28%		$28,175
Net amount:		**$72,452**

Roth Conversion IRA		
Current IRA account value	$10,000	
Account value at retirement, assuming 8% annual return	$100,627	
Total retirement income before taxes, assuming 8% annual return		$100,627
Future value of taxes ($1,500) paid on converted amount**		$10,795
Tax on distribution: 0%		$0
Net amount:		**$89,832**

Yes, by converting his regular IRA to a Roth Conversion IRA, Jim could receive *$17,380 more* retirement income.

Scenario #2

Kay Smith, age 40, is currently in the 28% tax bracket. She plans to take distributions from her IRA over 20 years beginning when she reaches age 60, when she still expects to be in the 28% tax bracket. She has made nondeductible contributions totaling $40,000 to her IRA, which is currently worth $100,000. Should Kay convert her regular IRA to a Roth Conversion IRA?

Regular IRA (no conversion)		
Current IRA account value	$100,000	
Account value at retirement, assuming 8% annual return	$446,096	
Total retirement income before taxes, assuming 8% annual return		$879,127
Total tax on distributions: 28%		$234,956
Net amount:		**$644,171**

Roth Conversion IRA		
Current IRA account value	$100,000	
Account value at retirement, assuming 8% annual return	$466,096	
Total retirement income before taxes, assuming annual 8% return		$879,127
Future value of taxes ($16,800) paid on converted amount**		$83,249
Total tax on distributions: 0%		$0
Net amount:		$795,878

Yes, by converting her regular IRA to a Roth Conversion IRA, Kay could receive *$151,707 more* retirement income.

**Assumes amount compounds at 8% annually in a taxable account and conversion taxes are paid at the first of the next year.

Scenario #3

Susan Anderson, age 60, is currently in the 28% tax bracket. She plans to take distributions from her deductible IRA over 20 years beginning when she reaches age 65, when she anticipates being in the 15% tax bracket. Her regular IRA is currently worth $100,000. Should she convert her regular IRA to a Roth Conversion IRA?

Regular IRA (no conversion)	
Current IRA account value	$100,000
Account value at retirement, assuming 8% annual return	$146,933
Total retirement income before taxes, assuming 8% annual return	$277,138
Total Tax on distribution: 15%	$41,571
Net amount:	**$235,567**

Roth Conversion IRA	
Current IRA account value	$100,000
Account value at retirement, assuming 8% annual return	$146,933
Total retirement income before taxes, assuming 8% annual return	$277,138
Future value of taxes ($1,500) paid on converted amount**	$64,474
Total Tax on distribution: 0%	$0
Net amount:	**$212,664**

No, by converting her regular IRA to a Roth Conversion IRA, Susan could receive *$22,903 less* retirement income.

Scenario #4

Ted Myers, age 55, is currently in the 28% tax bracket. He plans to take distributions from his deductible IRA over 15 years beginning when he reaches age 60. He anticipates being in the 15% tax bracket at that time. His regular IRA is currently worth $75,000. Should he convert his regular IRA to a Roth Conversion IRA?

Regular IRA (no conversion)	
Current IRA account value	$75,000
Account value at retirement, assuming 8% annual return	$110,200
Total retirement income before taxes, assuming 8% annual return	$178,813
Total tax on distributions: 28%	$26,822
Net amount:	**$151,991**

Roth Conversion IRA	
Current IRA account value	$75,000
Account value at retirement, assuming 8% annual return	$110,200
Total retirement income before taxes, assuming 8% annual return	$178,813
Future value of taxes ($1,500) paid on converted amount**	$42,308
Total tax on distributions: 0%	$0
Net amount:	**$136,505**

No, by converting his regular IRA to a Roth Conversion IRA, Ted could receive *$15,486 less* retirement income.

Summary

As you can see from these scenarios, your time horizon can be one of several key factors in determining whether a Roth Conversion IRA is right for you. That's because the power of tax-deferred compounding over time may generally outweigh the immediate tax bill you may face with a conversion. To help you decide whether you should convert your regular IRA to a Roth Conversion IRA, you may want to complete the worksheet on the next page.

**Assumes amount compounds at 8% annually in a taxable account and conversion taxes are paid at the first of the next year.

IRA Conversion Worksheet

This worksheet is designed to help determine if you would benefit from converting your regular IRA to a Roth Conversion IRA.

Step 1: Assumptions

1. The current value of your IRA. $_____

2. The total amount of your nondeductible IRA contributions. If all your contributions were deductible, enter "0." $_____

3. The annual rate of return (between 4% and 12%) that you expect to earn on your investments prior to retirement.   _____%

4. The annual rate of return (between 4% and 12%) that you expect to earn during retirement.   _____%

5. The number of years you have to save for retirement (between 1 and 30). Please use a number that would result in your retiring no sooner than age 59½.   _____years

6. The number of years (between 1 and 30) you plan on taking distributions from your IRA after retirement.   _____years

7. Your federal income tax rate prior to retirement (15%, 28%, 31%, 36% or 39.6%).   _____%

8. Your anticipated federal income tax rate during retirement (15 %, 28%, 31%, 36% or 39.6%).   _____%

9. Subtract your tax rate prior to retirement (line 7) from 1.00 (for example, 1.00 - 0.28 tax bracket = 0.72). Multiply the result by line 3.   _____%

10. Subtract your tax rate during retirement (line 8) from 1.00. Multiply the result by line 4.   _____%

Step 2: Future Value Factors

11. In the table below, find the number of years to retirement (from line 5) in the left-hand column and your expected rate of return while working (from line 3) across the top. The intersection is your future value factor.   _____

12. In the table below, find the number of years to retirement (from line 5) in the left-hand column and your expected after-tax rate of return while working (from line 9) across the top. The intersection is your after-tax future value factor.   _____

Rate of Return

Years to Retirement	2%	3%	4%	5%	6%	7%	8%	9%	10%	11%	12%
1	1.02	1.03	1.04	1.05	1.06	1.07	1.08	1.09	1.10	1.11	1.12
2	1.04	1.06	1.08	1.10	1.12	1.14	1.17	1.19	1.21	1.23	1.25
3	1.06	1.09	1.12	1.16	1.19	1.23	1.26	1.30	1.33	1.37	1.40
4	1.08	1.13	1.17	1.22	1.26	1.31	1.36	1.41	1.46	1.52	1.57
5	1.10	1.16	1.22	1.28	1.34	1.40	1.47	1.54	1.61	1.69	1.76
6	1.13	1.19	1.27	1.34	1.42	1.50	1.59	1.68	1.77	1.87	1.97
7	1.15	1.23	1.32	1.41	1.50	1.61	1.71	1.83	1.95	2.08	2.21
8	1.17	1.27	1.37	1.48	1.59	1.72	1.85	1.99	2.14	2.30	2.48
9	1.20	1.30	1.42	1.55	1.69	1.84	2.00	2.17	2.36	2.56	2.77
10	1.22	1.34	1.48	1.63	1.79	1.97	2.16	2.37	2.59	2.84	3.11
11	1.24	1.38	1.54	1.71	1.90	2.10	2.33	2.58	2.85	3.15	3.48
12	1.27	1.43	1.60	1.80	2.01	2.25	2.52	2.81	3.14	3.50	3.90
13	1.29	1.47	1.67	1.89	2.13	2.41	2.72	3.07	3.45	3.88	4.36
14	1.32	1.51	1.73	1.98	2.26	2.58	2.94	3.34	3.80	4.31	4.89
15	1.35	1.56	1.80	2.08	2.40	2.76	3.17	3.64	4.18	4.78	5.47
16	1.37	1.60	1.87	2.18	2.54	2.95	3.43	3.97	4.59	5.31	6.13
17	1.40	1.65	1.95	2.29	2.69	3.16	3.70	4.33	5.05	5.90	6.87
18	1.43	1.70	2.03	2.41	2.85	3.38	4.00	4.72	5.56	6.54	7.69
19	1.46	1.75	2.11	2.53	3.03	3.62	4.32	5.14	6.12	7.26	8.61
20	1.49	1.81	2.19	2.65	3.21	3.87	4.66	5.60	6.73	8.06	9.65
21	1.52	1.86	2.28	2.79	3.40	4.14	5.03	6.11	7.40	8.95	10.80
22	1.55	1.92	2.37	2.93	3.60	4.43	5.44	6.66	8.14	9.93	12.10
23	1.58	1.97	2.46	3.07	3.82	4.74	5.87	7.26	8.95	11.03	13.55
24	1.61	2.03	2.56	3.23	4.05	5.07	6.34	7.91	9.85	12.24	15.18
25	1.64	2.09	2.67	3.39	4.29	5.43	6.85	8.62	10.83	13.59	17.00
26	1.67	2.16	2.77	3.56	4.55	5.81	7.40	9.40	11.92	15.08	19.04
27	1.71	2.22	2.88	3.73	4.82	6.21	7.99	10.25	13.11	16.74	21.32
28	1.74	2.29	3.00	3.92	5.11	6.65	8.63	11.17	14.42	18.58	23.88
29	1.78	2.36	3.12	4.12	5.42	7.11	9.32	12.17	15.86	20.62	26.75
30	1.81	2.43	3.24	4.32	5.74	7.61	10.06	13.27	17.45	22.89	29.96

Step 3: Income Factors

13. In the table below, find the number of years you plan on taking distributions (from line 6) in the left-hand column and your expected rate of return during retirement (from line 4) across the top. The intersection is the factor that will determine your amount of annual retirement income. ________

14. In the table below, find the number of years you plan to take distributions (from line 6) in the left-hand column and your expected after-tax rate of return during retirement (from line 10) across the top. The intersection is the factor that will determine your after-tax annual retirement income. ________

Years in Retirement	Rate of Return 2%	3%	4%	5%	6%	7%	8%	9%	10%	11%	12%
1	1.00	1.00	1.00	1.00	1.00	1.00	1.00	1.00	1.00	1.00	1.00
2	1.98	1.97	1.96	1.95	1.94	1.93	1.93	1.92	1.91	1.90	1.89
3	2.94	2.91	2.89	2.86	2.83	2.81	2.78	2.76	2.74	2.71	2.69
4	3.88	3.83	3.78	3.72	3.67	3.62	3.58	3.53	3.49	3.44	3.40
5	4.81	4.72	4.63	4.55	4.47	4.39	4.31	4.24	4.17	4.10	4.04
6	5.71	5.58	5.45	5.33	5.21	5.10	4.99	4.89	4.79	4.70	4.60
7	6.60	6.42	6.24	6.08	5.92	5.77	5.62	5.49	5.36	5.23	5.11
8	7.47	7.23	7.00	6.79	6.58	6.39	6.21	6.03	5.87	5.71	5.56
9	8.33	8.02	7.73	7.46	7.21	6.97	6.75	6.53	6.33	6.15	5.97
10	9.16	8.79	8.44	8.11	7.80	7.52	7.25	7.00	6.76	6.54	6.33
11	9.98	9.53	9.11	8.72	8.36	8.02	7.71	7.42	7.14	6.89	6.65
12	10.79	10.25	9.76	9.31	8.89	8.50	8.14	7.81	7.50	7.21	6.94
13	11.58	10.95	10.39	9.86	9.38	8.94	8.54	8.16	7.81	7.49	7.19
14	12.35	11.63	10.99	10.39	9.85	9.36	8.90	8.49	8.10	7.75	7.42
15	13.11	12.30	11.56	10.90	10.29	9.75	9.24	8.79	8.37	7.98	7.63
16	13.85	12.94	12.12	11.38	10.71	10.11	9.56	9.06	8.61	8.19	7.81
17	14.58	13.56	12.65	11.84	11.11	10.45	9.85	9.31	8.82	8.38	7.97
18	15.29	14.17	13.17	12.27	11.48	10.76	10.12	9.54	9.02	8.55	8.12
19	15.99	14.75	13.66	12.69	11.83	11.06	10.37	9.76	9.20	8.70	8.25
20	16.68	15.32	14.13	13.09	12.16	11.34	10.60	9.95	9.36	8.84	8.37
21	17.35	15.88	14.59	13.46	12.47	11.59	10.82	10.13	9.51	8.96	8.47
22	18.01	16.42	15.03	13.82	12.76	11.84	11.02	10.29	9.65	9.08	8.56
23	18.66	16.94	15.45	14.16	13.04	12.06	11.20	10.44	9.77	9.18	8.64
24	19.29	17.44	15.86	14.49	13.30	12.27	11.37	10.58	9.88	9.27	8.72
25	19.91	17.94	16.25	14.80	13.55	12.47	11.53	10.71	9.98	9.35	8.78
26	20.52	18.41	16.62	15.09	13.78	12.65	11.67	10.82	10.08	9.42	8.84
27	21.12	18.88	16.98	15.38	14.00	12.83	11.81	10.93	10.16	9.49	8.90
28	21.71	19.33	17.33	15.64	14.21	12.99	11.94	11.03	10.24	9.55	8.94
29	22.28	19.76	17.66	15.90	14.41	13.14	12.05	11.12	10.31	9.60	8.98
30	22.84	20.19	17.98	16.14	14.59	13.28	12.16	11.20	10.37	9.65	9.02

Step 4: Calculations

Total Income From Roth Conversion IRA

15. Multiply the current value of your IRA (line 1) by the future value factor on line 11. $_____

16. Divide line 15 by the income factor on line 13. Multiply the result by the number of years you plan on taking distributions (line 6). $_____

17. To determine the opportunity cost of having to pay taxes on conversion, subtract the amount of nondeductible contributions on line 2 from line 1. $_____

18. Multiply line 17 by your tax rate while working (line 7). This is the amount of taxes you will owe upon conversion. For simplicity, we will assume you pay this amount out of an account other than your IRA. $_____

19. Multiply line 18 by the after-tax future value factor on line 12. $_____

20. Divide line 19 by the after-tax income factor (line 14). Multiply the result by the number of years you plan on taking distributions (line 6). $_____

21. Subtract line 20 from line 16. $_____

Total Income From Regular IRA

22. Multiply the current value of your IRA (line 1) by the future value factor on line 11. $_____

23. Divide line 22 by the income factor on line 13. $_____

24. Divide the amount of nondeductible contributions on line 2 by the number of years you plan on taking distributions (line 6) $_____

25. Subtract line 24 from line 23. $_____

26. Subtract your tax rate during retirement (line 8) from 1.00 (for example, 1.00 - 0.28 tax rate = 0.72). Multiply the result by line 25. $_____

27. Add line 24 to line 26. Then multiply the result by the number of years you plan on taking distributions (line 6). $_____

Result

Enter below the amounts on lines 21 and 27. The greater of the two indicates which option may provide the highest total amount of retirement income.

Roth Conversion IRA (line 21)	**Regular IRA** (line 27)
$_____	$_____

This is not a complete analysis and does not factor in any applicable state or local taxes. Therefore, we suggest you contact your investment representative and tax advisor for more specific information relating to your individual circumstances. For more information on your regular and Roth IRAs, call a Franklin Templeton Retirement Plan Specialist at **1-800/527-2020**

Rollovers

Rollovers have been around a while and remain intact. They are established by distributions you receive from qualified retirement plans when you change jobs, leave a company, or retire. Rollovers make wonderful sense for people who are receiving lump sum distributions from company plans, for several reasons. You can continue to benefit from tax-deferred growth until you withdraw from your rollover account. By directly rolling over your assets, you also avoid income tax and 10% IRS penalties for withdrawing before age 59½.

A rollover allows you to better control your tax situation as well. With a lump sum, your taxes are due for the year in which you take the distribution. When you roll over your retirement account, you leave the money in the account until, theoretically, you retire and start taking distributions as you need them. That means that you spread the taxes out over several years and, sometimes, when you're in a lower tax bracket.

To avoid tax penalties, you must place your distribution into a rollover IRA within 60 days of the date of the distribution of your funds. If you don't roll it over within this timeline, the distribution is treated as ordinary income and subject to the 10% penalty if you're under age 59½. An additional advantage to an IRA rollover is that, while many 401(k)s offer a limited menu of investment choices, an IRA rollover allows a wide variety of investment options, including stocks, bonds, and mutual funds. For this reason, many people opt for the rollover option even if their former employer would let them leave their money in the old 401(k).

Whatever you do, don't use this money for fun and games, because it could be some of the most expensive money you ever spent. Suppose, for example, you're in the 28% bracket and are age 50 when you leave your employer. Let's look at how this might affect you. If your distribution is $10,000 and you don't roll it over, you'll pay $2,800 in federal taxes and a $1,000 early withdrawal penalty. This means this money is costing you $3,800, which is 38%. As I've said before, it's hard to imagine even the worst credit card charging you this kind of interest. This doesn't even take into consideration the "opportunity" cost of having lost that money for your retirement, not to mention the potential return on the money. Despite this outrageously high cost, I've actually seen people use this money for additions to their home, trips, or new cars. Don't do this!

Education IRAs

This IRA can be established by anyone; it offers tax-free earnings and withdrawals for qualified higher education expenses. You may establish one Education IRA for any child under the age of 18. The income limitations for establishing this IRA are the same as for a Roth IRA. You may not contribute more than $500 per year per child. This limit has been widely criticized as being too low, as any of you with children in college would agree. Raising the limit is currently under consideration, because of the constantly rising costs of higher education.

Contributions are made with after-tax dollars and all earnings in the account accumulate tax-free if, at withdrawal, the money is used to pay for qualified higher education expenses. These include standard items, such as tuition and room and board. Any withdrawals of earnings not made in connection with these qualified expenses may be subject to income taxes and a 10% penalty. Exceptions to this penalty include the death or disability of the beneficiary.

Any earnings not used by the time the beneficiary of the account reaches age 30 would be subject to income taxes and the penalty unless the account value is rolled into a new Education IRA for a family member of the beneficiary. This new IRA is one of the few tax shelters available to parents who are seeking ways to fund their children's college education. In addition to being attractive to parents, this account can be established by anyone, including friends or relatives, wishing to provide for the educational needs of a child should the parents not be able to do so.

It's important to note that you may not make Education IRA contributions for a child who receives a same-year contribution to a prepaid state tuition program, regardless of the amount.

72(t) Distributions

Now that we've covered the ins and outs of IRAs, you know that you cannot take a distribution before age 59½ without receiving a penalty. But remember that I said there may be an exception to this rule. Now we're going to talk about that exception.

Within the Internal Revenue code, there is a provision for waiving this premature distribution penalty. 72(t) states that, if distributions are part of a substantially equal periodic payment (not less frequently than annually) made for the life or life expectancy of the individual or joint lives of the individual and designated beneficiary, the penalty shall be waived. The bottom line: this clause allows individuals to withdraw a stream of regular payments from their IRAs in compliance with certain rules without having to pay that 10% penalty.

All IRA and 403(b) account owners are eligible at any time for any reason, but participants in a qualified plan, such as a 401(k), are eligible only after they leave their job and the funds are in an IRA rollover account. You do not need to consider all retirement accounts when calculating the payment, which allows individuals flexibility to establish separate IRAs to achieve their desired income level.

How Are These Distributions Calculated?

The three major conditions to qualify for a 72(t) are:
- They must be part of a series of substantially equal payments made on a regular basis (at least annually).
- They must be calculated according to one of three IRS-approved methods.
- They must continue for at least five years or until the account owner reaches age 59½, whichever is longer.

The three methods used to calculate distributions are the life expectancy, the amortization, and the annuitization methods. While all three of these are based on the account owner's life expectancy or the joint life expectancy of the owner and a beneficiary, each method produces a different figure. It's important that you work closely with your financial advisor and your accountant to determine which of these methods is most appropriate for your needs. Once you select one of these methods and payments begin, you cannot change the method for five years or until the individual reaches age 59½. After that time, you can stop the distribution or modify the amount. You've probably noticed that the IRS isn't famous for its flexibility so, if you don't adhere strictly to the method chosen, you could trigger a significant tax penalty.

Who Could Benefit from a 72(t) Distribution?

This provision could work for anyone who wishes to take distributions from an IRA at any time prior to age 59½. You do not need to have any specific reason, such as early retirement. Obviously, younger IRA owners will have longer life expectancies and will therefore find their payments to be smaller than older account holders. The distribution requirements are set in stone by the IRS, so it's important to comply with these requirements. This provision does, however, provide a method of obtaining an income stream for a person who wants early retirement. Don't lose sight of the fact that you will now begin to spend rather than accumulate your retirement assets.

A common feature of every single type of retirement plan discussed in this chapter is that the government stipulates how much you can set aside. If you are like most Americans, whose greatest living fear is outliving their retirement money, you may be inclined to want to do something over and above these plans. One of the few tax-deferred investment vehicles that allow you to enhance your retirement planning is annuities. Stay tuned: we'll examine them in detail in the next chapter.

10 Estate Planning

*E*state planning is the fancy title given to the process you use to plan how to pass on your assets while minimizing the impact of taxes. Most people think of estate planning as something designed exclusively for the rich. As you'll see, that is not the case.

To most of us, estate planning ranks right up there in popularity with buying life insurance. Both are about planning for things that will happen after we die—not on our top ten list of fun things to do. While estate planning is not fun-filled and riotous, in this chapter you'll see that actions you take while living can have a profound impact on your loved ones after your death.

Wills

Usually the first thing that comes to mind under the general heading of estate planning is a *will*. A commonly asked question, and one that you may be wondering is, "How do I know if I need a will?" Generally speaking, many experts believe that anyone who owns property, has a family, or wishes to have control over the dissemination of his or her estate should have a will.

A will is simply a legal document in which you describe how you want your assets to be distributed after you die. It determines who inherits property that is held in your name without any beneficiary designated. Most wills are formal documents that usually require witnesses and a notarized signature. Many states will allow you to have a handwritten will in easily understood language. If you die without a will, your assets will be distributed according to the laws of the state. This is called *intestate*. If you don't plan for yourself, the state does it for you—and frankly they don't give a darn what your wishes were.

Some of the assets typically distributed through a will include stocks, bonds, bank accounts, houses, cars, and personal property. Proceeds from life insurance may or may not pass through a will. Life insurance is a contract between the owner of the policy and the insurance company. As part of this contract, the owner of the policy dictates who receives the proceeds by naming a beneficiary. In that case, the proceeds are paid directly to the beneficiary and would not pass through the will. If the insurance policy named the estate as the beneficiary, the proceeds would then pass according to the provisions of the will.

In addition to planning how you will distribute your assets, you can achieve other important goals with a will. For example, in a will you can designate a guardian for any minor children in the event that both you and your spouse die at the same time. Generally speaking, it is wise for both the husband and wife to have individual wills.

You can change your will at any time, and you should review it periodically. Tax laws may be revised, your personal situation may have changed, or you simply may wish to amend how you would like your estate distributed. You can make a simple amendment to your will; this is usually referred to as a *codicil*.

Don't be put off by what you perceive as great costs associated with writing a will. Many states allow you to complete a packaged "kit" to prepare your will. Check with your state; you may be surprised how flexible the rules are about writing valid wills. If you decide to meet with an attorney, ask up front what the approximate cost will be and go prepared with a list showing how you want your estate distributed. You don't want to die of shock when you receive your "will bill."

Trusts

The popularity of trusts as a way to establish control over an estate has dramatically increased in recent years. A trust is a legal entity established by individuals to hold and manage assets. As we'll soon see, different types of trusts have different tax consequences and levels of flexibility associated with them. There's a huge assortment of highly specialized trusts appropriate to various situations. These include charitable remainder trusts, marital deduction trusts, irrevocable life insurance trusts, and estate trusts. This area of estate planning can be highly complicated, so I would urge you to seek both legal and tax advice when choosing from the menu of trusts available.

> **Buys Briefs**
>
> A **trust** is an arrangement under which a person (or persons) or institution holds legal title to real or personal property for the benefit of another person (or persons), usually under the terms of a written document which states all parties' rights and responsibilities.

In this chapter, I'm going to provide you with a basic understanding of the major trusts and what they can and cannot do. To help us wade through the language of trusts, I'd like to define some key terms.

Grantor This is a person who is creating the trust and transferring assets to it. This person also outlines the terms under which the trust is to be managed and does so in the trust instrument.

Trustees The trustees manage the assets transferred to the trust and may do so only according to the terms of the trust agreement.

Term When a trust is created the grantor specifies how long it is to last. This is known as the term. It can range from years to lifetimes. During the term of the trust, the trustee has legal title to the assets.

Beneficiaries The trustee manages the assets of the trust for the benefit of another person or persons, known as beneficiaries, as named by the grantor.

Revocable and Irrevocable Trusts

The most common trust is *revocable*, which allows for amendments, modifications, or cancellation at any time, hence the name *revocable trust*. The catch is that assets disposed of by a will or by a revocable trust will be included in your gross estate for estate tax purposes. So you ask, why would you set up a revocable trust? The answer is that, since revocable trust assets pass to the beneficiaries you named in the trust document, they are not controlled by your will and so they avoid probate. A revocable trust would be particularly helpful, for example, if you own real property outside your state of residence. If so, probate proceedings may be required by each state in which you own such property. With a revocable trust, you avoid the hassle of having to deal with several states and probate. This may make a trust very attractive.

The possibility of having to probate an estate strikes terror into the hearts of most people. We envision a costly and lengthy process that we would do almost anything to avoid. Fortunately, this is not the case in a number of states. You may actually find that it can be more expensive and time-consuming to establish and convey assets to a revocable trust than it is to create and probate a will. Don't be "sold" on creating a revocable trust, which some people consider the attorney's "full employment act." Be sure to consider all the alternatives and the time and costs involved before making your decision.

> **Buys Briefs**
>   A **Revocable Trust** is a trust that *can* be amended, modified, or canceled at any time.
>   **Probate** is a court-supervised procedure for validating a will, paying debts, and distributing the property of a deceased person.
>   An **Irrevocable Trust** is a trust that *cannot* be amended, modified, or canceled.
>   A **Life Insurance Trust** is a trust established to minimize estate taxes by transferring life insurance policies and all incidents of ownership to your children or to a trust for your family's benefit.

An *irrevocable* trust, as the name implies, cannot be revoked or changed after you create it. The whole idea behind this kind of trust is to remove property and future income from your estate and it is usually created to help reduce income or estate taxes. Irrevocable trusts exist only if the grantor gives up all rights whatsoever over all of the assets in the trust.

Life Insurance Trust

Many of you may be aware that life insurance proceeds are received free from income tax. What you may not know is that they are *not* free from estate tax. Life insurance proceeds payable to your estate will be included in your total estate for estate tax purposes. Notice that I said "life insurance proceeds payable to your estate." By transferring the policy and all claims of ownership to a life insurance trust, the insured no longer has ownership, and this allows the benefits to escape estate taxes.

A good way to structure these types of life insurance trusts allows you to use your annual gift tax exclusion (up to $10,000 per recipient, to any number of people) to pay for premiums for the insurance in the trust. This means that you're enjoying the benefits of the gift tax exclusion and allowing the insurance proceeds to pass to your heirs without income, gift or estate taxes. To make this work, you put so called "Crummey" provisions in the trust.

These provisions, named after a court decision, give the beneficiary the right to demand payment from the trust. This right will never be exercised, though, because the trust needs the money to pay the pre-

	Gross Estate	Total Settlement Costs	Net Estate	% Shrinkage
Marilyn Monroe	$819,176	$448,750	$370,426	55%
W.C. Fields	884,680	329,793	554,998	37%
Humphrey Bogart	910,146	274,234	635,912	30%
Franklin D. Roosevelt	1,940,999	574,867	1,366,132	30%
Clark Gable	2,806,526	1,101,308	1,705,488	30%
Gary Cooper	4,984,985	1,530,454	3,454,531	31%
Elvis Presley	10,165,434	7,374,635	2,790,799	73%
John D. Rockefeller, Sr.	26,905,182	17,124,988	9,780,194	64%
Walt Disney	23,004,851	6,811,943	16,192,908	30%

Figure 10-1. The impact of estate taxes

miums on the life insurance policy. One of the main uses of this trust is to create an estate upon your death, as your heirs will receive the funds from your life insurance policies. Another use is to create a pool of money available upon your death to pay estate taxes without having to liquidate part of the estate.

If you think estate taxes can't destroy a nest egg, think again. Figure 10-1 shows some examples of a few prominent people and how much the value of their estate shrank after all expenses were deducted.

While many of us don't leave estates this size, it's clear that planning plays a major role in passing on the bulk of your assets.

Durable Power of Attorney

Durable Power of Attorney is a legal document prepared by a lawyer stating that you grant authority to one or more—known as attorney(s)-in-fact—to manage your affairs on your behalf.

Let's imagine that you've been very responsible in long-term planning and you've prepared a will that covers all of your wishes regarding the disposition of your estate after your death. You feel smug and think that now you can relax.

Not quite so fast. Suppose you become ill or incapacitated in such a way that you can no longer manage your affairs. Your family might have to get the court to appoint a guardian or a conservator to manage your finances. Not only can this be time-consuming and expensive but also the decisions made for you may not be what you had in mind. A good safeguard may be a durable power of attorney.

This is a document by which you appoint a legal representative to manage your affairs if you become incapacitated. You have the right to change or revoke the power at any time and it automatically terminates upon your death. A general durable power grants your attorney-in-fact authority to handle virtually all of your financial matters. A special durable power restricts this power to one or more specific functions you designate. It provides a simple, inexpensive way of continuing the management of your affairs should you become incapacitated.

Living Wills and Health Care Powers of Attorney

We are often fearful about what type of medical care we will be subjected to if we are unable to speak for ourselves. There are two instruments that can allow you greater peace of mind.

A **Living Will** is a written statement that expresses your wishes about prolonging your life by artificial, extraordinary, or heroic measures.

A living will is a written statement that expresses your wishes about prolonging your life by artificial or heroic measures. Using a health care power of attorney, you can appoint a person to make medical and health care decisions on your behalf if you are unable to do so. Most states have legislation recognizing both living wills and health care powers of attorney. States may have different legal requirements regarding the execution of these documents so it's crucial that you consult an attorney or someone familiar with the laws in your state.

There's quite a debate as to how much attention medical personnel really pay to these documents. Hospitals certainly do not want to face a major lawsuit and many feel they are protecting themselves by providing life-sustaining medical treatment in spite of the patient's wishes. Be sure to notify your doctor as well as your attorney and family regarding your wishes in this area.

Estate Planning Review

After you get all your ducks in a row, don't make the mistake of forgetting to periodically review your plan. If you already have an estate plan, you should reexamine some of the techniques you have used in the past in light of the Taxpayer Relief Act of 1997 and any subsequent tax changes. For example, the new tax laws raise the limit on the amount of the unified tax credit that effectively exempts assets from federal estate and gift taxes. The unified credit is available to each individual's estate so, with proper planning, a married couple would be able to transfer to their beneficiaries a total of $2 million, free of estate taxes

Buys Briefs
The **Unified Estate and Gift Tax Credit** is a credit applied toward both gift and estate taxes amounting to the tax generated by a transfer of $600,000 for each individual (husband and wife). No estate or gift taxes are assessed on the first $600,000 of combined taxable gifts and transfers at death.

when the increased exemption is fully phased in by 2006. Below are the new limits.

YEAR	EXEMPTION AMOUNT
1997	$600,000
1998	$625,000
1999	$650,000

YEAR	EXEMPTION AMOUNT
2000	$675,000
2001	$675,000
2002	$700,000
2003	$700,000
2004	$850,000
2005	$950,000
2006 and beyond	$1,000,000

In addition to tax changes, other considerations that should trigger a review of your estate planning include changes in family circumstances, changes in ownership of family property, and simply the passage of time.

In this chapter I've only scratched the surface of the complicated area known as estate planning. This is an area to which you should devote serious, careful attention. It is definitely not an area to be ignored. Think carefully about your particular situation. Should you have a will? Do you have one? Would a trust be appropriate for you? If so, what type? If you've done estate planning, is it up to date? Have you reviewed it lately? If you were incapacitated due to illness or injury, would your financial affairs be taken care of? Would you want to be on life support? If so, for how long? Make sure that what you want to happen actually happens via some of the tools I've reviewed in this chapter.

If you wish to learn more or you are interested in a particular type of trust or planning issue, I urge you to do more research yourself and seek the assistance of a professional. Money spent in this area may be more than returned in the form of tax savings and lessened aggravation for the loved ones you leave behind.

11 Insurance

When most of us hear the word "insurance," an involuntary shudder runs through our body and our mind turns off. I believe insurance is the most widely held and yet least understood investment. You don't believe me? The next time you get together with your friends, ask them what kind of life insurance policy they have and how it works. I can assure you that your question will be followed by several moments of silence. Then your friends will probably tell you that you need to get a life.

Today it seems that insurance of one type or another is everywhere. You can buy travel insurance, dental insurance, pet insurance, and an assortment of others designed to insure your every need. Like it or not, some form of insurance is a part of most people's financial life.

While we won't discuss all types of insurance, in this chapter we'll cover the basic ones you need to know. I'll also define the common terms associated with the most popular types of insurance, so you can be informed when evaluating your alternatives. I know this may not sound quite as exciting as a Tom Clancy novel, but I'll do my best to help you find your way through the insurance maze.

Life Insurance

I feel confident in saying this isn't your favorite topic. (It's not mine either, for that matter.) But life insurance is something that touches many people, so it's important for us to understand what we're talking about and how our choices will affect us. When you buy health, disability, or auto insurance, you're buying protection to cover a certain risk. When you buy life insurance, you're buying coverage for your eventual death, which—just like taxes—is a certainty. But even though death is inevitable, that doesn't mean everyone needs to have life insurance. This is a very individual decision that only you can make, within the context of your unique situation.

If you're considering life insurance, it's important to consider the reason for purchasing that insurance. This will guide you to choose the appropriate type of life insurance. Is your goal to leave assets to provide for your family? To establish a fund for settling your estate? To provide coverage for a business partner? It's important to identify your reason for buying life insurance and not simply purchase it because a life insurance agent recommends it.

How to Decide If You Need Life Insurance and How Much

You may have had the unsettling experience of calculating the death benefit you would need, using a sheet provided by your friendly insurance company. You fill in the numbers, then your agent takes this sheet to do an analysis and sets up an appointment to share the findings with you. At this follow-up meeting, you discover that you need "approximately $80 million" to keep your family afloat after your departure.

Although I'm being facetious about the number, I'm very serious about the outcome of these projections. Some of my clients have called me after such meetings, feeling overwhelmed and totally depressed by these numbers. I've also had some quality insurance agents tell me that they believe many of the projections to be outrageous. If insurance agents get paid based on the amount of insurance they sell, it's safe to say they have a vested interest in selling you a substantial chunk. Don't go on a guilt trip if you don't sign up for all of the insurance they tell you your loved ones will need to keep up their current lifestyle!

You need to sit down with your partner, if you have one, and discuss what your wishes are should something happen to one or both of you. Play out some scenarios and run the numbers.

Let's look at a way for you to begin to realistically estimate what your life insurance needs may be. Most people buy insurance to provide security for their loved ones after their death. With this in mind, the first step is to compute the current annual living expenses of your survivors. This would include items such as food, clothing, automobile expenses, education, housing costs, and so forth. A good way to do this in an informed manner is to look at your check register for the last six months. This is helpful in two ways: it shows you where your income is going and it helps you determine what expenses are essential. Don't forget to consider expenses that may be triggered by your death as a parent, such as child care costs. One school of thought says you should consider getting enough insurance to cover about 70% of the current family expenses.

Next you should consider what ongoing sources of income there will be after your death. This may include spousal income, Social Security, investment income, pensions, and other insurance. Once you've determined this figure, subtract the amount to come in annually from the amount that will be needed to cover expenses annually.

If you find you have an income shortfall, you need to consider how much more you'll need. Remember that this represents an annual figure, so you need to start considering how many years you feel you wish to provide for your family and what rate of return you expect to receive on your investments. Keep in mind extraordinary expenses triggered upon death, such as funeral expenses, estate administration expenses, and any taxes that may be due. After you've arrived at the total capital needed and are getting fairly depressed, you need to look at your resources.

Here you'll want to take into account investments, insurance you may have through work, retirement accounts, equity in your home, and generally anything you feel can be thrown in the pot as a resource. If your family's needs exceed the total resources available, you can use life insurance to fill the gap.

If you've made the decision that you need life insurance, you'll soon discover that there's a wide variety of types. All life insurance falls into two broad categories: term insurance and cash value insurance.

Term Insurance

Term Insurance is insurance covering a specific period of time. There are no savings or investment features associated with term insurance.

Term insurance is the least expensive and simplest form of life insurance. It's very attractive when your goal is to provide income for your family's needs. Frequently young couples who don't make a lot of money but do need insurance would favor this type. You pay your insurance company a fixed amount annually and it pays your beneficiary if you die during the term of the coverage, the period for which you paid for insurance. Once the term expires, you can't renew the policy unless you've paid for that as an option. You can purchase a new policy, but it will usually cost more because the fundamental rule of life insurance is that the older you get, the more it costs—and the rate of increase accelerates as you get older.

Annual Renewable Term Insurance

A very common type of term is *annual renewable term insurance*. The good news with this type of insurance is that the company must renew your policy every year. The bad news is that your premiums increase over time.

Level-Premium Policies

In contrast to this are *level-premium policies*. As the name implies, with this type of term insurance the premium remains constant year after year. While this sounds terrific, bear in mind that insurance companies are very wise and have figured a way to cover costs for themselves with this type of policy. With a level premium, you're apt to pay higher premiums in the early years than for annual renewable life insurance and less in the later years, leading us to believe that it all pretty much averages out.

Level Term Insurance

A variety of death benefits are associated with term insurance. With *level term insurance*, you are provided a specific amount of insurance for a specified period of time, so you may buy a $50,000 policy for 10 years and, if you die any time within those 10 years, your beneficiary receives $50,000.

Decreasing Term Insurance

Decreasing term insurance, as the name implies, pays a death benefit that gradually decreases over the term of the policy. Your premiums also decrease as the amount of coverage decreases. This type of policy is commonly used in association with financial obligations that reduce over time. The best example of this is with a mortgage. As the amount of the mortgage goes down, so too does the amount of insurance coverage. By purchasing decreasing term, you've provided a mechanism for paying off the mortgage in the event of your death.

Increasing Term Insurance

Increasing term insurance, as you would assume, provides for an increasing death benefit over the term of the policy. You're probably wondering why you would want your premiums and payout to increase over time. This might be appropriate, for example, for a couple with young children who know their financial obligations will increase as their children begin attending college. The increase may be in dollars or by a percentage. It may also be tied to a cost of living index, such as the Consumer Price Index (CPI).

Cash Value Insurance

Term insurance is the least expensive insurance alternative, because you're buying strictly insurance coverage (a death benefit) and no investment vehicles. Cash value policies, on the other hand, provide two things: death benefits and an investment. Your payment is divided between the insurance premium and the investment account. These policies allow you to accumulate the investment portion of the money as a reserve. This accumulation, commonly called the policy's *cash value*, increases each year the policy is kept in force. In later years, you may choose to let that money pay your policy premiums, to borrow against the policy, or to leave it to add to the death benefit.

> **Buys Briefs**
> **Cash Value Insurance** is a type of policy that's initially more expensive than term insurance but offers a wide variety of savings, investment, and payment options. Types of cash value insurance include variable, whole, and universal life.

I can't stress strongly enough that you must understand why you are buying insurance and what it will do upon your death. You do not want to focus on investment returns. The hard-core reality is that there are many other investment alternatives that will give you better returns and cost significantly less. With this thought in mind, let's look at a few of the more common cash value policies.

Whole Life

This type of insurance has been around for a long time. Essentially, as long as you pay your premium, you'll be covered. Since the payments remain fixed, it makes sense that the younger you are when you first buy the insurance, the cheaper it will be when you're no longer so young. The cash value of these policies typically increases based on the insurance company's general account performance. This account is usually invested in bonds or other fixed-income investments.

> **Buys Briefs**
>
> **Whole Life Insurance** is a type of cash value insurance with premiums and coverage associated with your "whole" life.
>
> The **General Account** is where insurance companies invest the cash values of a policy, which build on a tax-deferred basis for the policy holder.
>
> **Universal Life Insurance** is a type of cash value insurance that allows flexibility in determining the policy's face amount and premium payments.

Universal Life

Universal life is a variation of whole life, but with significantly greater flexibility. This product allows the policy owner to determine the amount and frequency of premium payments. It also allows the owner to increase or decrease the face amount of the policy. As premiums are paid and cash values accumulate, interest is credited to the policy's cash value. As long as this cash value is sufficient to pay the monthly mortality and expense costs, the policy continues in force, whether or not the owner pays a premium. If no premiums are received and the cash value is too low to pay the mortality and expense costs, the policy terminates.

A policy owner can elect to pay more into the policy, adding to the cash value. You're probably wondering why in the world you would pay more into an insurance policy than you have to. The answer is that a large percentage of the money withdrawn from an insurance policy, in the form of a loan, is tax-free. To make sure that you're really buying insurance for insurance purposes and not just creating a tax-free income stream, there are strict guidelines regarding the relationship between the face amount of the policy and the cash value.

> **Buys Briefs**
> **Variable Life Insurance** is a type of cash value insurance where the policy holder has the opportunity to invest the premium in the mutual funds provided by the insurance company. The performance of these funds will increase or decrease the amount of the death benefit.

Variable Life

This is a whole life contract with a twist: the person insured has the right to direct how the policy's cash value will be invested. In turn, the insured bears the investment risk in the form of fluctuations in the cash and the death benefit. The cash value fluctuates with the performance of the investments and, since they are market-related, the performance is not guaranteed. Depending on how the investments do, the variable life death benefit will increase or decrease, but a minimum death benefit equal to the face amount of the policy is guaranteed. This is patterned after the variable annuity, which I'll discuss later, and was created to overcome the risk of inflation through the use of growth-oriented investments.

> **Buys Briefs**
> **Universal Variable Life Insurance** is a type of variable life that allows more input. The premium payment may be increased or decreased within a given payment period. The policy owner also decides how the money will be invested.

Universal Variable Life

This policy combines characteristics of a variable life policy and a universal life policy. As in a variable life policy, the death benefit and cash value vary according to the performance of the investments. As with universal life, the policy owner may adjust the premium payments and death benefit according to changing needs. This policy also will not lapse as long as the cash value is sufficient to pay the mortality and expense costs, whether or not the owner makes a payment.

What's for Me?

To further clarify the differences, Figure 11-1 on page 146 provides the highlights of three major types of insurance products.

People comfortable with investing frequently prefer the variable type

Whole Life	Variable Life	Universal Variable Life
• Premium is level and fixed.	• Premium is level and fixed.	• The timing and amount of the premiums are discretionary.
• Premium is payable for life.	• Premium is payable for life.	• Fees and charges are deducted from cash value.
• Death benefit is guaranteed and fixed; it remains level.	• A minimum death benefit is guaranteed; benefit may fluctuate above minimum amount.	• Policy may lapse due to insufficient cash value.
• Cash value is guaranteed.	• Cash value is not guaranteed; it depends on performance of investment account.	• Death benefit may equal policy's face amount or face amount plus cash value. Face amount cannot be less than a predetermined percentage of cash value (100% to 250%).
• Premiums are held in general account	• Premiums are held in investment account(s).	
• Reserves are maintained in general account.	• Reserves are maintained in investment account(s).	• Investment experience affects duration of policy; earnings must be enough to pay for face amount.
• Expenses are paid from investment income.	• Expenses are paid from investment income.	• Policy owner may directly adjust death benefit by increasing or decreasing premium, subject to policy minimums and underwriting requirements (insurability).

Figure 11-1. The differences among the major types of life insurance

of policy, because they understand volatility and the potential growth of market-related investments. If this description fits you and you understand that your premium may change, you may want to consider one of the variable life products. On the other hand, if you consider yourself fiscally conservative and want to know precisely what your premium will be over a fixed period of time, whole life is probably your best bet. Whatever you do, be absolutely certain that you understand the differences among the various insurance products and are selecting the one that best fits your actual needs and comfort zone.

Disability Insurance

Disability Insurance is insurance coverage for an injury or illness that prevents the policy holder from working for a certain amount of time.

Could you or your family continue to pay the bills if you or your significant other were unable to work? That's really the question you need to answer to determine how appropriate disability insurance is for you. It's designed to provide part of your income when an illness or injury prohibits you from earning your living. This type of policy is equally as important for single people as it is for married people. If you're single and self-employed, disability insurance should be high on your list of priorities.

If you think this isn't big business, consider this: more than 23 million Americans over age 15 have severe disabilities, and a recent survey of adults with disabilities found that almost 75% had been disabled before age 55.

Buys Briefs

How likely am I to need disability insurance? Most of us believe these things happen to somebody else but studies show that men have a 43% chance and women a 54% chance of experiencing a disability during their working years.

When purchasing disability insurance, you will face a menu of options. What you choose will directly affect the amount of your premium and benefit. An initial distinction is between short-term and long-term disability coverage. Short-term will typically provide coverage for up to two years, whereas long-term may provide protection over your lifetime.

Cost of Living Adjustment (COLA) is a provision in insurance policies that allows an annual inflation adjustment in the amount of the protection you receive.

A tough decision you'll have to make is how much you want to receive in benefits. Most policies will not let you replace more than 80% of your current income. Obviously, the more of your income you choose to replace, the higher the cost of the policy. Similarly, the longer you plan to be able to wait before you begin collecting benefits if you become disabled, the lower your premium will be. As with other types of insurance, the earlier you buy disability insurance, the less expensive it will be.

An important option to consider is the Cost of Living Adjustment (COLA) rider. If you're purchasing disability insurance only to cover a short-term claim, this feature would not be as important to you. It's much more important for the long-term policies. What you're buying here is really protection against inflation. This provision generally allows an annual adjustment that will begin after your first year of disability. On that date, the monthly benefit will be modified to reflect any increase in inflation measured by the CPI.

Because you'll be relying upon this insurance to survive financially, it's imperative that you understand the specifics of what you're buying. Does the insurance cover accidents and illnesses? Is inflation factored into the benefit? How is the insurance defining "disability"? What do you have to do to trigger the beginning of payments? What exclusions, if any, are there in your disability contract? Is it job- or skill-specific? (Many policies don't kick in if you're able to work at any job, not necessarily just the one for which you're trained.)

Long-Term Care Insurance

This insurance isn't cheap and it's becoming more difficult to obtain because of abuses that have cost the insurance companies money. If you're employed by a large organization, you may have disability insurance available through your company inexpensively or at no cost. As I stated earlier, if you're self-employed, the potential benefits of this insurance may very well justify the expense.

Long-term care costs have become one of the major health care expenses that Americans face today. If you think this applies only to the elderly, you are sadly mistaken: 40% of those currently in need of long-term care are between 18 and 64.

In my state, Colorado, the average cost of a nursing home for one year is nearing $42,000, while the median annual income for those of retirement age is $27,000. With the increase in life expectancy and improved medical care, people are living longer. Studies show that 60% of the population will need long-term care. Medicare pays for less than 20% of all long-term care in the U.S. today and frequently state Medicaid programs make you spend down to poverty levels to qualify. Obviously, the cost of long-term care has reached a point where few individuals can afford the cost out of their personal resources. In response to this need, long-term care insurance was created.

Buys Briefs

Long-term care involves a wide variety of services for people with prolonged physical illnesses, disabilities, or cognitive disorders (such as Alzheimer's disease). It is not one service but many different services aimed at helping people with chronic conditions compensate for limitations in their ability to function independently. Long-term care differs from traditional medical care in that it is designed to help a person maintain the level of functioning, as opposed to care or services intended to rehabilitate or correct certain medical problems.

When assessing long-term care policies, one of the first questions to ask is how do you qualify for care? Most companies base your eligibility on a loss of *Activities of Daily Living* (ADLs) or cognitive loss. For example, some require a loss of two out of six ADLs for you to qualify. These activities are typically dressing, transferring, toiletting, continence, eating, and bathing. It's important to make sure your policy includes bathing, because that's frequently one of the first ADLs to be lost.

In purchasing long-term care, you want to make certain that you have coverage for a variety of services. Ideally your policy will cover nursing home, private home, and community-based care. You'll need to determine how much coverage you'll need in the form of daily benefits and how long you want your benefits to continue. Another initial decision is determining when you want your benefits to begin—20, 30, or 100 days after home care starts or you enter a nursing home. Equally important is inflation protection: many policies allow an optional provision for indexing your benefits for inflation.

As with any other form of insurance, the more bells and whistles you choose, the greater the cost. If you're interested in purchasing this type of policy, you may want to read "A Shopper's Guide to Long-Term Care Insurance," a publication by the National Association of Insurance Commissioners. You can obtain this publication from many insurance companies or by writing the National Association of Insurance Commissioners at 120 West 12th Street, Suite 1100, Kansas City, MO 64105-1925, or calling the NAIC at (816) 842-3600.

Tax-Deductibility

As an added incentive, the Health Insurance Act of 1996 provides that tax-qualified long-term care policies may be tax-deductible. The maximum annual deduction gradually rises from $200 for people 40 or younger to $2500 for people over 70. In addition, benefits received under tax-qualified policies are not taxable, up to certain limits. While this sounds great, bear in mind that premiums are deductible up to certain age-related limits as part of the medical deduction allowed for expenses over 7.5% of adjusted gross income—the same as for other health insurance premiums.

Age	1997 Maximum Deduction per Individual
40 or younger	$200
41 through 50	$375
51 through 60	$750
61 through 70	$2000
71 and older	$2500

Limits will increase annually, based on the medical care component of the Consumer Price Index (CPI).

Since women outlive men, they are more likely to need long-term care. In fact, more than 75% of the people over 65 in nursing homes are women. Remember: many people who require long-term care are not sick in the traditional sense. They are old and frail and, although not in need of medical services, they may need assistance in the activities of daily living. Given the costs of nursing home care, it's easy to see how quickly this type of care can deplete your resources faster than the lifestyles of the rich and famous, and only then will you find yourself eligible for Medicaid. Not a pleasant prospect, but it's one that you can plan ahead to avoid.

Annuities

Many of you are probably wondering what annuities are doing in this section. They have become so popular as investment vehicles that it's easy to lose sight of the fact that an annuity is an insurance contract that provides periodic payments for a specified period of time. Another misconception about annuities is that they are viewed as very conservative or very aggressive. In fact, as you'll see, they can be pretty much structured to meet any objective.

Buys Briefs
An **Annuity** is a contract between an insurance company and an individual. The insurance company promises to make a series of payments for a fixed number of years or over a lifetime. Payments may be delayed or begin immediately.

Annuity Contract Terms

When you complete an application for an annuity, you will see some terms that may be confusing to you. Let's take a look at a few of them and I'll provide some simple definitions.

Owner/Participant This is the person or entity who has complete control over the annuity contract. The death benefit is triggered upon the death of this person.

Co-Owner/Co-Participant This person would share equally in the contract with the primary owner. The death benefit is triggered upon the death of either the owner or the co-owner and the death benefit will be paid to the beneficiary, not the surviving co-owner.

Annuitant Most often this is the same person as the owner of the contract, but not necessarily. This individual receives the payments from an annuity plan.

Beneficiary This person receives the death benefit upon the death of either the owner, co-owner, or—in the case of ownership by an entity—the annuitant.

Annuities are very popular. Variable annuity sales reached $87 billion in 1997, which represented an 18% increase over 1996 sales. The single biggest reason for this popularity is because they are one of the few tax-deferred investment alternatives available on an *after-tax* basis.

What does this mean to you? Basically, you can put any amount from $1,000 or less to a million dollars in an annuity and it will grow tax-deferred until you begin withdrawals. As with other retirement vehicles, you can't begin withdrawals until 59½ without triggering a penalty.

A wrinkle with annuities is that they typically have surrender penalties. If you withdraw assets before a specified period of time, often seven years, you will be hit with surrender charges. These charges typically decline every year. This table is an example of how that would work.

Deferred Sales Charge Schedule

Length of Time Since Purchase Payment	Percentage of Purchase Payments Being Liquidated
0–1 year	7.5%
1–2 years	7.0%
2–3 years	6.0%
3–4 years	5.0%
4–5 years	4.0%
5–6 years	3.0%
6–7 years	2.0%
7 + years	0%

The two key timelines to keep in mind to avoid any penalties are age 59½ and the designated surrender period. This is *not* a case of either/or: you must be 59½ *and* wait the designated time.

Fixed Annuity

A **Fixed Annuity** is a contract between an insurance company and an individual that guarantees a fixed payment.

A fixed annuity is considered one of the more conservative investment alternatives. As the name implies, the return on your money is fixed and grows tax-deferred. An insurance company will guarantee you prevailing interest rates over a fixed period of time. You know exactly what your return will be and precisely what the value of your annuity will be at a fixed point in the future. The guarantee can be for periods as short as one year and as long as 10—you make the choice. XYZ insurance company, for example, may guarantee you a 6% return over the next seven years. You may be wondering why you wouldn't want to guarantee the rate for as long a period of time as possible. The reason is you're betting on the direction of interest rates. If interest rates go up, you're locked in at a lower rate. If interest rates go down, you look like a champion.

Notice that I mentioned the word "guarantee." These returns are guaranteed by the insurance company issuing the policy, not the FDIC. That says to you that the quality of the insurance company is of utmost importance. Insurance companies are frequently rated as to their credit quality. Some of the best-known rating services are A.M. Best, Duff and Phelps Credit Rating, Moody's Investor Service, Standard & Poor's, and Weiss Ratings. Information from these services can be obtained on the Internet or at many local libraries. In addition, any insurance company that you're considering should be able to provide these ratings to you.

A fixed annuity may be an appropriate investment for conservative investors who don't want to experience any volatility in the value of their account. Many people purchase these as an alternative to a CD, because interest from a CD is taxable, while interest in an annuity grows tax-deferred. Remember: fixed annuities, unlike CDs, are not insured by the FDIC.

Variable Annuities

This form of annuities is increasingly popular. They are called variable because the return isn't fixed. Instead, it varies according to the performance of the investments you select. Your choices include a variety of

A **Variable Annuity** is a contract between an insurance company and an individual by which the amount of the payout will vary depending on the value of the account.

professionally managed portfolios that invest in stocks and bonds and behave much the same as mutual funds. Since these investments are frequently market-related, you can expect the higher risks and rewards associated with the markets. Unfortunately, you can also expect the volatility.

Mutual fund companies, realizing the popularity and business potential of annuities, have joined forces with many insurance companies to offer their products within the annuities. You can expect to find the likes of Putnam, Franklin, Fidelity, Janus, T. Rowe Price, Oppenheimer, and many other prominent fund families among your investment choices in variable annuities. Keep in mind that variable annuities grow tax-deferred, so you don't receive one of those ugly 1099s on your capital gains and dividends.

The tradeoff is that these are long-term investments and the same rules apply as with a fixed annuity: don't touch 'til you're 59½ and your surrender period is over. Unlike with a fixed annuity, the return from a variable annuity is not guaranteed by the insurance company. Your money is actually placed with the fund companies (e.g., Janus, Invesco, or Oppenheimer) and not kept by the insurance company. Therefore, your return is based on the performance of the funds you've chosen.

Bells and Whistles

Death in a Down Market is a benefit provided by an insurance policy that states that the beneficiary will receive the initial investment or the current market value of the account, whichever is greater.

As with other insurance products, you'll find an assortment of features available within the annuities of different insurance companies. A common one is called "death in a down market protection." That has a great sound, doesn't it? What it means is that your estate will receive either your initial investment or the current market value, whichever is greater.

Let's say that you place $25,000 in an annuity and you select aggressive investment choices. Then the market value plummets to $15,000. Your luck is clearly lousy: you book the only cruise that hits an iceberg in the Caribbean. Instead of focusing on your poor choice of cruises, your heirs will be eternally grateful, since they will receive $25,000, which is the greater of the two amounts.

Another common feature is a "stepped up death benefit." Many insurance companies, either annually on your anniversary date or on another specified date, "step up" the minimum death benefit your beneficiaries can receive, based on the current market value. This benefit becomes the new minimum amount they will receive, if the amount is higher than the value upon your death. In view of the market's recent record years, these death benefits have become more significant.

If you had placed $100,000 in a variable annuity that at the end of year one was worth $128,000, that would become your new death benefit, based on an annual "step up" in value. Should you die two years later and your annuity is worth $118,000, your beneficiaries would get $128,000. If, on the other hand, when you die it's worth $135,000, that would be the amount distributed to the beneficiaries. They receive whichever value is greater.

> **Buys Briefs**
>
> A **Stepped Up Death Benefit** is a benefit provided by the insurance company whereby on an anniversary date (annually, every five years, etc., as determined by the company) the death benefit is determined by the account value on that date. If the account value has dropped by the next anniversary date, you would receive the prior anniversary account value as the benefit. If, on the other hand, the value is higher on the next anniversary date, that becomes the new death benefit amount: the benefit is "stepped up" to the new level.
>
> An **Immediate Annuity** is a contract between an insurance company and an individual whereby a lump sum is invested and the payments start immediately.

Immediate Annuity

With fixed and variable annuities, your goal is to build assets so that you will have a nice nest egg down the road from which you could derive income at a later date. An *immediate annuity*, in contrast, is purchased with a single payment and, as the name implies, you may begin receiving income immediately. These contracts pay you a set income for life or a fixed period of time. The most common use of this type of annuity is after retirement. They appeal to conservative investors who like to know that they have a regular income stream in an exact dollar amount. A disadvantage is that they typically have low rates of return, so you may suffer the loss of higher returns for the sake of predictability of income.

Payout Options

Now that we've looked at the options in setting up an annuity, let's take a look at the most common options for getting your money out. Originally, annuities were designed to be converted into an income

A **Payout Option** is the method by which you decide to receive your benefits from an annuity.

stream and paid over the course of years. This was called annuitizing. In fact, less than 1% of annuity owners take this route each year. This is due to some serious issues involved in annuitization.

Generally, once you annuitize, you can't draw more money from your account than your predetermined systematic payment, which effectively eliminates the liquidity, since you can't get more money than the stated payment. Another very troubling aspect of annuitization is that, under some circumstances, when you die your assets are left to the annuity company rather than to your heirs. In the future, I believe you'll see greater and greater revamping of annuitization by the insurance companies and more innovative options to make this alternative more appealing.

Studies show that the average age of annuity owners is 52 and they're using the instrument only to accumulate money tax-deferred. Because of this, insurance companies are trying to give investors more choices in what are commonly referred to as "payout options" that allow you access to your money without annuitization.

Lump Sum Distribution With this option, you receive your entire account balance in a single payment. The downside is that the earnings will be taxed at regular income tax levels. That could be a big tax hit all at once.

Systematic Withdrawals This is one of the more popular options. You receive periodic payments while the balance of the account continues to grow tax-deferred. Many companies will allow you to receive monthly, quarterly, or annual payments in a certain amount or percentage of your holding.

Annuitization Options

This is the process by which you determine a method of receiving payments in a fixed dollar amount for an extended period of time, usually life. Once you determine the method of payout, you cannot change. It's a very important decision, because it determines how you will receive your money for the rest of your life.

Life Only This option provides a series of guaranteed payments for as long as the annuity owner lives. When the owner dies, payments stop and any money left over is forfeited to the insurance company.

Life with Period Certain This features the life only option in combination with guaranteed payments for a certain number of years, usually in increments of five. If the owner dies during that fixed period, payments go to a beneficiary for whatever time remains in the specified period.

Joint Life and Survivor This option provides an income stream for two people—the annuity owner and a beneficiary. All payments cease upon the death of the second party. This can be combined with a period certain feature.

Term Certain Payments are guaranteed for a specified number of years. If the owner dies during the period of time selected, the beneficiary receives the money for the remainder of that period.

As you can see, annuitization options are fairly cut-and-dried. You know what will happen and for how long. Once you decide to annuitize, there's no turning back—no flexibility in how much you'll receive from year to year. Weigh your options carefully before making a final decision.

While we may not want to acknowledge it, insurance is a necessary part of our lives and we are profoundly affected by the choices we make. We have health, car, homeowner's, and other types of insurance to minimize our risk in a variety of areas. Although I did not cover those types of policies, that does not mean that I don't think they're vitally important. My intention has been to present enough information on the types of insurance that can have a great impact on us and our loved ones. Having a sufficient comfort level with these products can give you confidence to further explore those that are appropriate for your needs and allow you to make the right decisions when buying insurance.

12 | Life's Uncertainties

For most of us, any major change involves stress and emotional turmoil. The greater the change and the more emotionally charged it is, the greater the discomfort. Probably the two most difficult times of our life are divorce and the death of a loved one. Unfortunately, while we are going through emotional turmoil, we're expected to keep our financial feet on the ground and make important monetary decisions that will affect the rest of our life.

While we all know statistically that divorce is very common and death is a certainty, this knowledge isn't "real" until it happens to us. We know that close to 50% of all marriages end in divorce, yet how many of us believe, when we're walking down the aisle, that we'll be a part of that statistic? Divorce, at any age, is almost always a traumatic experience. Terminating a marriage is often gut-wrenching for both spouses, their children, their families, and their friends.

In spite of the emotional upheaval, it's a time when we have to look at the financial aspects of divorce, which may be equally troubling. If you're going through a divorce, you can bet your financial situation will change; if you're a woman, that change is very likely to be for the worse.

On average, newly divorced women suffer a 75% drop in their standard of living. This is a truly amazing and sad statistic. The lesson to be learned is that you need to pay very close attention to your divorce settlement and your assets.

The Need to Know

I meet with many women well after their divorce who indicate that they had no idea where the money was going when they were married. Few knew what investments they had made jointly and how the investments worked. They were equally unaware of their debt obligations and their tax situation. When it came to the financial settlements, many of them were at a loss in understanding the difference between an illiquid, semi-worthless limited partnership and a high-quality mutual fund. Guess what many of them ended up with?

This is not an exercise in male-bashing, because a large part of the problem is that the women allow this to happen. Women should not be passive recipients of total financial guidance from their significant other or an attorney. We must assume responsibility for taking an active role in all aspects of our family's finances.

The first step in taking this active role is to begin learning about financial matters before a crisis forces you to do so. Ideally, you and your spouse should be equal partners in financial matters. This includes not only investment decisions but also anything relating to money. A top priority is understanding the cash flow in the family—what comes in, what goes out, and where it goes. The more organized your family finances are, the easier they will be to manage both before and during a divorce.

Be responsible about participating in your retirement plan at work or, if you're not employed, know how your retirement needs will be met. Life and health insurance are other areas about which you need to become informed. I can't stress enough the importance of knowing about investments and your overall family financial picture. Whether or not you end up being a divorce statistic, there is no question that knowledge of these matters is empowering and essential.

Divorce and Financial Planning

A commonly asked question is about the tax treatment of child support. These payments are neither deductible by the spouse who pays them nor included as income by the spouse that receives them. On the other hand, if you receive cash payments of alimony or separate maintenance, you must include them in figuring your gross income. The person paying the alimony or separate maintenance may deduct the payments from her or his gross income.

Another area of concern is the status of qualified retirement plans in a divorce. Most states regard the present value of retirement plan benefits as marital property subject to distribution. An important point for women to remember regarding retirement is that you can receive Social Security benefits based on your former spouse's work contribution if you were married for 10 or more years. How can this benefit you? Not only does it establish your eligibility, but your ex-husband may qualify for higher benefits than you would and this provision allows you to collect at his higher benefit level. This is a law and does not diminish your ex's Social Security benefits at all.

If they haven't done a lot of homework while married, most women should seek advice from financial professionals while in the process of divorce. We are frequently quick to seek necessary legal advice, but not so quick to seek necessary financial advice. In addition to helping you understand your current holdings, a financial professional can help assess the financial planning consequences of alimony, child support, and property division. There may also be insurance and estate planning issues associated with divorce. Don't wait until your settlement is cast in concrete before seeking assistance.

Death of a Loved One

Much of what we have been discussing in terms of divorce is equally true when a spouse dies. The emotional tidal wave that accompanies the loss of a loved one can be so powerful that people are frequently left unable to make even the most basic of life's decisions. Yet again, we are called upon at that very difficult time to make some of the most profound financial decisions of our lives. Often we receive a large lump sum of money from life insurance. As if you don't have enough on your plate, you now must decide what to do with this large sum of money. If you haven't managed financial affairs in the past, the decisions you are called upon to make can be terrifying. Should I pay off the house? If I can't pay off the house, will I be able to afford living here? What kind of income will I receive? Can I live on that amount? How long will it last? How will I pay for child care? Will I have to go back to work or school?

These are very important, anxiety-producing questions that need to be answered. It's our natural inclination to act quickly to reduce the stress they cause. But one of the worst things we can do is to act too quickly after the death of a loved one. I'm not advising that you delay these decisions indefinitely; I'm just saying that you need to allow yourself some breathing space, a time when you can calm down, look at your situation, and weigh your options. Some investments and investment advisors are targeted to widows and you may be urged to act quickly when it's not in your best interest to do so. If you're being pushed and it doesn't make sense, back away.

Again, it's very clear that you want to learn about financial matters *before* you are forced to do so and are least able to handle these responsibilities. Be proactive, not reactive. There are some things you can do to help ease you through this period, in addition to pursuing your financial education.

A basic but often overlooked necessity is to be organized and know where all the important documents are located. Do you know where your wills and life insurance policies are kept? Do you know how to reach your attorney and life insurance agent? Do you know where your financial statements are? Do you have a relationship with the family's financial advisor? Are you aware of your family's financial obligations? Obviously, there are many questions like this; the more of them you can think of and answer, the more prepared you will be.

In the discussions of both death and divorce, the common thread is the need for financial advice and knowledge. Neither of these situations would be an appropriate time for you to let Uncle Harry give you his investment wisdom—unless Uncle Harry is more than an amateur. There are other life events, such as inheritance, job loss, and serious illness, that may trigger the sudden need for financial advice from a professional.

Financial Advisors

Unfortunately, this arena appears highly confusing to most people, because there are so many types of financial advisors and so many titles given to investment professionals. Frankly, I do not agree with a lot of the advice you get in this area in many investment books. Some portray the financial planner as always being noble and a stockbroker as a villain. Others say that a Registered Investment Advisor is the ideal and an insurance agent is terrible. This, my friends, is a bunch of hooey! The fact is that, behind all those various titles, you find the good, the bad, and the ugly.

Below I've listed some of the common designations and credentials for your reference.

- **CFP – Certified Financial Planner** The Certified Financial Planner Board of Standards in Denver issues these credentials to those who have passed the 10-hour CFP exam and agreed to abide by the CFPB code of ethics.

- **CLU – Chartered Life Underwriter** The American College in Bryn Mawr, Pennsylvania issues this designation to applicants, mostly life insurance agents, with three years' experience and 10 college-level courses who sign the CLU code of ethics. Agents can also acquire a Chartered Financial Consultant (ChFC) certificate by taking three more courses.

- **MBA – Master's of Business Administration** This graduate degree normally provides a good, solid background for financial occupations.

- **Registered Representative** This is typically a stockbroker who has successfully completed the necessary exams approved by the National Association of Securities Dealers (NASD). There are also ongoing continuing education requirements by the firms they work for and the NASD.

- **Series 7** This is an examination that qualifies a candidate for the solicitation, purchase, and/or sale of corporate securities, municipal securities, options, direct participation programs, investment company products, and variable annuity contracts. There are continuing education requirements.

- **General Securities Principal, Series 24** This is an examination that qualifies a candidate to register as a general securities principal. This license is required to manage or supervise the member's investment banking or securities business (including sales supervision) for corporate securities, direct participation programs, investment company products, and variable annuity contracts.

- **CPA – Certified Public Accountant** This designation requires passing a national exam and completing a specified level of financial and accounting education. There are continuing education requirements as well.

- **RIA – Registered Investment Advisor** These financial advisors are registered with the Securities and Exchange Commission (SEC). They file a form that contains a summary of their background and fees.

Paying for Advice

Don't believe that once you've picked the right title (whatever that is) you've done all you need to do. Within the world of these advisors, there's a great deal of variation as to how they are paid. No matter which one you choose, rest assured that they're getting paid. None are volunteers.

One of the methods of payment is fees. These fees may involve an hourly rate or a certain flat fee for developing a financial plan, for example. Traditionally, many professionals have been paid by commissions generated from the sale of a variety of investment products. Others receive a set fee, commonly around 1½% of the assets they manage for you. These fee structures are not mutually exclusive: you may find that your advisor can use all three or some combination. No reputable advisor will mind discussing her or his fees with you, so ask about them—and then ask questions until you understand.

What Does Your Gut Say?

When I teach, almost without exception, the question arises about selecting an advisor. One of my first rules of thumb is to go with your gut. Women generally have a good sense of who they think will be honest and trustworthy. If you're meeting with someone and something doesn't ring true, listen to that inner voice and move on. Since your relationship with your financial advisor affects one of the most important areas of your life, you need to give time and attention to selecting that individual.

In many investment books, the author provides a list of questions that you're supposed to take in hand as you begin interviewing prospective advisors. Some of the questions provided are inappropriate at best. For example, some tell you to ask the average return that advisor has produced for her or his clients. Speaking as an investment advisor, I can tell you I have my 93-year-old conservative clients in very different investments than for my 27-year-old aggressive ones. You'd hardly expect the same return for both.

What questions do I feel you should ask? First, I think it's important to know something about the advisor's background and credentials. The wider the variety of licenses and credentials, the better. If you're meeting with someone who is registered only to sell insurance, guess what might be the one product they may feel will meet your every financial need?

Do They Listen?

I think the questions *they* ask *you* are every bit as important as the questions *you* ask *them*. If in your initial meeting the advisor does all of the talking, something's wrong with the picture. A good advisor will have to know a great deal about you to provide the kind of guidance you need, customized to your unique situation. They can't get this information without asking questions and listening to your responses. At an absolute minimum, they should be interested in your investment experience, your risk tolerance, your investment goals, and your tax situation. In turn, you need to be able to provide this information. As with any relationship, this is a two-way street and information needs to flow both ways to make it work.

Do You Need a Formalized Plan?

After you've shared with them a profile of your situation, feel free to ask what their general advice would be. If they immediately leap to selling you an expensive financial plan, I'd quickly excuse myself and depart. Many people simply don't need these deluxe plans to move forward with their financial life. Often these plans are primarily designed to generate revenue for the firms selling them. Once the plan is completed, they're then likely to ask you to buy their proprietary products. That sounds like a good thing for the firm, doesn't it? It is. But not necessarily for you.

Let me hasten to add that there are times when a financial plan is a legitimate and necessary expense. In fact, the more complicated your financial picture, the more appropriate a plan may be.

> ### Buys Briefs
> **Proprietary** refers to products offered and controlled exclusively by a financial company, normally a brokerage firm.

You may not need a formalized financial plan—but you certainly need a plan. Frequently that plan does not have to be any more complicated than what you can outline with a pencil and a pad of paper. One way or another, you need direction and goals for your financial future. Then you should monitor your plan and adapt it on an ongoing basis.

Red Flags

In addition to what I've said above, there are some red flags to look for when seeking an advisor.

- **Flag 1** Don't buy something over the phone from an unknown cold caller. How could this person possibly know your personal situation and goals?

- **Flag 2** Beware of the advisor who wants to sell you only her or his "in-house" proprietary products. Whose interest do you think that person is serving?

- **Flag 3** If advisors are vague about their methods of receiving pay, that's not a good sign.

- **Flag 4** If they can't explain the investment they're proposing to you, shame on them, not shame on you. Get someone who explains things well.

- **Flag 5** If it sounds too good to be true, it is. Beware of guarantees that you'll get rich quick.

- **Flag 6** Every investment has risks. Make sure you're informed about what they are.

- **Flag 7** This is the biggest, blood-red flag of all. If any advisor treats you in any manner that appears patronizing or condescending, run, don't walk, to the nearest exit. I have heard horrible stories of women being treated in this manner by their brokers, yet for some unknown reason they continue doing business with them. You don't have to put up with that and there's a simple solution—fire the jerk. Whether the advisor is a man or a woman, this treatment is unacceptable. By putting up with it, you're allowing it to continue and shortchanging yourself.

Resources to Help Find an Advisor

There are some resources to use when looking for an advisor. A very good way to begin would be by asking your friends or family members. This way you get a referral from someone who actually knows the advisor and is theoretically pleased with her or his services and approach.

You may also wish to attend classes and seminars offered by professionals, so you can decide if you might enjoy working with this person. Professional resources are also valuable. Your attorney or accountant may be able to recommend someone. Once you obtain a few names, you can get information about certain disciplinary actions and other matters through the National Association of Securities Dealers, Inc. (NASD) by calling 1-800-289-9999 or your state securities division.

Obviously women must become knowledgeable about money matters. Too many of us wait to begin learning until we're in a vulnerable state and forced to make decisions.

The choice you make in selecting a financial advisor is very important. You've seen that advisors come in a variety of flavors. Watch out for those red flags and trust your gut in making your selection. If it doesn't work as you intended, you can always change to someone more suited to your needs—and you owe it to yourself to do so!

13 *Financial Potpourri*

*J*ust as its title implies, in this chapter we're going to look at a variety of financial transactions and situations you might find yourself involved in, from real estate to ESOPs and more.

Real Estate

One of the subjects that raises the most questions, in my experience, is real estate. When I was young and early in my career, I would answer these questions with my most professional and well-reasoned financially based answers. Now that I'm a little later in my career (and still young, of course!), I have come to understand that questions surrounding real estate are every bit as emotional as they are rational. There's no question that most people still have that image of home ownership making their life complete, whether or not it makes financial sense. Let's take a look at when it may or may not make sense to buy a home.

Buying vs. Renting

As with most things, there are advantages and disadvantages to both buying and renting. An obvious advantage of renting is that you have freedom to come and go as you wish. Your payment is perhaps lower than if you were purchasing and you normally have no maintenance cost. That gives you greater cash flow potential and an ability to invest those other dollars if you wish to do so. There are typically fewer hassles with renting and you couldn't care less about the upturns or downturns in property values. An obvious disadvantage to renting is that you're not building any equity and you don't receive any of the tax benefits associated with home ownership.

Equity is the difference between the amount a property could be sold for and the amount owed on that property.

When you buy a home, the tax advantages associated with ownership are an important benefit. Unlike other debt interest, your mortgage interest and property tax payments receive favorable tax treatment. In addition, you're building equity in your property and also enjoy the intangible but very real sense of security that is associated with owning your own home.

There are significant advantages to owning a home, but if you currently own a home you know that there are also some definite disadvantages. The older I get, the less interested I am in the time and expense associated with maintenance. Make no mistake: home ownership requires plenty of each. In addition to these expenses, you also need to concern yourself about property values and the overall economic conditions in your community.

Real estate is *not* a highly liquid investment. If any of you have lived in a community that has gone through a recession, you understand this point very well. In Colorado we've had a series of boom-and-bust economies. During the boom cycles, you enjoy tremendous appreciation, but during the bust cycles, it's difficult to even give a property away.

Getting Qualified

Since almost all of us end up buying homes, there are a few things we must do to be prepared. Once you've decided that you want to buy a home, do yourself a favor and get prequalified. This process tells you the approximate maximum amount you can afford to pay for a home. This will save you and your realtor time, energy, and the frustration of looking for properties that cost much more than you can afford. It will also allow you to act quickly once you find the property you wish to purchase.

Check Your Credit Report

Studies show that about a third of all credit reports contain errors serious enough to prevent the consumer from getting a home loan. In addition to containing incorrect negative information, some reports fail to mention positive information. Whether or not you plan to buy a home in the near future, it's a good idea to look at your credit report and ensure that it's accurate. There are three major credit reporting agencies. They are Experian (1-888-397-3742), Trans-Union (610-690-4909), and Equifax (1-800-997-2493). These companies generally charge for a copy of an individual credit report. Some states have now mandated that you must be provided a free copy of your credit report every year, while others regulate by law the cost of obtaining the report.

If you find errors in these reports, you can either use the form the credit reporting agency gave you to correct the mistake or circle the errors directly on the report and write next to them the reasons you believe them to be incorrect. You then return your corrected report with a short cover letter. If you don't hear back from the credit agency within 60 days, follow up. Laws require these firms to promptly investigate any reported discrepancies and correct all errors.

Mortgage Loans

Once you find that dream home, always shop for the best interest rate available. Mortgage lending is an extremely competitive business and you want to do comparison shopping, since you can save yourself thousands of dollars. The importance of the interest rate cannot be overstated. It not only changes your monthly payment but also dramatically affects the price you'll pay for your home over the term of the mortgage.

Be sure to compare all the costs involved. The interest rate is only one aspect of what you'll pay when you purchase that home. Make certain you understand the *total* cost structure by requesting a "good faith estimate," which will break down your final costs.

In periods of relatively low interest rates, you may want to consider refinancing. A rule of thumb has been that it's in your interest to refinance if you can lower your interest rate by two percentage points or more. Also consider how long you will continue to live in your current home, to justify the expenses associated with refinancing. Your new rate needs to be low enough so that your new payments compensate for the cost of refinancing in a relatively short period of time.

15 Years or 30 Years?

If you're looking to buy the most house that you can afford, you may very well need a 30-year mortgage, since your monthly payments will be lower. Also, if interest rates are very low, you may want a longer term to lock in these rates for a long time. On the other hand, if your goal is to build up equity rapidly and to pay off your mortgage sooner, a 15-year mortgage may be more appealing. Obviously your payments will be higher, but if you look at saving that extra 15 years of interest, you'll see that it translates to an astounding amount of money saved. You'll typically also enjoy a slightly lower interest rate on the 15-year. When choosing between the two terms, you want to consider the after-tax interest cost on your mortgage. If you want to pay your home off early but can't afford the payments associated with a 15-year mortgage, you can go with the 30-year and simply make additional payments on the principal whenever you're able to do so.

Paying Off a Mortgage

Don't always assume that it's in your best interest to pay off your mortgage. I've met with widows who have taken the lump sum of money they'd received from their husbands' life insurance and paid off a low-rate mortgage. This left them with very little resources to provide an ongoing income. In seeking security, they essentially made themselves "house poor."

Remember also to calculate your after-tax mortgage costs. This is important, not only in deciding on the mortgage term but also in deciding whether or not to pay off the mortgage. Let's look at this more closely. To use a simple example, let's assume you have a 7% mortgage and are in the 33% tax bracket. After tax considerations, your mortgage is essentially costing you about 4.7%. So ask yourself the question, can you outperform 4.7% in other investments? If the answer is yes, you may want to continue using your lender's 7% money, knowing that it's costing you less than 5%, and invest in such a way that you will outperform the cost of that money.

A final thought on real estate. While we all may dream of owning that home with the white picket fence, don't buy more than you can handle. You'll frequently find that you can qualify for more house than you can actually afford, if you enjoy other basic necessities, such as eating. Don't make yourself "house poor." It's common to hear that you should buy the most house that you can afford because theoretically your earnings will increase and you'll become more comfortable with your mortgage payment. This may be true theoretically, but in practice there can be problems. I work with young couples whose house payments are so restrictive that these people find themselves unable to do many other things they'd like to do.

Buying a home is one of the biggest financial decisions most of us will ever make. While we all want to own our little piece of turf, there are serious financial factors that you need to consider when making this purchase. Don't plunge into a decision without thoroughly studying your situation.

Other Real Estate Investments

Any decision about purchasing real estate for rental or other investment purposes should always be discussed with your tax advisor. If you don't have a tax advisor, this would be a real good time to get one. The types of real estate available are limitless; you should choose according to your particular situation and tax goals.

Buys Briefs

A **Real Estate Investment Trust** is a company dedicated to owning and, in most cases, operating income-producing real estate, such as apartments, shopping centers, offices, and warehouses in order to earn profits for shareholders. A REIT is legally required to pay virtually all of its taxable income (95%) to its shareholders every year.

REITs

People who are interested in investing in real estate but who don't want to buy property directly often turn to real estate investment trusts (REITs). These trusts pool cash from investors and issue shares that can be bought or sold on a stock exchange or in the over-the-counter market. REITs don't pay taxes, since they pass through to shareholders the income from rents, interest, and gains from any property sale. *Equity* REITs own interests in real estate developments or various types of properties, such as apartment buildings or hotels. *Mortgage REITs* offer mortgages or building loans. Since real estate is a valuable component in an asset allocation mix, this type of investment allows people to have exposure to this category without having to invest a great deal of money in purchasing properties directly.

Our Merry Oldsmobile

In addition to our homes, there is nothing that many Americans take greater pride in than what they drive. Unfortunately, many people seem to think they *are* what they *drive*. As an investment advisor, I feel honor-bound to briefly address this subject here.

With alarming regularity I meet with people who tell me they feel they can't put away enough to fund their retirement or they can't start saving for their child's education—yet they feel that driving the latest-model Lexus is a necessity. If they can't afford to buy the car of their dreams, they lease it. In fact, some people become downright indignant if I suggest that they could purchase or lease a less expensive vehicle and free up some of their money for other purposes.

If we choose to spend a significant portion of our income on our vehicles, we need to at least be honest and admit that it's a choice. In spite of all the money we spend on them, they are depreciating assets, unless we're purchasing a vintage, collectible vehicle, which is generally not the case. You're paying a price for looking really spiffy driving down the highway. It's up to you to make that choice and deal with the consequences.

Investing in Your Employer

Many companies offer programs to get their employees to purchase company stock. These plans are usually in the interests of both parties, since they frequently allow you to invest at a discount and, in return, your employer hopes that you'll have a more vested interest in the company and stay there for a long time. Since there are a variety of plans, it's important that you talk to your human resources department to see how yours works.

Employee Stock Ownership Plan (ESOP)

The first of these plans is called an Employee Stock Ownership Plan (ESOP). This is a qualified plan that allows you to invest in your employer's stock. The benefit of purchasing employer stock through this program is that, up to certain maximums, the amount of money you spend to buy the stock isn't subject to income tax until the stock is distributed from the plan to you. Tax on the capital gain can be put off even longer, until you decide to sell the stock; the profit would then be subject to regular capital gain tax rates.

It's dangerous to have most or all of your money in company stock, whether it's in your retirement plan or not. Even if your stock has appreciated 500% in the last three years, you are precariously non-diversified and this can have disastrous results if your company stock declines. Keep in mind that the greatest key to risk management is diversification in both your retirement and non-retirement accounts.

Employee Stock Purchase Plan (ESPP)

This plan allows employees the opportunity to buy their employer's stock at a reduced price, up to certain limitations, outside of a qualified account. It gives you the right to buy your company stock on a future date for an amount that's no higher than the current price of stock. For example, your company may allow you to buy stock on December 31 each year for the price the stock was selling at on January 1 of that year. In addition, some employers also allow you to purchase the stock for less than what the stock sold for on the day the right was granted. The discount may be up to 15%. These purchases are made throughout the year, according to company policy.

Stock Options

Another very attractive employee benefit is stock options. These plans allow you to purchase company stock at specified prices and dates. Typically the exercise dates (the dates on which you're allowed to make the transaction) are several years in the future, so the price of the stock would likely have appreciated greatly. For example, your company might give you today the option to purchase 300 shares of its stock at $30 a share in five years. If at the end of that five-year period your company stock is selling for $130 a share, you would make a very hefty profit.

Even after being taxed at ordinary income levels, this can be a substantial company benefit. If the stock of your company is going up and you have confidence in its future, this can be a great incentive for staying where you are—and that's exactly why companies offer stock options.

Futures

In Chapter 8 I discussed asset allocation and mentioned that there are many different asset classes. One of these asset classes not covered there is commodities. These are things like pork bellies and gold futures and other "commodities" items such as soybeans, wheat, coffee, and crude oil. You can also speculate on the direction of global currencies, interest rates, and stock indices.

> **Buys Briefs**
> **Commodities** are bulk goods such as grains, metals, and foods traded on a commodities exchange.

To participate in this market, you don't go out and buy a thousand pounds of coffee or five thousand bushels of soy beans and you don't invest half a million dollars in the Mexican peso. Rather, you invest in something called "futures contracts." These contracts are an agreement to buy or sell a specific amount of a commodity or financial instrument at a specified price on a specified future date.

Although futures contracts are highly sophisticated, they actually began as a way for farmers to lock in prices for their crops before the crops were ready for delivery. As recently as 1974, over 80% of the futures market was involved in the agricultural area. By 1997, almost two-thirds of all activity in the futures market was directed at financial futures. These include things such as interest rate futures, currency futures, and stock indices. There are now 75 distinct futures markets, ranging from agriculturals in Chicago to financial instruments in Tokyo. Trading is conducted 24 hours a day.

If all this sounds pretty complicated and risky, that's because it is. This is one area where you don't want to venture without the assistance of an expert. In fact, a study several years ago by the Chicago Mercantile Exchange found that 90% of individual investors who traded the futures market on their own lost money.

Since I've emphasized in this book that you don't need to chase speculative investments to do well, you may be wondering why I've included futures here. In discussing asset allocation, we saw that the idea was to hold investments that behave differently in different economic situations. True diversification means that you hold a lot of non-correlated investments. The commodities market has virtually no correlation to the stock market! What this means to you is that, by adding exposure to this asset class, perhaps through the use of a managed futures investment, you may actually be helping to protect your investment portfolio.

Studies have indicated that, by including managed futures in your portfolio, you can actually reduce portfolio volatility at many levels. A common rule of thumb is that aggressive investors may wish to have 10% of the equity portion of their portfolio in managed futures. For example, if you decided you wanted 80% of your portfolio exposed to stocks, you could take 10% of that 80% for an investment in managed futures. Although futures are an aggressive investment, they can be a valuable asset class for your portfolio, if you handle them properly.

Investment Clubs

With the popularity of the Beardstown Ladies, interest in investment clubs has boomed. These clubs can enable you to learn in a group setting about a variety of stocks. Pooling money makes investing cheaper for everyone and it allows you to learn inexpensively. Many of the clubs do extensive stock analysis and rely heavily on Value Line for data. The guidelines for forming a club are provided by the National Association of Investors Corporation (NAIC). If you wish to begin an investment club, you may contact the NAIC at 1-800-583-6242.

I believe that it's important for you to learn and enjoy yourself at the same time. Often these groups become so analytical that members find the activities overwhelming and tedious. Investors have told me that they've left their meetings in tears because they became so intimidated by all the information and research involved. If you're looking into an investment club, you may want to attend a few meetings before committing to that group, to make sure its style feels comfortable to you.

14 Real Women Real Stories

What follows is a series of interviews with women dealing with an assortment of situations that affect their financial lives. By sharing their stories, they're providing a unique opportunity for us to learn from their experiences. I believe you'll find some ordinary and some extraordinary, but you'll see common threads. It's my hope that in reading these pages you'll see yourself reflected in some of the tales and gain knowledge from the way others have handled their situations. I find many of these stories inspirational and hope you will as well.

These women come from different geographic locations and represent a wide variety of backgrounds. The stories are true, but the names have been changed to "protect the innocent." In some instances, identifying information has been omitted that may affect the financial planning considerations provided. In all instances, I would encourage these women to establish or review key legal documents, such as wills, durable powers of attorney, and medical powers of attorney.

Each profile will begin with an overview and will be followed by an interview with the woman profiled. At the end of the interview, I provide a brief summary, lessons to be learned from each scenario, and a sample of financial planning considerations that may be appropriate from each case. The intent is not to provide an in-depth analysis, but rather give you an idea of some of the financial issues in a variety of situations.

Profile 1
Name   *Jamie*
Age   *39*
Occupation   *Medical Sales*
Marital Status   *Single*
Annual Income   *$55,000*
Overview   *At age 25, totally unexpectedly, Jamie became the sole support of her parents and sister. At that time, she was earning $25,000 and did not own a home.*

Interview

Kathy: Jamie, could you share with us how you happened to become the family's sole support at such a young age?

Jamie: My family was in the farming business and they were doing well. My mom and dad were persuaded to take loans on the farm to acquire additional land. They weren't very sophisticated and didn't understand all of the risks that were involved. In the early '80s they were foreclosed on and lost everything. My immediate thought was, "Oh my God, here I am the full supporter of a family!"

Kathy: What did that do to your financial planning?

Jamie: Remember, I was 25 years old, so this kind of responsibility was the last thing on my mind. We grew up with the thought that you always needed to save for retirement so the only thing I was doing at the time was saving for retirement through my paycheck. My family had been very, very conservative. Now all of a sudden I had to buy a house and be the major support at a time that I was earning $25,000 a year. I provided the roof over their head and everyone had jobs to help support with all the utilities and food.

Kathy: This must have turned your world upside down.

Jamie: Exactly. My thoughts on security became even stronger. At that young age I had to understand that any type of move I made, whether it was career changes or savings, not only affected me; now it affected a lot more people. It also made me rethink my finances.

Kathy: In what way?

Jamie: As time went by, I realized that passbook savings wasn't the way to go. I wasn't getting ahead and I knew that in order to provide for unexpected happenings in the future, like nursing home or nursing care for my parents, I had to look at a more lucrative way of earning money.

Kathy: How did that go for you?

Jamie: Unfortunately I made a lot of mistakes. I bought some universal life insurance policies, which sounded good but I didn't know anything about. I also bought some stock that was connected to the place I work. I knew I needed to do something; I just didn't know what. My idea in buying the insurance was to pay off the house for my parents in case something happened to me.

When I met with the insurance salesman, he made the life insurance sound great and I thought, "OK, this sounds good: it's going to earn money and I just let it sit there." What I didn't understand were the expenses involved and how he came up with the numbers he had.

Kathy: Now you are as committed as anybody I know to serious planning and you're willing to branch past that security issue. How do you explain that?

Jamie: I realized I had to get educated about investments because I had a clear goal in mind. I want to have enough money to pay off my current home for my folks to live in and finally buy my own home.

I took money that I already had and invested that. I then watched for a little while and got comfortable with it. I'm now investing more.

My thoughts were always to save up front. I had my retirement money taken out of my paycheck and lived off of what was left because when I tried it the other way I never had any money at the end of the month to save.

Kathy: You're 39 now. When do you see yourself buying your own home?

Jamie: If I'm very successful in my current job and keep getting bonuses, I'm hoping to be able to buy within two to three years. I originally bought the house and then refinanced for a 15-year loan and went to a biweekly plan to pay it off so that I'm getting the biggest bang for my buck.

Kathy: Jamie, generally speaking, is there any message you'd like to relay to other women?

Jamie: I think they need to be a little bit selfish and think about their futures themselves. There's a lot of things out there that tempt you by now. I think you need to take a look at what your future is going to be. Women live a long life and they need to think about that. I don't care what age you are; you need to plan and the sooner the better.

Kathy: And maybe be a little disciplined?

Jamie: Exactly. You'd be surprised how fast you can accrue money, but you have to be very, very disciplined and make up your mind that that's a priority.

Kathy: Are you seeing many of your peers planning for their future?

Jamie: I would say the majority—no. I think even the ones that get paid well are living paycheck to paycheck. I always wonder what's going to happen if a disaster hits them or when they retire.

I know firsthand how life can deal you unexpected blows and it taught me to be prepared as much as possible. To make investing work, you have to either be scared or have a goal in mind. If you don't have that, you'll never be disciplined.

Kathy: Jamie, your story is remarkable. You've turned a family tragedy into a success story. Look where you've gone, from being 25 years old making $25,000 a year to now being almost at the point where you're able to buy another house. You're also managing to participate in your company's retirement plan and put a few dollars away. Great job. Thanks for sharing with us.

Summary

This story provides us several lessons. The first of these is what tragic consequences there can be when you make financial decisions without understanding all of the risks that are involved. In this case it ultimately cost Jamie's family their farm and livelihood. Obviously they didn't understand the inherent dangers of the loan paperwork they were signing. The bottom line here is that, if you don't understand what you're signing, don't sign it. If you're not equally clear on all of the ramifications of what you're agreeing to, seek professional help. It's well worth the price you might pay for this advice to potentially save you everything!

Jamie is a remarkably resourceful and responsible young woman. Her willingness to step up to the plate saved this family. When it came time for Jamie to make some financial decisions, notice that she indicates she made some mistakes, such as buying a life insurance policy she didn't understand, but quickly sought additional knowledge.

The theme of this story, as well as many to follow, is that life deals us many unexpected blows, and the better prepared we are financially, the greater our ability to cope. Place yourself in Jamie's shoes. Do you or your family have a cash cushion in the event of even the smallest of disasters? While Jamie faced a major disaster, often it only takes a broken appliance to break our financial backs. Pay yourself first.

Lessons

- Never sign documents you don't fully understand.
- Seek professional advice before making a complex legal and financial decision.
- Always have a cash cushion.
- If your first financial experience didn't meet your needs, cut your losses and move forward. Don't dwell on your mistakes. Turn the negative into a positive by resolving to learn more.
- Start planning for your financial future early and have specific goals in mind. It's hard to achieve something when you don't know what it is you're going after.

Financial Planning Considerations

- **Life insurance:** Provide for her parents in the event of her death.
- **Long-term care:** Protect her parents in their later years.
- **Retirement planning:** Continue full participation in 401(k) and consider other retirement-oriented investments (e.g., variable annuity or IRA).
- **Down payment for a home:** Establish monthly systematic savings

plan into a money market in conjunction with the bonus checks saved.

- **Investment plan:** Once target goal for down payment has been achieved, continue dollar amount of monthly savings into a mutual fund, using the principles of asset allocation, and increase as wages increase.
- **Review overall asset allocation:** This should include her 401(k), to make sure that the selections are in line with her overall financial objectives.
- **Estate planning:** This process should begin with establishing a will.

Profile 2	
Name *Peggy*	
Age *36*	
Occupation *Lieutenant in Fire Department*	
Marital Status *Married*	
Annual Income *Combined: $90,000*	
Overview *Peggy dropped out of high school and ran away from home at age 15. After being nearly beaten to death, she made a dramatic lifestyle change.*	

Interview

Kathy: What a tale you have to tell. Where do we start?

Peggy: My dad worked and my mom stayed home. She was both emotionally and financially dependent upon my dad. He was successful in his own business but never saved a penny. Whatever he made was what he spent. He was an absolute "playaholic."

I dropped out of school and started out on my own when I was 15. I didn't do this so much to get away from my parents; in fact, I'd even hitchhike home on weekends to visit them and I lived over 300 miles away. I thought I was grown up and wanted to prove my independence.

The first year and a half was a struggle. It was tough just being out on your own and learning about victimization and how vulnerable you are when you're not prepared.

Kathy: At 15 it's hard to be prepared.

Peggy: I made some bad choices that sometimes led to me being taken advantage of and when I was about 16½ I was almost beaten to death.

Kathy: What a nightmare at any age, let alone a teenager on her own.

Peggy: Yes, and it was at that moment a big shift took place and over the next three to five years a big change happened to me. I realized that I had to get control or I was going to die. Over that time I started to realize I had to make better choices and be more responsible. For instance, you can't just quit a job because it wasn't fun and you just can't hang around people you knew might get in trouble.... You know, stuff like that.

Kathy: How did you come to complete high school?

Peggy: I was fortunate enough to be bright and when I was 19 I got a job as a nanny with a great family. The woman encouraged me to go down and get my G.E.D., which I did. I did go to one semester of college, but felt I was going just for the sake of going and didn't know what I wanted to do yet. I learned a lot by living with this family and watching them. They encouraged me a lot and served as a role model, seeing how they did things I had never seen before in my life.

Kathy: Sounds like they were a great influence. Did they influence your views about money?

Peggy: Yes. They were wealthy and I could see they struck a balance. The balance I needed was learning how to play and enjoy money like my dad but at the same time saving and being responsible. My grandfather was so responsible he squirreled away every penny that he ever made. He lived so conservatively that his life was really sad. He couldn't enjoy it because he was always worried about savings. My mom knew nothing about money, my dad was a wild spender, and my grandfather couldn't spend anything.

Kathy: You really got some confusing messages there.

Peggy: Yes. I really didn't want to be like any of them.

Kathy: At what age did you get married?

Peggy: At 21 and we are financial opposites. It has been one of the bigger struggles in our marriage over the last 14 years. He's somewhat like my dad. He works really hard, but has no problem being deeply in debt and doesn't wait until tomorrow to buy things. He's really great at living beyond his means.

Kathy: Doesn't this drive you crazy?

Peggy: Yes, sometimes I feel like I'm carrying the financial weight. Not that he doesn't work, but he doesn't want to plan for anything. The problem got so intense we separated for a year and he didn't balance his checkbook for the whole year.

Kathy: What does he do for a living?

Peggy: He's a sheriff.

Kathy: You've clearly had a great career path. How'd you happen to get in the fire department?

Peggy: I spent a number of years working with juvenile delinquents. I got into martial arts for about 12 years and fought in tournaments around the country, but there was no money in it. At that time I heard about an opening in the fire department and that really appealed to me. The more I looked into it, the more I realized that was what I was looking for my whole life.

Kathy: So you got your job then?

Peggy: No, it took me three years. I thought I'd get on in a few weeks, but I knew I really wanted to do it and focused on getting hired until I finally did.

Kathy: You took my class and clearly have quite an interest in investments. What awakened that interest?

Peggy: I like being in control of my future. It's very important to me to take care of myself. I think this goes back to those earlier experiences when I was so vulnerable. I also know I'd like to retire at 50 and I plan to live to be 120!

Kathy: You better be saving a lot of money! What are you doing now to prepare yourself for this goal?

Peggy: I have three investment properties and I'm doing some mutual fund investments. In addition, I'm putting $300 a month into my retirement plan at work. I'm a slow mover. I like to study things, so now I'm spending more time learning about the stock market.

My husband has had his job for 10 years and has not gotten started yet. He's promised he'll start with $100 a pay period within the next month.

Kathy: You've come a long way emotionally, financially, and professionally. What message would you like to give women?

Peggy: The first thing is that women have to get over this fantasy of a guy on a white horse who's going to take care of them and make their life work out wonderfully. My mom certainly had that thought when she got married.

She was married at 18. My dad had a huge double standard, like most men of that generation did. My mom, finally after 26 years, drew a boundary with my dad for the first time and my dad packed his bags and left that night. Now they're divorced.

My white knight is a great guy, but he can't do it financially. I think women are independent in some ways but I think we've got a long way to go in other ways. One of them is becoming realistic about our future.

Kathy: It's incredible what you've done with your life. It should inspire a lot of women who are feeling hopeless because they think the deck is stacked against them. Thank you very much.

Summary

You must admit this is a fairly remarkable story, from being on the street at 15 to having a successful career at age 35. As you can tell from her story, she had a lot of conflicting role models financially, none of which she felt comfortable with. She was fortunate enough to come upon a family that changed her life emotionally, financially, and intellectually. While she continues to struggle with striking a balance financially and the attitude of her husband, Peggy has experienced a dramatic evolution and persists in her efforts to take care of her financial goals.

Lessons

- You can mold your own financial life in spite of the role models you've had.
- Never believe your situation will forever be hopeless.
- You can form and implement life directions personally and financially.
- It's important to be proactive and not be a cork on the water.
- Spend time discussing with your future partner what his or her perceptions are regarding money and money management and understand their importance in a relationship.
- Be open to learning from your environment and evaluate advice from others.
- Don't wait for somebody to come along to take care of you. Take care of yourself.

Financial Planning Considerations

- **Money management:** Negotiate an agreement with her spouse regarding future financial management and decisions.
- **Retirement planning:** Participate fully in retirement plan at work and encourage her husband to do so as well.
- **Goal setting:** Establish financial goals and strategies to reach them.
- **Diversification:** Review asset allocation, as she's highly concentrated in real estate.
- **Cash reserves:** Set up systematic investment plan, contributing to a money market on a monthly basis. This will create an emergency fund as well as provide a focus for her monthly cash flow.
- **Estate planning:** Both are in potentially dangerous occupations and should minimally have a will in place.

Profile 3
Name   *Stella*
Age   *43*
Occupation   *Pharmaceutical Sales*
Marital Status   *Divorced*
Annual Income   *$60,000*
Overview   *Stella went from her parents' home directly into marriage. Her ex-husband was a successful stockbroker with a major brokerage firm. When divorce hit, she knew nothing about their financial situation.*

Interview

Kathy: Your story is not uncommon in some ways but unique in others. Can you give us a little background?

Stella: I got married very young, in my early twenties, to a person who had his master's degree in business and became a very successful stockbroker. I was a nurse and he took care of all the finances in the family. This suited me fine because, to be honest with you I didn't have an interest in finance and I figured he was the expert in that field.

Kathy: How did that work out?

Stella: Fine—until the marriage ended in divorce after nine years. I knew I was in trouble because I had no clue what we had. I had no idea how much money he made, which is really sad. I could write checks and I had a credit card, but past that, as far as financial information, I was dead. I didn't know where our assets were tied up. I had no idea what the house was worth. I didn't even understand the terms such as "mutual funds" and "limited partnerships." When it came to dividing the assets, I pretty much left it up to him. I did hire a lawyer and, knowing what I know now, I realize he didn't do a very good job either.

Kathy: If you had known what you know now, would you have taken the same financial assets out of the marriage?

Stella: No. I would have tried to take them all! Seriously, my ignorance cost me. I would have taken more assets and different assets. I ended up with limited partnerships, which are a pain taxwise and next to impossible to get rid of.

My husband always made me feel that we really didn't have that much money, even though he was making well over $100,000 a year and I was working as well. I just felt like I could never spend the money and really never understood where it was going.

We had just moved into a nice home and I knew we had a big mortgage, but I didn't know how much. After the divorce, I had no idea how much I could afford or what I could or could not do. I had to learn all the basics of money.

Kathy: So here you were married to an "expert" in investments and yet you knew nothing.

Stella: Exactly. And part of that was my fault, for several reasons. First, I took no interest or responsibility in learning these things. On this account I must say he didn't want to teach me either, saying that he did that stuff all day and didn't want to talk about it at night. Second, I had not lived on my own and learned anything. I went from being taken care of by my parents to being taken care of by my husband. When we divorced, I didn't even know how to open a bank account. One of my good friends went with me to help. Sad, isn't it? Here I am in my early 30s and that's how little I knew.

Kathy: So your lifestyle changed dramatically after that?

Stella: I learned the art of downsizing quickly. While I eventually bought another home, it was certainly not in the same league as the one we had when I was married.

Kathy: What would you tell other women to help them avoid the pitfalls you faced?

Stella: I think women need to learn a great deal about financial planning, just for their own mental health. I also believe they should get themselves a financial planner, even if they're just starting out in a career. I read someplace that 50% of marriages end in divorce. I never thought that would be me—and probably neither do all those other women. If you don't have one before that, you'll probably need one then.

Kathy: What steps have you taken to turn your situation around?

Stella: I have established a couple of goals for myself. I want to be sure I'm taking care of me and that I have adequate money for retirement. I've taken classes and read books and my work provides me a lot of information. Since my divorce, I've gone an entirely different career direction after receiving my MBA.

I've gotten a little obsessive about savings, because I want to retire at a young age and enjoy life. My goal is to retire at age 55.

I recently saw on *The Today Show* the Secretary of the Treasury. She was talking about how Americans are still not saving enough for retirement and will be in for a rude awakening. I am just the opposite. My goal is to save 20% to 25% of what I make from my gross income.

Kathy: What specifically are you doing?

Stella: I max out my 401(k) at work and put some money into a money market and some into a mutual fund every month. If I get any bonuses, I try to take at least a portion of that bonus and invest it in something that my financial planner feels is appropriate. I always contribute to an IRA, even though it isn't a write-off for me.

Kathy: What about your mortgage?

Stella: I'm prepaying it even as we speak. I'm trying to put an extra amount of money every month and make it automatic. I just consider that paying myself first and use whatever money I have left over toward other things.

Kathy: What you're telling us is quite a transition from the woman who didn't know about money. What do you think brought about this dramatic change?

Stella: One of the biggest influences in my life was my friends. They were emotionally supportive and helped me learn a lot. Also, knowing that I'm the one responsible for myself made me take some action. I'm also lucky in that my job has allowed me to save, because I am making good money and that has helped.

Kathy: What other things do you think women can do to help themselves?

Stella: They can go to their local library and get any type of basic investment book. Try to read up and learn, because I believe women are very intimidated by financial markets and usually aren't exposed to things that help them learn. I just implore women who have children, girls in particular, to encourage them to invest and learn about investments

They also don't need a lot of money to start; they just need to start. I think that the number one thing that women should do is invest in their retirement plans at work. After that, you slowly write yourself a check, even if it's only $10 or $20 a month.

Kathy: You ought to feel very good about yourself. You may have learned a lesson the hard way, but you certainly learned the lesson. Thanks for talking with me.

Summary

For those of you in the mid-40s and beyond, Stella's scenario could be that of many women you probably know, perhaps even you. Going from one's parents' home to marry someone who then becomes highly successful sounds like a fairy tale. Here we learn that this type of story does not always have a happy ending if we don't assume personal responsibility.

It's important to note that Stella is willing to assume the responsibility for her lack of financial knowledge. While her stockbroker husband wasn't very interested in teaching her, she most honestly states that she wasn't very interested in learning. In this, as well as in many other aspects, Stella has now changed dramatically.

Lessons

- Practice financial independence prior to getting into a relationship.
- Establish the rules for mutual knowledge and management of financial resources in serious relationships.
- Learn about finances and assume personal responsibility for handling your money. You don't have to become a guru, but you do need a basic understanding and the freedom to ask questions.
- Teach your children about money. This can range from balancing a checkbook to learning about a variety of investments.
- Don't relinquish total control of your finances to your significant other, even if he or she is the "expert."

- Waiting until there's a crisis to learn can be "hazardous to your financial health."
- Invest in yourself. Stella realized that she wished to move from nursing into a more lucrative field. By earning her MBA, she was able to achieve her career goals.
- Rather than being overwhelmed by them, Stella has demonstrated an ability to grow and learn from her earlier mistakes. She has assumed full financial responsibility, has clearly defined retirement goals, and is taking steps to pay off her mortgage early. In addition, she is involved in a systematic investment and is actively pursuing building her non-retirement portfolio.

Financial Planning Considerations

- **Diversification:** Regularly review her asset allocation and portfolio performance in both retirement and non-retirement accounts. Her goal of early retirement necessitates a high return on investment. She needs to be monitoring her portfolio performance against that goal at least on an annual basis.
- **Disability insurance:** Learn the specifics of her company-sponsored disability insurance and assess if that meets her coverage needs.
- **Estate planning:** Begin process, including establishing a will.

Profile 4
Name   *Marie*
Age   *33*
Occupation   *Administrative Assistant*
Marital Status   *Single*
Annual Income   *$35,000*
Overview   *Marie began working immediately after high school. She attended college briefly, but never completed her degree. From a family of eight, she began adulthood with no financial resources.*

Interview

Kathy: Marie, tell me a little bit about your family background.

Marie: I'm from a large family and we never really had any money. My father was a blue-collar worker and my mother didn't work, obviously. Both of them were from farm families and believed in having a lot of kids. My dad was laid off from several jobs. I remember at age 9 being very aware of how little money we had. At that time all of the kids who worked were expected to pay half of any money we made to my dad. In spite of all of the mouths to feed, we were always able to make ends meet because all of the kids who worked shared their income.

Kathy: Was this expected to continue after high school if you lived at home?

Marie: Absolutely. In addition to the money, I had to "rent" the family car to get to and from work.

Kathy: What do you mean by "renting" the family car?

Marie: At 17, when I got my first job, I was expected to pay $10 a week to use the car.

Kathy: It seems to me that that arrangement would sure be an incentive to get out on your own.

Marie: At that time I was working full-time and going to school full-time, so I didn't have much choice. Within a few years, my sister and I were able to move out together so we could afford to get an apartment.

Kathy: When you got out on your own, how did you handle your money?

Marie: This was my first real taste of having any substantial money and I blew a lot of it. I reveled in the ability to do whatever I wanted with my money and probably spent my way through the restrictions of those years where it would have been out of the question. Shopping became my hobby and I hit the stores every weekend. I not only bought things for myself; I spent a lot of money on gifts for the family. I also bought my first new car.

I was very busy enjoying life and earning money. My best friend worked for an airline, so we were able to go on a lot of trips cheaply. Needless to say, college was the last thing on my mind and I eventually dropped out after 2½ years.

Kathy: When did you start to get interested in investments?

Marie: I was ingrained with a sense of being responsible. Although I had a couple of good spending years, I knew that couldn't last forever. Finally my dad said I had to get a new hobby, referring to my shopping. I remember feeling embarrassed and took his words to heart. If you read the paper or watch TV or talk to women, it's not a big secret it's an extremely important issue.

At work, my boss was looking into getting a 401(k) plan and I thought that was a great idea. My second job did have a retirement plan and the people who worked there were very interested in investments and willing to teach me. I joined the retirement plan and started investing.

Kathy: What exactly did you do?

Marie: During those years, I continued to learn more about investing and came to understand the need for growth of my money. I wasn't making tons of money, but knew I needed to find some way of saving. My venture was in the retirement plan at work. Throughout my career I have always participated in my company retirement plans. I bought my first mutual fund at 20 with $500. Shortly after that I bought my first stock, Waste Management, with $200. I know now that the stock wasn't such a good idea, because buying so little probably cost me a lot in commission.

Kathy: You started investing at the age of 20 and now you are the ripe old age of 33. How's your portfolio look today?

Marie: Well I have $35,000 in my IRA Rollover. This mostly came from 401(k) when I left my job. I also have a SEP worth about $11,000. My current retirement plan at work is worth about $15,000. You can tell I'm worried about retirement, because I also have an annuity with about $1,300. I just opened a Roth IRA with $500.

In my non-retirement account, I have $2,000 in a money market and about $3,300 in Eli Lilly stock, $2,150 in Pepsi, and $2,700 in Merck.

Kathy: You have done an incredible job of building your assets. You've got about $63,000 in retirement money and about $10,000 in non-retirement money. Can you believe you've done this?

Marie: I do feel great about this. I even had more which was in mutual funds, but I sold them to come up with a down payment on the town home I purchased. I don't want to be dishonest: I'm not a slave to my investing. I still enjoy the occasional trip and shopping. Now it's much more balanced.

Kathy: You really have done a remarkable job, starting with nothing and working yourself now to the point where you have a nice asset base and still managed to buy your own home. If anybody's entitled to give advice, it should be you. What would you like to tell women who are reading this?

Marie: If you wait for the right time to start investing, it will never come. There are more "excuses" to not invest than anything I've ever heard. I'm living proof you don't have to have a lot of money to get going and build, but you do have to actually do it. You have to quit making excuses and do whatever you have to do to take responsibility for your financial life.

I also believe that ignorance is not bliss. Whether or not we plead ignorance will not have much effect on the realities of poverty in retirement. People I know plead poverty all the time, yet manage to eat out a lot, take trips, and drive nice cars. How can they say they can't put $50 into a mutual fund when they do this? Maybe we can't have it all. We need to decide what is important to us and at least be honest about it, instead of making excuses.

Kathy: Marie, do you have any specific tips?

Marie: I'm big believer in having whatever amount you decide to invest, for retirement or not, be taken directly out of your paycheck or debited from your checking account. What you don't see you don't miss and it becomes like any other payment. Start with something, however small, but just start. If you think it's costing you a lot right now to put fifty bucks away a month now, think about how much it will cost you when you're 65 and pushing a grocery cart on the streets.

Kathy: You've taught us it's not necessarily how much money you make, but what you do with it. Keep up the good work! And thanks for your time.

Summary

As you read Marie's story, you probably think she's wise beyond her years and so do I. While not highly salaried, she has managed to invest for both retirement and non-retirement purposes. She has developed a focus that many people considerably older and more highly paid never quite achieve. In addition to the investments, she's also purchased a home and had some fun along the way.

Lessons

- You don't need a lot of money to get started. Just get started! The earlier you start the better you are. Look how much Marie has put together at the age of 33. Part of that nest egg is due to the factor of compounding. Also, she is developing excellent financial habits in that savings and investing have now become a routine part of her life.
- After normal, youthful, consumer spending ("shop 'til you drop"), Marie changed her habits and took charge of her finances. She is fortunate in that she didn't spend money she didn't have, so didn't dig herself a hole with credit card spending.
- Without being given anything, by parents or others, with determination and planning you can build your own wealth.

Financial Planning Considerations

- **College funding:** Plan for completion of college education through a systematic investment into a money market account.
- **Goal setting:** Establish financial goals, including the purchase of a larger home and a new car. She currently is purchasing a town home and knows she would eventually like to own a single family home. Her car is 8 years old and she is likely to purchase a new one within the next five years.
- **Investing:** Consider adjusting her systematic investment as she receives pay raises.
- **Disability insurance:** Examine the economic viability of purchasing disability insurance. It is not currently provided by her employer and may prove cost prohibitive for her to purchase directly.
- **Estate planning:** Begin basic estate planning, including establishing a will.

Profile 5
Name   *Erin*
Age   *27*
Occupation   *Assistant Manager, manufacturing firm*
Marital Status   *Single*
Annual Income   *$35,000*
Overview   *Erin has been out of college for four years and is currently pursuing an MBA. She just bought her first home and is establishing her financial goals.*

Interview

Kathy: As you first got out of school, what was your top financial goal?

Erin: When I graduated from college, I was really concerned about finding a job that paid enough to make ends meet and still let me save a little. My biggest goal was to purchase a house. I went through some trial and error as far as managing my money and learning how to budget. I think a lot of people fresh out of college have a real hard time doing that.

When you first get out of college, you have all these demands on your money. You rent an apartment, you may have to furnish that apartment, and you need to buy professional clothes for that first job. The 19K I made a year right out of college didn't finance a lot of that. I was lucky; at least I didn't have a college loan.

Kathy: How did you handle those expenses?

Erin: Unfortunately, many of my friends and I got in trouble with credit cards. They're just screaming at you to use a credit card. At that time you don't have a bed, couch, or TV, and those are all things that are essentially necessities of life when you start out. I and another friend actually ended up financing consumer loans to pay off that money so that we could get into a situation where we could save money. I think it takes a lot of discipline and you have to be able to identify how much you can afford and be willing to accept that you can't just buy anything.

Kathy: What happened after you got serious about your money?

Erin: Unfortunately I'm job-turnover happy, so I haven't been able to participate in a lot of companies' retirement plans, but I do when I'm eligible. I knew I wanted a house badly and started saving for that. I did that by an automatic withdrawal from my checking account into a savings account. That way I never saw it and what's not there wasn't missed.

I had to be willing to accept the house that was in my price bracket, as opposed to looking at all the houses that I couldn't afford. I figured if you have to buy a $50,000 townhouse because that's what you can afford, it's better than paying the rent.

Kathy: Did your mom and dad teach you about investing?

Erin: No. My interest in investments was mostly self-generated. My parents were big savers and they were very conservative with their money and that was definitely instilled in me. Up until the age of 18, my parents had a savings account for me and any gift that I got in the form of cash or a check went into that account. I never saw any of that money and I used to really resent them from keeping it from me until I was 18 and then I was very grateful because I used that money to go to Europe and part of it to buy a car.

Kathy: How have your peers been doing financially since they finished college?

Erin: I know a lot of guys who were equally as irresponsible with their money as women. Most of my women friends are pretty progressive and are career-oriented, so I don't think that their attitude is that they are going to be taken care of. A few of them are even doctors.

Some of the other ones are in positions where they will max out at 35 or 40 thousand a year. They are very complacent because they think their needs will be met by somebody else's income when they need it. I think that's a big mistake. I've never presumed that I would ever be taken care of and, as far as my career ambitions go, I've always thought that it's just going to be me. I never expect that five years down the road I'll probably be married and somebody else will be taking care of me.

Kathy: What are your next financial goals?

Erin: Buy a bigger house! I've been putting money in my house, so I need to get back on track to putting money away on a consistent basis. I've just become eligible for my retirement plan at work, and I'll start that.

If I marry, I feel 100% responsibility to provide a college education for any kids. That's one goal I'm not too worried about now.

Kathy: Do you feel now your debts are pretty well under control?

Erin: Oh yeah. I have no debt except for my mortgage.

Kathy: Do you have any investments besides your home?

Erin: I have about $4,000 in an IRA and a little bit in mutual funds and money market, but I plan to add to those.

Kathy: Now that you've achieved wisdom with age, what advice would you give?

Erin: I think that the whole nature of Wall Street is "old boy school" and it's intimidating, and being afraid to ask questions or make the right decision is all a part of that. I think women need to educate themselves. It's obvious you get better returns on your money by investing than if you just buy a CD. Financial advisors really should take a role in making their clients understand what they are doing. I have a friend who just gives her advisor money and has no idea what it's going into or why.

Kathy: It sounds like you've learned some valuable lessons at your tender age and you are well on your way to sound financial management. Thanks for your insights.

Summary

Erin initially fell into a trap that many young women do. She was seduced by the call of the credit card. Although she built up a lot of debt, many of the things she charged were for legitimate reasons. Thankfully, she quickly came to see the dangers of credit card debt. Her goal became the purchase of a home and ultimately that dream came true.

Her propensity toward frequent job change has made it very difficult for her to become involved in a company retirement plan. She plans to add this as a focus of her financial life, as well as being in a career that is financially rewarding and allows her to lead the lifestyle she wishes while remaining independent.

Lessons

- Don't ever depend on credit cards to finance your lifestyle. Seek help if you are overwhelmed by this debt, as Erin did by obtaining a credit consolidation loan. View these cards as your enemy, unless you can pay off the balance monthly, or for use in an emergency situation.
- Understand that you are essentially "cheating" building your assets for retirement if you change jobs too frequently to take advantage of a company's retirement plan. If this fits you, or your company doesn't offer a plan, be certain that you are doing other things, such as funding an IRA, to compensate.
- You can achieve a goal, such as home ownership, by taking specific steps and making that goal a priority.
- Erin knew her limits when purchasing her first home. Looking outside your price range can only lead to frustration and depression.
- Even without guidance, you can become educated about investments. While Erin's parents were savers, she realizes she has to become an investor to meet her targeted goals.
- Take advantage of educational opportunities provided by your employer. Obtaining her MBA is a win/win for Erin. She gets her degree and her employer is paying the cost.

Financial Planning Goals

- **Retirement planning:** Participate in company retirement plan as soon as she is eligible. Until then, fund IRA.
- **Budgeting:** Review her cash flow to help determine where she's spending her money, such as on her home, to get a much better handle on what's happening to her money.
- **Goal setting:** Further refine her goal of purchasing a larger home, including price range, required down payment, and timeline. Once she has these established, she can set up an investment plan that will help her meet this goal. Establish other financial goals and investment objectives.

Profile 6	
Name *Suzie*	
Age *45*	
Occupation *Flight Attendant*	
Marital Status *Divorced with one child*	
Annual Income *$40,000*	
Overview *Instead of the dream marriage that Suzie had imagined, she found herself married to a man who was an addict. After finally dealing with these emotions and obtaining a divorce, she received another blow when he died two years later.*	

Interview

Kathy: Would you mind sharing with us a little history of your marriage?

Suzie: I was married for 10 years to a man who was an addict—not just alcohol, but drugs as well, and I just didn't know it. I made good money and he made good money, but for some reason we could never meet our needs and I could never understand why. I would put money in savings and he would take it out. When I asked him where the money was going, he said he had no idea what I was talking about. We both worked for an airline, and one situation where we went on strike we almost didn't make it through financially because we literally had no money.

Kathy: How did you ultimately discover what was going on?

Suzie: Ultimately it got pretty violent and a lot of abuse happened between us. I just thank God our daughter didn't see it. I realized then what was going on and that I had to get out.

Kathy: How was it for you financially at that time?

Suzie: I worried a lot about money. In my line of work, we don't get raises except for contractual raises. I needed to review how much money I made, whether I could stay at the townhouse where we were currently living. At that time, I was also so mad at myself for having been so ignorant about my husband and all this financial stuff as well. I really doubted my intelligence level. At least he didn't go through my money at that time, just his. I found I could survive with financial assistance from him. It was small, but it was enough to get us by.

Kathy: Did he contribute financially after you were divorced?

Suzie: After the divorce I was afraid he wouldn't because of his financial status, so I went to the courts and had the child support made directly to the court from his paycheck. It was an automatic withdrawal to the court and the court paid me directly. This made me feel more secure. We did maintain a relationship because of our child—she was very close to her father. I still cared very much about him too.

Kathy: He died shortly after the divorce?

Suzie: Yes, he was 41 and died from alcoholism. By that time he had gone so far downhill that he was $30,000 in debt and slept in a room in a house where he didn't have anything. It was sad to see that he'd gone from living with me and having nice clothes and such a different lifestyle to living in a shack in one room.

Kathy: What effect did his death have on you?

Suzie: The death was a major upheaval in my life. I learned to stand on my own two feet and say, "What do I need to do to help my daughter and I survive?" I found out about Social Security survivor's insurance and applied for that for my daughter. I get that monthly payment now until she's 18, and she's 10 right now.

Kathy: I know you had some issues about his life insurance. Would you tell me about that?

Suzie: He had life insurance through his work and he kept me as the beneficiary. That was his wish after the divorce. He felt that way if anything happened to him it would take care of our daughter. I also knew that we had another life insurance policy from many years ago. We had been paying on it for 10 years and when I called them to ask about it they told me he hadn't made the last premium payment. Both his doctor and I explained to them that at that time he was so sick he didn't even know who he was. I tried to talk to the insurance company; they just kept hanging up on me. They said, "We're not liable, we don't have to pay you." They didn't care, so I got a lawyer and it took nine months of fighting and I had to settle for 90% of the amount because they just wouldn't pay. Then I had to pay lawyer fees on top of it, but I learned a lesson.

I learned a lesson the hard way. In order to sustain yourself as a woman, you better know where everything is. You need to know how much money there is for you, how much is in life insurance, how much will my children get, and where will money come from to meet our needs. I didn't have the answers to any of these.

Kathy: How did you decide what to do with the insurance money?

Suzie: The work policy was for $86,000. I didn't know what to do with the money. I was afraid I would just blow it, because I was so desperate and needy. My ex-husband's uncle was an insurance person, so he took most of it and put it into an annuity. It paid low interest, but at least it was out of my sight and out of my mind and saved for my daughter's college education.

I did take some of the money and did some things to the house, because whenever I would walk into the house all I could see was him. So a little bit of it went to rearranging the house so we could visually walk in there and not see him all the time.

Kathy: What did you do with proceeds from the other policy?

Suzie: At first I put it in the bank in an account earning 4% interest and not going anywhere. I knew this wouldn't do. I believe you meet the right people at the right time and I met someone who mentioned a financial advisor that they liked very much. I called that person and started investing—but only after it was clear this person could guide me. I knew I needed this guidance because I didn't have any background, but I wanted someone to treat me as a quality person and take the time to teach me.

I ultimately put the money in a diversified portfolio.

Kathy: I know you've become a believer in managing your money. You're in a job where you work with a number of women. Are they taking money seriously?

Suzie: They're living in yesterday. They have rose-colored glasses on regarding finances. They believe there's going to be a man coming along for them and he's going to take care of them. I just sit back saying, "Oh sweetheart, I hope there is, but please don't bet on that because I know you got to take care of yourself. That man may come but he may also go and with him goes everything." Most of them get their paycheck and it goes toward clothes, phone bills, travel, and pleasure. If I say to them, "What are you going to do to help maintain this lifestyle for tomorrow?" they look at me with this deer-in-the-headlights look. They don't have a clue what I'm talking about.

Kathy: If they'd listen to you, what advice would you give them?

Suzie: The most important thing is not to wait for a crisis to learn. Know where your money is going. Don't be stupid and think that it's the man's job to handle the money and you just have to float around going to cocktail parties and having a bunch of fun.

Your emotions are in such turmoil when something like this happens to you that I suggest you put any money away for three to six months and don't even think about it. Just pretend it doesn't exist. Everybody goes through a different time frame, but eventually your emotions settle down and you're more able to deal with it. Put it away: hide it, all of it. When you are ready, get a financial person who has your well-being at heart. It's a huge decision, so wait 'til your head is clear.

Maybe 10% understand how important a 401(k) is for their retirement. People don't understand the great amount of money we need to save for that and they should. I increase my contribution every time I get a raise.

Kathy: What did you look for in a financial advisor?

Suzie: I wanted somebody, a reputation. I wanted someone who I could talk to and they could talk to me. I've been talked down to and I met with people who wanted to talk technical things and I got absolutely nothing out of that because they talked over my head. I wanted someone who, if I called them with a really stupid question, would say, "Let me explain that to you." I asked around a lot and I got the same name from several people. When I met with that person, I knew it was a fit because everything was explained in layman's terms and I understood why we did what we did.

Kathy: You've overcome some major financial and emotional traumas while keeping life on track for you and your daughter. I hope women will pay attention to the lessons in your story. Thanks for reliving these difficult times for us.

Summary

Suzie's tale is a truly tragic one. She married the man of her dreams, lived in comfortable surroundings, and had plenty of money. As she realized the money was disappearing and why, the marriage became more violent and ultimately ended in divorce. As if she didn't have enough trauma in her life at that point, her ex-husband died shortly after the divorce from alcoholism at age 41. While totally devastated emotionally, Suzie then had to muster enough strength to fight the insurance company, which was initially unwilling to pay his death benefit. This is indeed a story of strength and courage under a great deal of adversity.

Lessons

- Know as much as possible about your family's finances. It took Suzie years to realize that their money was "disappearing." She knew nothing about any financial assets that they had, including whether or not the premiums were being paid on a life insurance policy.
- Participate fully in your retirement plan at work. If you are married, both of you should be contributing.
- Even though Suzie was emotionally devastated, she found the strength to battle the insurance company for the sake of her daughter. Don't give up. Suzie sought the help of an attorney. If you can't do it on your own, find the resources you need to help you.
- When you're on an emotional roller coaster, don't rush to make financial decisions that could affect the rest of your life. As Suzie says, "Hide it until your head is clear." No decision needs to be made until you feel you are ready to make that decision.
- Do your homework when choosing a financial advisor. Suzie asked around a lot, got a number of referrals, and interviewed advisors until she found the fit that was right for her.

Financial Planning Considerations

- **Retirement planning:** Continue to increase 401(k) contributions as she receives pay increases and monitor portfolio.
- **Estate planning:** Purchase life insurance and make other plans for meeting the needs of her daughter.
- **College planning:** Establish a plan for her daughter, using the life

insurance proceeds as well as ongoing contributions into a diversified mutual fund portfolio.

- **Disability insurance:** Review the provisions of company-provided disability insurance. Supplement as necessary.

Profile 7
Name *Vera*
Age *50*
Occupation *Government Manager*
Marital Status *Married with two children*
Annual Income *$80,000*
Overview *Marrying an artist seemed very romantic to Vera and she never felt that discussing finances was the "right" thing to do until years later when it was too late. A divorce is pending now that Vera sees there will be no resolution to the different views she and her husband hold about money.*

Interview

Kathy: I wonder if you could start by telling us a bit about what your situation was with your husband over the years in terms of finances.

Vera: Problems probably started right off the bat, right after we got married. For some reason, I had it in my head that it was the husband's job to pay the bills and keep the finances. It was apparent within a matter of months that he couldn't even pay the utility bills on time, which doesn't seem like rocket science stuff.

Kathy: Were you both working at the time?

Vera: I was working full-time and he was in school and working part-time as an artist. He's a really good artist. When he was graduating from school, he had a very successful show. He was involved in an art league and I thought, "Gee, how romantic, how nice. Why doesn't he just paint?" Never thinking what that would really mean monetarily.

So he painted and I worked. He eventually got really uncomfortable that he wasn't bringing in any income and got a "real" job. That led him to getting his own graphic shop, where he's been a sole proprietor for the last 21 years.

Kathy: Was your frustration with him that he didn't want to deal responsibly with the finances?

Vera: He completely refused to manage his own income. It didn't matter if we had money; he always wanted to do something other than what we needed to do with it—pay bills. He never, of all of the income he made, never put money aside for the taxes his business incurred, and that's what finally made me snap.

I had to remind him time and time again to pay his quarterly taxes. Even though he never did manage his money, he was insistent on being in charge of it, and I guess that's understandable. We had various accountants counseling him the same way I did, trying to get him to put "X" amount aside every time he got paid. Of course he didn't, but he always had cash in his pockets on the weekends.

Kathy: If he didn't pay his taxes, he probably didn't do any retirement or financial planning as well.

Vera: Not really. We did contribute a couple years' worth of IRAs, but he never would be consistent about putting anything aside. If he took $2,000 and contributed to his IRA, he wouldn't have money for the household expenses.

Kathy: Were the household expenses your responsibility then?

Vera: Yeah, he was supposed to pitch in, but I always—I mean always—had to ask him for money. He'd just complain that I was constantly bugging him.

Kathy: Did you make about the same income?

Vera: At some point his salary equaled mine. I always had a steady income and paid the health insurance through work. I found out that he had a couple of really good years when I started filing my taxes separately. He had made $80,000 net. Keeping careful records in the household checkbook, I knew he had only given me $25,000 that year. I asked him what in the world he did with the rest of the money. He was always scrambling for money to pay the taxes, and when he didn't make the payments on time he had massive penalties and interest piling up and that was usually in the first quarter.

Kathy: Would you say that this eventually got to be a major problem in the marriage?

Vera: Yes, because for me it was a trust factor. I could never trust that he was going to hold up his end of the bargain. There was no solid ground for us to be planning a future together. I got to the point where I really resented the fact that he wasn't even conscious of our money situation. His inability, for whatever reason, to be a grownup drove me nuts. I knew that it would be my retirement that kept us afloat.

Kathy: Vera, if you could have seen ahead, what do you wish you would have known that you didn't know financially?

Vera: I think maybe, had the lightbulb gone off sooner that you can't change people, maybe I would have isolated my own finances sooner. It wasn't until my accountant pointed out to me that, if I didn't file separately, I would be liable for his debts. After I did begin filing separately, liens were placed on our joint accounts. Again, I resented that, because most of that money was from my parents' trust.

Kathy: Basically you were contributing all of the monies to the retirement accounts and general savings?

Vera: Yes. I couldn't count on him for any money. There would be times that I held my breath until my next paycheck because, although I would ask him for money, he'd never come through. He'd just say, "Yeah, yeah, yeah, you're always on me."

Kathy: Your frustration seems to come not only from him being irresponsible but also his unwillingness to change his behavior.

Vera: Yes. I never minded that he had his bills to pay, but having to always ask him for money and that he always dropped the ball was hard to swallow.

Kathy: What would you like, looking back on your life, to say to someone starting out in a marriage?

Vera: You have to have balance and communicate. I stayed with my husband as long as I did for the kids, and whether that was the right decision or not, time will tell. I needed to have a comfort level, knowing that I didn't need to scramble for my next cup of coffee. It was probably clear from the beginning that this wouldn't work, but being romantic about him being an artist took over.

Kathy: What would you have done differently then?

Vera: Talk about it more and talk about it early on. Develop a philosophy together.

Kathy: To know where they're coming from before you get to this point, you mean?

Vera: Yes. Try to talk about it and learn together. He didn't know any more than I did. Classic—he's a banker's son.

Kathy: I think all of us want to have a comfort level when it comes to our finances and know that we can rely on our partner. Your points on talking about finances prior to marriage are important and I hope women will heed your advice. Thanks for your sharing your thoughts, Vera.

Summary

The central problem in this situation was a total lack of communication prior to and during marriage regarding financial roles and responsibilities. Vera was swept up in the romantic notion of being married to an artist and never considered what an area of conflict this could potentially become. Eventually this became a trust issue, because Vera felt she "could never trust that he was going to hold up his end of the bargain."

Lessons

- Although it's not very romantic, discuss financial roles and responsibilities prior to marriage. This should encompass attitudes and perceptions about money, because money means something very different to each of us.
- Don't make assumptions. It's unfair of us to assume that all men enjoy or are good at paying the bills and handling financial decisions. Although Vera's husband was a banker's son, he had no desire whatsoever to deal with any type of monetary responsibility.
- Never underestimate the power of monetary issues to disrupt a marriage. If left unaddressed, these issues can lead to anger, resentment, and ultimately the termination of a marriage.
- Contrary to popular opinion, you frequently can't change people. When financial responsibility became an issue, Vera assumed, with counseling from accountants, that her husband would change his behavior. Obviously this was not the case.

Financial Planning Considerations

- **Divorce settlement:** Seek quality legal and financial assistance prior to agreeing upon a financial settlement, so as not to lose her government retirement.
- **Estate planning:** Determine disposition of assets, after divorce is final. A primary concern is the children's college education.
- **Retirement planning:** Once finances are settled, continue to maximize contributions to work-related retirement plans.
- **Investments:** Establish a non-retirement portfolio, perhaps beginning with a systematic investment program.

Profile 8
Name   *Melissa*
Age   *55*
Occupation   *Social Worker*
Marital Status   *Divorced*
Annual Income   *$40,000*
Overview   *Nearing retirement, Melissa finds herself the legal guardian of her 10-year-old grandchild. Then her daughter is sent to prison and wants Melissa to take care of her second child, who is 18 months old.*

Interview

Kathy: Would you briefly review your marital history for us?

Melissa: Shortly after college I married the man of my dreams. We both worked and he handled the money. His idea of handling money was that, as long as he had a charge card, he could buy anything he wanted. It then became my job to figure out how to make the payments each month on all of his "little toys," but I never knew what was in the checking account because he never wrote down any withdrawals he took out of the account.

He was a systems analyst for a major bank and we had good

income. It's just that he had more outgoing than incoming. Whenever I'd ask him about money, he would become belligerent.

Kathy: Did you do any investing at that time?

Melissa: When I would manage to save up a little, he would invest it in penny stocks and nine out of ten times they weren't worth what we paid for them.

Not only did I not get anything out of the investments when we divorced, what I did inherit were half of the bills, even though it wasn't things that I bought or were for me.

Kathy: How did you do financially after the divorce?

Melissa: In addition to the marital debts, I had to borrow money from my mom for the divorce and pay that back. By that time our daughter was nine years old. My ex insisted he would not pay child support through the courts. It had to be directly to me, so he could harass me by paying me whenever it suited him. He'd pay each month, but it might be the 10th or the 25th, so if I was banking on paying a bill that month with that money, I couldn't count on when I'd get it.

It took me about two years to get everything straightened out and start saving on a regular basis. The only thing I had going for me was my retirement plan at work. Once I got out of debt, I signed up for deferred comp.

Kathy: About the time you started to get your life back on track financially, I know you began to have other difficulties.

Melissa: Yes, my daughter essentially dropped out of high school in the 9th grade and ended up becoming pregnant at 17. Because of my daughter's emotional problems, I ended up being custodian for my grandchild, who is now 10 years old and has basically lived with me all her life.

Kathy: This whole situation must have been emotionally and financially draining.

Melissa: True. Most people at 55 aren't paying daycare. This has obviously impacted my finances. I save less for retirement and do fewer things for myself, like travel. For example, in the summer I pay $400 a month for daycare. That doesn't include karate, clothes, and gymnastics. Before I was able to be named legal guardian, I had to pay all of her health and dental expenses out of my pocket, because I couldn't claim her at work until it was legalized. That has only been for the last two years.

Neither her father or mother provide any assistance and, since she is only 10, I'll have this for a long time to come.

Kathy: Now I understand your daughter recently had another child. What is the plan for that child?

Melissa: Yes, the child is 18 months, but my daughter lost custody in another state. Now she wants me to take care of that child as well. I just don't know what I'm going to do at this point.

Kathy: So it would be safe to say that at 55 you're not building retirement assets, but you're actually projecting a greater need for cash outlays in the future.

Melissa: Yes, but I would get some from social services for the younger child.

Kathy: Given your life situation, what would you have done financially if you would have had any clue how life was going to play out?

Melissa: For starters, I definitely would have kept my money separate from my ex-husband's. I would have made certain that it was his problem to pay for his toys. I would like to think I would have saved enough money that I wouldn't have had to go to my mom to borrow money for the divorce. To give you an example of how bad he was about money, he went out once and bought a car without telling me a thing about it. First I knew about it was when there was a Toyota Land Cruiser in the driveway.

Investments need to be a two-way thing. I would never again let someone invest my money without me knowing what we're investing in.

Kathy: Is there any one thing that sticks out in your mind that you'd like to tell other women?

Melissa: Yes. Get yourself educated. Know where your money is going and understand the different investment choices you have. I put money in the retirement plan at work and didn't know much, and thank heaven it's worked out for me. You never know what turns life will take, and the more informed you are the better.

Summary

In addition to dealing with financial issues and a divorce, Melissa provides an excellent illustration of coping with the unexpected. At age 55 she finds herself the guardian for her 10-year-old granddaughter while her daughter is in prison. At the time that most people are dealing with retirement, she is dealing with the emotional and financial issues associated with raising a child.

Lessons

- Like many women of her era, Melissa was excluded from knowledge of or participation in the family's finances. It was her husband's belief that she had no right to make any inquiries about money or how it was spent. I may be beating a dead horse, but I repeat that you should know where your money is going and demand an equal partnership. Your responsibility in this is to get yourself educated regarding money and investments.
- Life deals you many unexpected events with which you are forced to cope. Although you can't plan for the unexpected, don't put off funding important goals, such as retirement, because a life crisis may intervene. As soon as possible, participate in your retirement plan. Do all you can to secure your financial future while you can. When Melissa divorced, she had no financial assets, even having to borrow money for a divorce from her mother.
- It's never too late to start learning. When she was out of debt, Melissa signed up for her retirement plan at work and began to educate herself about different investment choices.
- If forced to deal with a sudden care-taking situation, seek advice from all potential resources. These circumstances cause severe emotional trauma and can disrupt many aspects of your life, including finances.

Financial Planning Considerations

- **Retirement planning:** Change her plans to reflect the demands of her unexpected caretaker role. The additional demand on her finances necessitates that she cut back for herself or lower the amount of money she's placing in retirement accounts. She may need to work longer than she'd planned to do so. In retirement she'll continue to have increased expenses, so she'll need a greater income than she'd originally anticipated.

- **College education:** Prepare to put her granddaughter through college. She has eight years until the child graduates from high school.
- **Goal setting:** Establish priorities for her goals and decide on structuring the funding for each. Funding strategies may range from a systematic savings or investment program to adding to IRAs and other retirement-oriented investments.
- **Estate planning:** Because of her daughter's emotional problems, structure her estate planning to provide a trustee to take care of the needs of her granddaughter. She may wish to explore trusts to protect her assets as well as analyzing her life insurance to ensure her policies are adequate.
- **Cash flow analysis:** Carefully analyze her cash flow and future cash needs, before making a retirement decision, so she has a realistic picture of what her retirement situation may be.

Profile 9	
Name *Vanessa*	
Age *54*	
Occupation *College Professor*	
Marital Status *Married with two children*	
Annual Income *$100,000*	
Overview *Like many parents today, Vanessa and her husband find their children are still requiring financial assistance beyond their expectations. Conflicting demands on their finances have led to difficulty in retirement planning.*	

Interview

Kathy: Tell us a bit about your situation if you would.

Vanessa: I'm married with two children, ages 24 and 21. The one who is 24 has still not gotten through college, but we're trying to minimize our financial responsibilities to him. The second boy is now a sophomore at college, because he didn't start school right away. This means neither will be out of school for sure for two and possibly three more years.

Kathy: How has this affected your ability to plan for retirement?

Vanessa: It was our plan years ago that when the boys got out of college we would live on one salary and sock the other one away. My husband is a self-employed clinical social worker. That field has changed a lot and he's not making the money he used to and he is also not happy in his work anymore. We also had some things we were planning to do. These things were not important 10 years ago—or at least we didn't see the urgency of our retirement at that point.

Kathy: Aging brings on that urgency, doesn't it?

Vanessa: Right. The last five years look very different than they did 10 years ago. I don't think it's total doom and gloom because we still have some options. One of the things we did was renovate a very old home a long time ago, with the intention of selling that at some point. Now I have emotional ties to the home and I am not as willing to give it up. I know it's a larger home than we need and the money can go toward our retirement, but I'm just not at a place now where I'm ready to sell.

Kathy: You say your husband is not happy in his job. Is he looking to change careers?

Vanessa: No. The financial demands we have now put a kink in his options and we feel he needs to stay where he is until the kids have finished college.

Kathy: Did you plan for the kids' college education?

Vanessa: Not really. We were just going to pay for that when the time got here. I made a decision when the children were young to work part-time so that I could be with them and have a career. Now I am working full-time to put them through school and work toward retirement.

It's also a mistake to assume your kids will go to an inexpensive college and finish in four years. My oldest son went to an extremely expensive school for a couple of years and for what we paid for his years there he could have been in and out of a couple of state schools and been over and done.

Kathy: How has your image of retirement changed?

Vanessa: One thing for sure, I've come to grips with knowing that I can't retire before 65, because we just haven't put enough away. I wish both my husband and I could put as much away as we possibly could in our retirement. It's not like we haven't done anything, but we need more.

Kathy: In retrospect, what would you have done different in planning for college or retirement?

Vanessa: I wish we would have started far enough ahead so it isn't really a sacrifice. If you start early enough, the amount isn't as painful. I think a lot of people are doing that now with college education, because there's just no way people are going to be able to afford what my husband and I did.

If you plan to pay for a big expense this way, you can't have any variables come into play. What if somebody gets hurt and can't work or they're in a company that gets downsized? There are too many variables in life that we are too naïve about early in life but that can and do occur.

Kathy: Did either of you have much exposure to finances or financial planning?

Vanessa: No, and I definitely think that plays a part. Not just for us but for teaching the kids as well. One set of our friends have absolutely insisted on their children putting away a certain amount of their money and now they're teaching them about investing. We didn't have that exposure or help, but they did from their parents.

My youngest son had a really great personal finance class in college last year and they made him take a certain amount of money and actually invest it. My husband and I never had that kind of exposure. I think the biggest thing is planning ahead and having some sort of a model, whether it's a parent, a teacher, or a friend.

Kathy: Thanks for your insights. These are clearly issues for a lot of parents.

Summary

How many of you actually know people whose children have finished college in four years and were on their way? More and more, rare is that child. This is the story of two parents who found that seeing their children through college was a longer-term and more expensive obligation than they had bargained for. The problem was exacerbated by their lack of financial knowledge.

Lessons

- Parents need to make a decision regarding their financial commitment to their children's college education. Are you willing to provide four years at a state school? Private schooling? Graduate education? Medical school, etc.? There's no right or wrong answer, but it's important that both the parents and children be clear about financing college education.
- If you're saving for your child's college tuition, target more than you feel you will need. That way if it's more expensive, you'll have the assets. If it's less expensive, it's a bonus in your pocket.
- It's very difficult to fund college tuition out of cash flow. Vanessa thought they could pay for college when the time arrived. In addition to being costly, this strategy is dangerous, because it assumes no one will ever get hurt or laid off or have any other emergency.
- You can't safely put off retirement planning. They now find, in their mid-50s, that they're paying for tuition when they had intended to fund their retirement. It's clear they won't be able to retire before age 65 or later, because they just haven't put enough money away.
- Teach your children about money. Neither Vanessa nor her husband had exposure to finance and investing. She now is a strong advocate of education in this arena.

Financial Planning Considerations

- **Retirement planning:** Focus on retirement, as soon as they can stop paying for college. One major resource for retirement money is the large, renovated home that they may sell to downsize.
- **Disability insurance:** Protect the husband's income. Since he's self-employed, it's very important that he have disability insurance.
- **Estate planning:** Review their plans, including life insurance and wills, as their situation continues to evolve.

Profile 10

Name	*Clara*
Age	*79*
Occupation	*Retired*
Marital Status	*Married*
Annual Income	*$160,000*
Overview	*Winner of $5 million lottery.*

Interview

Kathy: The first question I have to ask you, because everybody will want to know, is how in the heck did you manage to win the lottery?

Clara: My husband and I bought two tickets for a Wednesday lottery and one of them had three of the winning numbers. On Friday it was a beautiful day and we decided to go for a ride and turn those lottery tickets in and buy a few more. We got four quick picks from a local grocery store. On Saturday, the night of the lottery drawing, we had guests and went out to eat and played cards. After they went home we watched TV and we saw the numbers on the screen. I didn't even know how much it was until I glanced up and saw that it was five million. We couldn't believe it and checked the numbers again. Even after we knew we'd won, we didn't know if we'd have to share the jackpot with anybody.

Kathy: When did you find out you were the single winner?

Clara: The next morning on TV, an announcer said, "Somebody's probably wondering whether to go to work tomorrow because they just won $5 million and there was just one winner."

Kathy: How did you actually collect your money?

Clara: On Monday morning I called and said that my husband and I had the winning ticket—what is your procedure? They said, "Come on down and get your money." We went downtown and they had called all four TV stations to watch us get our money.

Kathy: Which one of you was the official winner?

Clara: They wouldn't let both of us sign the ticket, so I signed it. My husband said he wanted it in my name because he can't hear very well, he can't write very well, and he sure can't talk like I do!

Kathy: How was your payout structured?

Clara: The first check was $140,000 and we were set up to receive a payment a year for 25 years, the last one to be better than a quarter of a million dollars. We kept the payment that way for five years.

Kathy: What did you do at the end of five years?

Clara: We went to an attorney to see if we could do any better because taxes were killing us. He called in an insurance man right away and he right away wanted to sell us an insurance policy that cost $65,000 per year. I about had a fit. We did more research and found another attorney.

Kathy: What did this attorney recommend?

Clara: He recommended a bunch of trusts. We now have six trusts: one for me, one for my husband, and one for each of the children. We redid our wills, our power of attorney, and the whole ball of wax. He told us we would have been a lot better off if we would have set up a family corporation, because we would have saved a bundle in taxes, but it was too late now.

Kathy: What did you do with the money as it started coming in?

Clara: First thing we did was buy a car. We put some in CDs, gave some to our children, and used the money to redecorate the apartment and so forth. A neighbor man taught my husband about mutual funds, so he started buying some of them.

Kathy: I know you recently sold the lottery annuity winnings. How did you come to do that?

Clara: The whole time we had it, we had all kinds of people calling wanting to buy it. Three or four companies specialize in this. At the time in my state, it wasn't legal to sell. Finally, our governor signed a bill that allowed us to sell, but it had to be approved by the IRS, so we waited until it went through. We aren't in great health and are getting up in years and were told when we die our children would have to pay about a million-dollar tax bill in nine months. We knew they couldn't afford to do that.

Kathy: What happened when the IRS approved this?

Clara: We still didn't sell right away, because I liked the security of knowing we had that income for medical expenses and so forth. To make a long story short, one of the outfits upped to 42% of the remaining $5 million that they were willing to pay. After all was said and done, we ended up getting $1,800,000, out of which we had to pay taxes.

Kathy: Now you've received this large amount of money, how did you handle it?

Clara: We knew we couldn't handle it and at that time we decided we better meet with a financial advisor. I didn't know what I was going to do when they put $1,800,000 in our checking account, so I said we better find out.

Kathy: How did you go about selecting your financial advisor?

Clara: My son and daughter-in-law had an advisor that they liked very much, so my husband and I decided to tag along on a meeting they had with her. We liked what we heard so much that we set up an appointment before we left for just the two of us to meet with her.

Kathy: Did you have any financial experience before this happened to you?

Clara: Very little. We never really had big money like this. My husband was a tool and die maker and I didn't work much. My husband was in an investment club years ago at the foundry and learned a little from that. He had some Sears stock from years ago and it ended up being a godsend. We never touched it and it really appreciated. After 23 years, my husband didn't have a pension and the stock kept us going for many years.

Kathy: I know you've learned a lot. Any advice you'd like to give people?

Clara: Oh definitely, especially women. Kathy, I have had too many friends whose husbands pass away who knew absolutely nothing. Most of them have never even written a check. Their husbands always did all of it. My own sister never had a checking account in her whole life. She didn't drive, she had no identification, and she had to have a special card to cash her Social Security check.

Lastly, if people come into any money, they really should seek legal and financial advice. A mistake in either area can cost you a lot of money.

Kathy: You've been great and I hope you manage to win the lottery again. Maybe lightning will strike twice!

Summary

This is a wonderful, elderly couple who experienced the American Dream—they won the lottery! They found out quickly that this windfall was accompanied by a lot of financial and legal issues with which they were ill-prepared to deal. They were smart in seeking the help they needed and planning wisely for the future.

Lessons

- Don't use the lottery as your sole source of retirement planning vehicle. While it worked for this couple, we all know the odds against winning are astronomical.
- Seek professional help when faced with issues beyond your realm of expertise. Clara and her husband realized they made a mistake by not seeking legal advice before picking up their lottery winnings. They learned from this and have subsequently sought out the legal and financial advice they needed.
- Take your time before making financial decisions. This couple waited until they received a lump sum of money and needed assistance; in the process, they were wise shoppers in their search for a financial advisor.
- Enjoy yourself, but don't blow all your money when you receive a windfall. Notice that, in addition to buying a new car and redecorating, this couple put money in CDs and gave some to their children. The rest they invested in mutual funds.

Financial Planning Considerations

- **Estate planning:** Determine the disposition of their assets. This is the single biggest issue for this family, because of their ages and the sizable asset base. The major goal is that their children receive as much as possible and are able to pay estate taxes. They have revised their wills and established a number of trusts. They should review their estate planning tools regularly.

• **Portfolio monitoring:** Allocate their assets in line with their risk tolerances and monitor their portfolio for balance and performance.

Profile 11
Name *Patty*
Age *50*
Occupation *Senior Management*
Marital Status *Married*
Annual Income *Combined: $175,000*
Overview *Patty has been very successful in her career. She entered this, her second marriage, in her late 30s. As she and her husband begin retirement planning, they have very different perceptions on how to approach it financially.*

Interview

Kathy: Patty, could you give us a quick family profile?

Patty: I was originally married right out of college and the marriage lasted about six years. I remarried much later in life. My husband is 50 years old and this is his first marriage. Neither of us have ever had children.

Kathy: I know both of you were well-established when you got married. At that time, how much did you discuss finances?

Patty: Yes, we were both established in our careers and we both had homes. We were both used to pretty independent lifestyles. Sadly, we did very little talking about money before marriage. In terms of perceptions about how things were going to work out, they were quite different. He felt that our finances would be comingled and I felt that our finances would be kept fairly separate.

Our first financial decision was deciding to sell our two homes and building a new one. We had to figure how we wanted to handle the mortgage. So we set up a household account to which we both contributed and we kept separate accounts for our own expenditures. Everything from utilities to groceries comes out of the household account.

Kathy: When did you realize that your ideas about retirement income differed?

Patty: I had always anticipated that I was going to retire much earlier than my husband, because I have stayed with my current employer all of my professional career. My husband has changed jobs a number of times and didn't build the retirement assets as I have. Nowhere, in my mind, was it ever written that husband and wife always have to retire at the same time. I was perfectly content that I was going to retire and he'd be working. When his mother died, he inherited a sizable amount of money and it became clear that he planned on retiring when I did. At that point he contacted a financial planner with whom we both met.

Kathy: So without knowing it, each of you was headed to that meeting with a different set of expectations?

Patty: Yes. The planner immediately had assumed that everything that we had was to be mixed and we were going to work out our retirement plan from that pool of money. He had no concept that my husband had his money and I had my money. When the plan became clear, I said, "Whoa, that's my money." The planner took for granted that I would pay the majority of the expenses initially.

Kathy: What was your husband's response at that time?

Patty: My husband essentially agreed with the planner. After that we had some very heated discussions, because my feeling was, if he wanted to retire at the same time I retired, he was going to have to figure out a way to have enough money to cover his portion of the expenses.

There were other things about the meeting with the planner that I didn't like at all. First of all, he brought in a stockbroker who looked at the investments we had and of course wanted us to consolidate everything. He wanted me to sell all my stock and contribute those proceeds to a consolidated joint account. I also didn't like that he was immediately interested in selling us life insurance. We ended up having a disagreement in the office. I told my husband that if he wanted to keep going to this guy that was fine, but I was not going to have any part of it and wouldn't go back.

Kathy: It's clear that you have strong feelings that assets don't have to be pooled in a marriage. Can you tell us more about that?

Patty: I think a lot of my feelings come from watching my mom and dad when I was growing up. My experience was that my mom didn't work and my dad had control over all of the money. There seemed to be nonstop battling every time my mom would buy clothes or put anything on a credit card. It was fight, fight, fight. I just developed this thing about having my own money and not having to answer to anybody about what I do or don't do with my money.

My beliefs were reinforced during my divorce. At the end of that marriage, I had no credit and had to establish it. I wasn't about to go back to that mode.

Kathy: After all this time, do you feel that your husband is comfortable with your philosophy?

Patty: No, actually I think he's a little miffed because he still does not understand all this independence stuff. He's gotten better and he's not pushing to merge our investments or anything like that.

Kathy: How do you see this issue being resolved?

Patty: I don't know that it is going to be resolved until we get to the point where we're near retirement and have a better sense of what our expenses are going to be. At that time it may be that initially I'll end up kicking in more, because he won't be able to get at some of his things until he's 59 and we both want to retire at 55. That's one of the options we've discussed.

Kathy: Is there any special advice you'd give women who have assets of their own and are entering a second marriage?

Patty: First of all, I think having the household account is a key thing to do. I know some people in second marriages who have not set things up this way and have actually gotten into major financial battles over covering household expenses. As far as assets beyond your house, I truly believe it's better to keep things separated both in life and in death.

Kathy: Could you explain that death part a little to us?

Patty: Both my husband and I will leave assets to each other, but we won't be the full beneficiary of each other's assets. For instance, I have specific wishes for my side of the family as to what they should inherit. If our money was comingled now, I think it would be harder to divide our assets that way upon death.

I think there's a certain pervasive attitude out there that somehow if you're a woman and remarry all your assets somehow merge with those of your new spouse. I know several women who feel as I do and don't want to have it that way. It's probably an emotional thing, but financially it works for me. I believe it's OK if women have been through a divorce and have assets they want to protect that it's fine to keep them separate.

Kathy: I really do appreciate your being so honest with us. I know your thinking goes against the more romanticized version of marriage, but you raise valid issues that women should consider.

Summary

Patty represents many women in that she is in her second marriage. Success in her career and lessons from her first marriage make financial independence highly important to her. Like most people, she and her current husband did not talk about finances prior to getting married. Their varying opinions of roles and responsibilities would later lead to conflict.

Lessons

- As we've seen throughout many of these scenarios, you must always, always, always discuss financial matters prior to entering a relationship. I can't stress enough the emotional component of money and the dramatic difference in perceptions we have in this area. There's a good reason that the overwhelming source of conflict in a marriage is money.

- What we think is the "obvious" way to handle money may be obvious only to us! Both the financial planner and her husband assumed that their finances were to be comingled before and during retirement. We all know what happens when we assume. Again, there are no right and wrong ways, but there are different ways and we need to be very much aware of that with our partners. Patty clearly feels strongly about how she'll manage her own money and what her responsibilities are financially.

- The old rules don't always apply. Years ago, when I would meet with a married couple, I assumed that they wished to open a joint account and the man's name would be listed first. After being severely beaten about the head and shoulders, I've learned the error of my ways. Very commonly couples, whether in first or subsequent second marriages, wish to maintain separate accounts.

- It really does pay to do serious retirement planning. Because of Patty's longevity with her employer, her upward mobility, and her participation in her retirement plan, she will be able to retire comfortably at age 55 if she chooses to do so.

Financial Planning Considerations

- **Retirement planning:** Understand how they will handle finances in retirement and define the responsibilities of each party. This is currently at the top of their list of financial goals. Because their perceptions differ, they need to be highly specific in this regard and not simply deal on the conceptual level or it will be an ongoing source of unresolved conflict.
- **Housing:** Decide whether to purchase a smaller home, buy a second home, or stay in their current home.
- **Estate planning:** Set up wills and perhaps arrange for trusts. Since neither spouse intends for the other to be the full beneficiary of his or her estate, they should clearly specify their wishes in a will. As their estate grows, they may wish to consider the pros and cons of trusts.
- **Asset allocation and portfolio monitoring:** Ensure that their diversified investments are repositioned as their lifestyle changes, in order to meet those changing needs.

Financial Professional Interviews

Annie and Debra are financial professionals. Annie has been in the business 18 years and Debra 20. They have given hundreds of seminars. I asked them to draw from their wealth of information and share with us their perception of women and investments.

Profile 1 *Financial Professional*	
Name *Annie Moberly, CFP*	
Title *Regional Vice President*	
Firm *Liberty Financial Investments*	

Interview

Kathy: Over the years have you seen a shift in women's interest in investments?

Annie: I'd say that over the years women are definitely taking a stronger interest in their financial futures, but it's definitely not across the board. The older women who are realizing they are outliving their husbands or are going through divorces are definitely more interested in educating themselves about financial affairs than the younger women.

Kathy: Why do you think that is?

Annie: I don't know if younger women aren't as trusting of advice or just not as concerned as older women. They seem to look into investments but lose interest because they don't understand. I think intimidation is a big factor. Younger women who are just beginning in the workforce probably don't have a lot of money to invest, but it does surprise me that coming out of college they don't have more roots in the financial area. I'd say women in the 50+ category are the ones who are becoming much more aware and interested.

In fact, last night I had dinner with a couple of women friends and, knowing I had this interview today, I asked them their feelings about investing. One was fresh out of college and the other is single, never married, and 46 years old. Both of them said they had no interest in investing. They aren't comfortable reading the financial pages and so forth and they're not gravitating toward educating themselves. This really surprised me.

Kathy: Based on your experience, what would you recommend that women do to take control of their money?

Annie: The number one thing is education. It could be from a book or some course, but they have to understand the basics of money. Once they understand some of these things, they'll be much more comfortable.

The other thing I think they need to do is become less concerned about cost. I know these questions have been drilled in their heads from magazines. Instead of asking, "What is it going to cost me?" I think a more appropriate question would be "Where can I get the help I need?" Most of them need someone to sit down and work with them. I have people ask me about mutual funds, "Is there a load?" As I talk to them, it becomes clear they don't even understand what the question means, but they read about it in *Money Magazine* or something.

Kathy: What do you think are some of the fears women have about investing?

Annie: I think the single biggest fear is "Am I going to lose my money?" I also think they tend to be too short-term in their thinking. I think they need to look at their assets and decide what money could be treated as long-term and then invest that in more aggressive investments. If they view their money as short-term, they don't want to take any risks with it and we know that costs them a lot over time.

Another big fear women seem to have is the fear of making the wrong decision. Many of them are so concerned about making the right decision that they make no decision at all.

Kathy: Have you seen much of a gender difference in the way people view money?

Annie: Yes, I have. I've seen it professionally and personally. I know a successful couple who make excellent money. She can't stand the thought of losing any money and wants to be very conservative. Her husband is the opposite. He's willing to gamble and has no interest in keeping his nest egg safe. He figures, "If I make the wrong decision, so be it, I'll overcome it, I'll make more money…whatever."

Kathy: Where do you think these differences originate?

Annie: Men are used to being team-like. They play baseball and team-oriented sports and, if they get into an argument, by the time things are over they're all backslapping and going to the bar for Miller time. Women, on the other hand, do more solitary activities. We play dolls or jacks or hopscotch. I think this overlaps in the field of finance. How many times do you get in a women's social group and talk about financial affairs? Guys, on the other hand, whether they know much about it or not, are going to wing it. I think investment clubs are one of the best things that have happened to a lot of women.

Kathy: In terms of specific action steps, what's your advice to women?

Annie: The first I would say is to get started. The reason I say that first is because they're never going to have the comfort of knowing it all and, even if they get educated, the biggest risk of all is procrastination. I'd recommend starting with a systematic investment plan, whether it's $50 a month or whatever they can afford. I'd put that into a broad-based mutual fund so they can start to understand the concepts. From that point they should continue getting educated, so they get comfortable with other important financial areas, such as insurance.

I think women are a lot more auditory than they are visual and I would suggest they get books on tape that are investment-oriented.

Many women should seek out and find a professional that they are comfortable with. One of the best ways to find a person is through referrals. I believe it is very important that, when you ask someone for a referral, you outline your own situation to them to allow them to better help you. If you're a beginner, tell them so. If you don't have a lot of money to invest, tell them so. Realistically a big producer won't have a lot of time to spend with a small, beginning investor. On the other hand, if you are referred to someone who is just maybe starting out in the business, they will be able to take more time and educate you. Sometimes new people in the business are very good and very diligent. If you have a lot of money, you may not want a new practitioner because they don't have the depth of knowledge that an experienced person may have.

Kathy: In this book I've given the readers a few red flags to look out for when selecting an advisor. Do you have any red flags you'd like to share?

Annie: The first red flag should be that you never have to do something today. Don't be pushed into doing something right away that you don't understand. I've watched women ask drilling questions of their doctors in selecting a physician, yet they'll let a lawyer, CPA, or stockbroker walk all over them because that's an area that they don't know enough about. They might be dealing with a very abrasive personality or someone they just don't jive with, yet they just keep working with them.

The next red flag is that if your advisor is more a talker than a listener you have a problem. Go with your gut in this selection. If you don't feel that the person you go with is right for you, make a change, even if the person is highly regarded and often referred. Women have good instincts—I wouldn't ignore them.

Another red flag is not returning phone calls. They may not be able to return them immediately, but certainly within a day or so. How much interest do they have in working with you if they don't return your calls?

Kathy: I think you're right on the money about those flags. Any closing messages?

Annie: Yes, you have to become educated in these matters, and with that education will come confidence. If you entrust all your financial concerns to a significant other, you can be in trouble. I've seen through my years of experience that frequently things go wrong, and then we're always pointing the finger—"It wasn't my fault, it was their fault," "I was a victim of ..." whoever or whatever. So my feeling is just to get out there and take matters in your own hands. If you don't understand the tax return you're signing, ask. If you don't understand an investment or why you're making that investment, ask. Start asking questions and go with your gut.

Kathy: Thanks so much for sharing your perceptions with us.

Profile 2   *Financial Professional*
Name   *Debra Carter, CFP*
Title   *Vice President*
Firm   *Franklin Templeton*

Interview

Kathy: In your 20 years of experience, how many seminars do you think you've presented?

Debra: About a zillion!

Kathy: I'm sure you've gained a lot of insights during these zillion seminars and I know you get a lot of questions from women. What do you think are some of the common pitfalls that women fall into with their finances?

Debra: It's so varied, but something that I think is a general blanket statement is that we just don't pay enough attention to this part of our lives. I've seen this in a variety of women, ranging from highly compensated professionals to blue-collar workers. They just haven't educated themselves on finances and I stress the word they. They've simply ignored it.

Kathy: What reasons do you think there may be for that?

Debra: I think there are a lot of reasons for that. You can go back and look at the way women have been brought up. Finances were always something women just chose to leave to the man in their life. That's one reason. Another reason is that women are just intimidated—and with justification. Investment products are becoming more numerous and complex, so we're comfortable to turn it over to someone else or just ignore it completely. There's always that theory that some people are waiting for that prince to come and save them from all these awful things.

Kathy: This behavior can lead to disastrous results down the road.

Debra: Yes, it can lead to a very bleak financial future and, again, for a variety of reasons. All you have to do is look at the statistics for the life span of the average woman. The fact that we tend to make far less than men, that many women leave the work force, temporarily at least, to raise children, makes it clear that women will have fewer retirement resources. Unless she takes control of her own financial future, she is going to be in difficult financial straits at some point in her life. Remember: even if we have that wonderful spouse, it's likely we'll outlive him. It's a virtual guarantee that, at some point in her adult life, every woman will be responsible for her own financial future.

Kathy: If you were speaking to a group of 100 women and they didn't have a lot of investment experience, what would you want to say to them?

Debra: Put all of this under the heading of "being a good consumer." Women are good consumers in so many areas. A lot of women are in charge of the family checkbook, shopping for the family, seeing that the medical needs are met, etc. I think that, because it's so intimidating, we just lose sight of the fact that finance and financial products are just another consumer product. If you look at it this way, it becomes a little less intimidating and you take it one step at a time. Our goal is simply to become educated consumers.

Kathy: How would you advise women become educated consumers?

Debra: There's a lot of financial information out there and the number one thing to do is to take advantage of that information. You can't pick up a financial publication without seeing something about finances, stock markets, and so on. There's a lot of information available at the public library; start there. You can network with your friends or other women generally who have an interest in the same thing you do. One way to do that may be through an investment club. What you have to bear in mind is to take one step at a time.

I put the responsibility for education back on the shoulders of the women. We can't sit back and wait for somebody to come to us with an education. That's something we have to do for ourselves.

Kathy: Being a professional in the business, do you think people in the financial industry have been responsive to women?

Debra: No, I don't. There's a statistic that shows the high number of brokerage accounts owned by women versus the low percentage of female advisors out there. *Money Magazine*, a couple of years ago, presented an article dealing with the way that brokerage firms treated women differently than men in the products they recommended, even though both presented the same investment goals. The women were always given the conservative choices. In addition to this objectionable treatment, I think the industry has overlooked the fact that the first-in-line beneficiary is the surviving spouse, AKA the woman.

Kathy: I've included a section on the book about selecting a financial advisor. What tips would you give?

Debra: Here's my number one rule when I do a seminar—and I put this in big letters: NEVER, NEVER, NEVER INVEST IN ANYTHING YOU DON'T UNDERSTAND. It's amazing the number of people I meet who have a 401(k) investment and have no idea what it is. I believe you should be able to articulate each of your investments in 25 words or less.

In selecting an advisor, find out if that person is involved in any litigation or has any charges pending against him or her. The selection process goes back to being an educated consumer. Ask questions. Look at their professional certifications and standing.

Lastly, you must find somebody you are comfortable with because—make no mistake—this is a relationship. It is not simply a transaction. It's a business relationship that presumably will last for many, many years. So find somebody you're comfortable building that relationship with.

Kathy: As usual, you were brilliant. I certainly appreciate your input.

Bottom Line

I think we can learn a number of lessons from these stories. Probably the most important is that with courage and determination we can overcome many adverse situations. Without exception, these women have all stressed the need to become involved and gain an education. These women make it clear that we must assume responsibility for our own futures and they emphasize the importance of doing it before a crisis develops. No one denies that this can be an intimidating area but certainly one that you can manage through knowledge.

After reading these stories, I'm sure you can tell that it was painful for some of these women to share their experiences. They did so in the sincere desire to help other women learn from their situations. I am truly grateful to all of them for their contributions.

Graduation

Congratulations!

You've finally reached the end of the book. Don't spend too much time congratulating yourself, because it's now time to put our thoughts into action.

I said at the beginning of this book that I thought there were two things that kept women from taking control of their financial life—the emotional issues surrounding money and the lack of knowledge and confidence about investment concepts. In this book we've taken a look at both. If you're a beginner, you should now be ready to get started. If you already have some assets, you're now prepared to branch out.

I never give a speech without mentioning what I call "analysis paralysis." As women we like to do our homework and understand investments before we leap forward. Unfortunately, we also use this as an excuse to do nothing. It's not enough for us to find a good mutual fund that will meet our needs. Instead, we spend weeks and weeks agonizing over what to do and searching for that investment that is divinely inspired, preferably managed by God. And so we miss out on opportunities. Let's face it—some of the more mediocre mutual funds have outperformed our savings accounts. Don't use the search for perfection as an excuse for spending too much time studying and no time investing.

You've seen the effects of taxes and inflation and should now have a better understanding of the various types of risk. I hope that you now understand that one of the greatest risks is doing nothing. As you've discovered, the world of investments is approachable and understandable. We've seen the numbers and realize it's imperative that we as women take control of our financial lives.

If you think about what I've been saying in the book, you have no doubt realized that sometimes investing calls for you to step outside your comfort zone. If we were honest with ourselves, most of the time our comfort zone would leave our money plopped right at the bottom of the investment pyramid in CDs and savings accounts. With any luck at all, you've discovered that over the long haul, when you factor in taxes and inflation, these investments may actually cause you to lose ground in building money.

If you're honest with yourself, you have to admit that you know a heck of a lot more now than when you started the book. If you really want to be sure that you don't lose momentum, I'd suggest you begin by leaving this book on a table and dusting around it until you do something. You don't need a fortune or an advanced degree to get moving— and I promise you'll feel better when you start to take control of this aspect of your life. I wish you every success and, as Mr. Spock says, "Live long and prosper."

Financial Information on the Internet

*I*f you look for financial information on the Internet, you'll find more material than you know what to do with. To help you narrow your search and give you a general idea of the information available, I'm going to provide some World Wide Web sites. The search engine locations may be general, but will provide you a number of additional sites for specific topics that you're wishing to research. In addition, I'll provide you some Web site addresses that I like and think you may find useful.

Search Engine: Infoseek
http://www.infoseek.com
Enter keyword: *Investing*

This will lead you to a screen called *Infoseek Personal Finance*. This page will then show you a variety of investment topics that you may click on to bring up those specific pages. These include Personal Finance, Investing, Financial Services and Reference, Financial Market Analysis, Personal Investment, and Stock Investors Advice and Services. Also provided is a heading **stock links**, under which you may get a quote or a chart or track your stocks.

By clicking on the topic *Investing*, you may find some of the following sites:

Sallie Mae
Guide to finding student financial aid.
http://www.salliemae.com/

Dollar for Dollar
Links to personal finance resources on the Web.
http://www.dollar4dollar.com/

NAIC (National Association of Investors Corporation) Home Page
Investment information, services and professional support for members.
http://www.better-investing.org

Bloomberg Online
News, markets, financial analysis, and Bloomberg Radio
in Real Audio.
http://www.bloomberg.com/

Quicken Financial Network
Resource for investments, financial planning, and tax information.
http://www.qfn.com/

Financenter Home Page
Interactive calculators and connections to financial services.
http://www.financenter.com/

Financial Players Center: A Center for Financial Learning
Online newsletter and financial learning tools.
http://fpc.net66.com/

Retirement Planning: Frequently Asked Questions about IRAs
Extensive information about this personal retirement plan.
http://www.vanguard.com/educ/lib/retire/faqira.html

Kiplinger's Retirement Report
Articles on retirement planning and money management issues.
http://kiplinger.com/newsletter/retire.html

The Gilbert Links: Financial
A listing of World Wide Web and Internet resources in the Financial category.
http://www.gator.net/ ~ james/finance.html

Retirement Benefits
From the Social Security Addminstration comes this online booklet designed to help you make important decisions regarding retirement.
**http://www.ssa.gov/programs/retirement/
publications/retirement.html**

Retirement Planning
Comprehensive introduction to the major issues of retirement planning.
http://www.bus.orst.edu/faculty/nielson/finplan/retire/retirmt.htm

Roth IRA
Technical and planning information on Roth IRAs for professional planners and individual investors.
http://www.rothira.com/

Women and Pensions: What Women Need to Know and Do (PWBA)
Advice from the Department of Labor, Pension and Welfare Benefits Administration.
http://www.dol.gov/dol/pwba/public/pubs/women/women.htm

ThirdAge.com Money Matters
Financial advice and discussions for active adults over 50.
http://www.thirdage.com/rd/dir/money.html

Financial Planning Calculator
Download a financial calendar to your desktop. This calendar for small and home-based business is full of expert planning advice.
http://www.hpcalendar.com/

Glossary of Insurance and Financial Planning Terms
Reference guide from a professor of insurance and risk management.
http://www.ucalgary.ca/MG/inrm/glossary/index.htm

101 Questions to Ask Before Investing
General questions and questions about risk, business ventures, stocks, options, tax shelters, commodities, and other investments.
http://mosl.sos.state.mo.us/sos-sec/101que.html

How to Avoid Investment Fraud
Consumer education resources for recognizing investment fraud from the Kentucky Department of Financial Institutions.
http://www.dfi.state.ky.us/fraud/scamalert.html

Mutual Funds: A Guide for Beginning Investors
A primer on mutual fund investing from the Missouri Securities Division
http://mosl.sos.state.mo.us/sos-sec/mufunds.html

Tools
Calculators and quizzes: compare mortgages or buying vs. renting, calculate retirement expenses or life insurance needs, and test your risk tolerance, financial aptitude, and knowledge of mutual funds.
http://www.infoseek.com/Topic/Personal_Finance?sv = IS&nh = 10&svx = related

The engine Lycos search (**http://www.lycos.com**) also features many investment-related topics, including money, investments, taxes and planning, insurance, and banks and loans. Using this search engine, I located the following Web sites.

Welcome to Divorce Online
This site features articles on the financial, legal, and psychological aspects of divorce and referrals to professionals who specialize in these areas.
http://www.divorceonline.com

Wall Street Coffee Company
Price-weighted average of the 30 stocks that make up the Dow Jones Industrial Average. Also features an investment and insurance glossary and links and other useful information.
http://www.wallstreetcoffee.com

Stock Wire
Stock quotes, research reports, SEC filings and so on.
http://www.stockwire.com

Investing Hot Links
Favorite links from the Illinois CPA Society.
http://www.icpas.org/invest.htm

Stock Tip Radio
This site provides a forum for sharing tips and discussing stocks, with links to sites related to investing.
http://www.submit-a-page.com

Stock Talk
Silicon Investor: "the largest financial discussion site on the Web."
http://www.techstocks.com011

The New York Stock Exchange
http://www.nyse.com

The American Stock Exchange
http://www.webpoint.com

NASDAQ
http://www.nasdaq.com

Stocksite | research
Stock market reports, quotes, and links to a wide range of market tools, including business news and stock picks.
http://www.stocksite.com

BigCharts
Chart stocks, check indices, follow the markets, and find out about the Big Movers.
http://www.bigcharts.com

Using the search engine Excite (**http://www.excite.com**), you'll find a major heading, Money/Investing. At that location you'll find more investment sites that you can select. These include bonds, brokerage firms and advisors, columns, DRIPs, getting started, investing styles, mutual funds, retirement, and stocks and women.

If, like me, you're not an experienced Web surfer, you'll still find this a very easy process. Essentially, if you go to any of the major search engines, enter your key word or phrase, such as "money" or "investments," you'll pull up tons of sites. Simply start by clicking on one that sounds best to you and keep going until you find a site that fits your needs.

A word of warning: Many investment sites have commercials and sales pitches for a particular product, newsletter, or whatever the sponsor is selling. Ignore the self-serving part and gather whatever information you can find.

Key Sites

One of my personal favorites is Yahoo Finance. At this location you can find an incredible assortment of information, quotes, and news about financial markets. I go directly to **http://quote.yahoo.com**.

If you're just looking for stock quotes, many people use **http://www.quote.com**. Here you can get free quotes with a 20-minute delay and can create a portfolio with up to 10 ticker symbols. You may input your date and purchase price and simply click the mouse to update your portfolio value, showing profits and losses.

Another prominent site is **http://www.quicken.com**. This Web site provides information about a variety of financial topics including investing, insurance, and mortgage information. You can even do your income taxes online at this site if you wish.

Sites Specifically for Women

The two standouts specifically targeted to women that provide good information for everyone are the following:

http://www.moneyminded.com
http://www.womenswire.com/money.

Moneyminded
http://www.moneyminded.com
The site is sponsored by Hearst Communications and is designed to make finance fun. The site offers advice on mortgages, work life, investing, debt and credit, and retirement planning. You may participate in forums, calculate a number of financial futures, and discover innovative ways to budget.

Women's Wire Money
http://www.womenswire.com/money
This is the money channel for the Women's Wire site. It was developed with the Bloomberg News Service and covers all kinds of information regarding personal finance for women. It provides informa-

tion about mortgages, budgeting, investing and savings, and whether to buy or lease an automobile.

Other sites for women worth exploring include:

http://www.onegroup.com/women/education.shtml
This is a Web site for The One Group family of mutual funds. This site offers an entire section on women and investing and includes many investment calculators, ranging from retirement planning to planning for your child's college education.

http://www.stpt.com/women/investing.html
This Web site, Starting Point, features a section called Women's View, sponsored by **www.women.com**. This is an index of Web sites for investing women, so you can do some major exploration at this site.

http://www.women.com.
This is a generalized site for women, with information on careers, style, health, and money. The money section features a great deal of information, including calculators and tools to use for almost any investment scenario.

Key Real Estate Sites

http://www.quickenmortgage.com. This site features a section entitled Home & Mortgage Center. Here you'll be able to input your financial information and compare actual mortgages offered from some of America's leading lenders. You can shop and actually apply for a mortgage or refinancing on line and get an immediate answer from the lender.

http://www.homeshark.com
http://www.eloan.com
These are well-established, independent sites that allow you to submit a loan application online.

Major lenders, mortgage brokers, and most real estate firms maintain sites. For additional search tools, check the following sites:
http://www.loanpage.com
http://www.mortgage-net.com

Media Sites

If your time is limited and you want to go to one site that will give you many, many choices, the two that I would recommend are **www.cnnfn.com** and **www.cnbc.com**. Both of these are prominent, independent financial news networks. They give you current news information and a variety of market statistics, including most active stocks, biggest gainers, biggest losers, etc. This is your basic one-stop shopping for financial information.

Major financial publications have Web sites, among them **www.wsj.com** (*The Wall Street Journal*), **www.nytimes.com** (*The New York Times*), and **www.kiplinger.com** (*Kiplinger's*). These sites feature subsites. For example, at **www.update.wsj.com**, *The Wall Street Journal* presents a guide to investing. It offers investment analysis and reports and has links to other investing-related sites.

Most major newspapers also have Web sites. If you go to the newspaper site, you can usually then click on the business section and obtain information of a local nature.

This should give you a good series of beginning points in your search for information on the Internet. In addition to what I've discussed here, there are a number of brokerage firms and mutual funds with Web addresses that tell you the specifics of their products or funds as well as other information and interactive tools. You can even make investment purchases on the Internet through a variety of discount broker Web sites. If you get interested in online trading, you'll find their Web sites in advertisements in most financial media. Proceed with caution.

Good luck and good "surfing"!

Index